ILLUSIVE SHADOWS

ILLUSIVE SHADOWS

Justice, Media, and Socially Significant American Trials

Edited by
LLOYD CHIASSON JR.

Westport, Connecticut
London

Library of Congress Cataloging-in-Publication Data

Chiasson, Lloyd, 1947–
    Illusive shadows : justice, media, and socially significant American trials / Lloyd
Chiasson, Jr.
        p.   cm.
    Includes bibliographical references and index.
    ISBN 0–275–97495–2 (alk. paper)—ISBN 0–275–97507–X (pbk. : alk. paper)
    1. Trials—United States. 2. Crime—Social aspects—United States—History. 3. Crime
and the press—United States—History. I. Title.
    KF220.C52   2003
    345.73'02—dc21   2003046962

British Library Cataloguing in Publication Data is available.

Library of Congress Catalog Card Number: 2003046962
ISBN: 0–275–97495–2
        0–275–97507–X (pbk.)

First published in 2003

Praeger Publishers, 88 Post Road West, Westport, CT 06881
An imprint of Greenwood Publishing Group, Inc.
www.praeger.com

Printed in the United States of America

The paper used in this book complies with the
Permanent Paper Standard issued by the National
Information Standards Organization (Z39.48–1984).

10 9 8 7 6 5 4 3 2 1

This book is dedicated to Lloyd Sr., Helen, Susanne, Mary Shannon, Marnie and Cassidy. Chiassons all.

CONTENTS

ACKNOWLEDGMENTS

A heart-felt thanks to all the contributors. Special thanks to my Fulbright brother, Bob Dardenne, a dear friend who has endured me over countless projects. Although his writing and research always have been a hallmark of the edited volumes with which we have been associated, never has it been so superb as in this book.

THE OPENING STATEMENT

Ladies and gentlemen of the jury, as you read this, the prosecution and the defense ask only that you weigh all the facts as fairly as possible. As you will note during the presentation of the 10 exhibits, earlier juries have already spoken, and your duty is not to assign guilt or innocence to those previously charged. Your task is larger in scope, perhaps more difficult than that of the original juries. But let us not meander in the proceedings. You will receive your charge soon enough. First, the events you are to read about and ultimately make judgments upon require a preface.

It is the stuff of news. High drama. Life and death. That rare moment when justice, or a reasonable facsimile, is meted out. And what offers up more high drama, or melodrama, than a highly publicized, juicy "whodunit"? Most news events live short life spans. They happen; they are reported; they are quickly forgotten. A trial, however, often is a lingering, living thing that builds in tension. It is, every once in a long while, a modern Shakespearean drama with a twist: The audience becomes members of the cast because, every once in a long while, society finds itself the defendant, and justice is deaf and dumb, as well as blind.

As you perhaps already know, a jury may hand down a legal judgment, but the larger court of public opinion usually determines the final verdict in terms of social and historical significance of the crime, the trial, and the accused. This was true when John Proctor faced charges of witchcraft in 1692, and it has proven true for every socially significant trial since. The reason is relatively simple: Trials are media happenings, and a media happening is a self-fulfilling prophecy. The more coverage, the more important the trial. And the crime. And the accused.

This is not to say that trials have no lasting importance beyond how the public perceives them. A trial can have long-reaching significance if it changes the way people think or how institutions function or if it shapes public opinion. Ten such American trials covering a span of 307 years are herein presented. In each, the sociological underpinning of events often has greater significance than either the crime or the trial.

Now, a glimpse at the facts:

In the early years of America, in the years before science would claw its way into the public's consciousness, fear of a dark evil permeates the colonies. One small village, in particular, becomes both infatuated with, and stricken by, demonic thoughts. Suddenly, neighbor is pitted against neighbor, family against family, and, as many see it at the time, good against evil. Before the year 1692 is history, 24 people die in the conflagration. That we know. How it happened, and what it all means, we leave to you.

A century and a half later, a kidnapping case finds its way before the American public. The issues are as bizarre as they are provocative. What is the status of a kidnapped African on American soil? Moreover, just what is the legal status of a slave? Is he a human being with God-given human rights, or is he chattel? Can a man murder to prevent his enslavement, or is that action illegal when perpetrated by a piece of property?

Minnesota in 1862: A land of hope inhabited by grizzled residents, adventuresome Easterners, and hope-filled immigrants. One small problem exists, however. The land—but not the hopes and dreams for a better life—has to be shared with those who came before. The red man and the white man are a combustible mixture producing predictable frustrations with unpredictable results. Broken treaties, broken promises, and, ultimately, broken peace. A microcosm, perhaps, of how the West was won?

Now, we arrive at the twentieth century, a pompous hundred years littered with trials of the century. As Americans enter that modern epoch, increasing numbers come to loathe capitalism. In their eyes, it is oppressive control at worst, a failed experiment at best. What follows is a battle of ideas, some familiar, some different, some novel. These new ideas take fresh names and many forms: organized labor, the Wobblies, socialism, communism. Although people die, the most notable one being a former governor, the battle is fought, as is so often the case, on the battleground of public opinion at the front known as Idaho.

Across the country at the same time, old wounds reopen when a black man is convicted of raping a white woman. The place is the South, where it has been said old ideas die hard. Perhaps events flow from a righteous indignation born from an act of unspeakable violence. Or perhaps they flow from a rekindled racism, smoldering, perhaps, since the slave ships sailed years before.

Then, in 1921, 12 Americans decide the fate of two European immigrants. The questions before them, and now you: What is the case about, and what does it prove? Is it about murder or ideology? Does it prove that an immigrant can be executed for being from the wrong part of Europe? Or that under some circumstances and in some situations, some Americans—like those from distant Salem—are executed for the convenience of the majority?

Just four years later, in 1925, old wounds reopen when a black man is found guilty of location by his white neighbors. The place is the North, where it has been said old ideas die hard. Perhaps events flow from a righteous indignation borne from a belief in property values. Or perhaps they flow from a rekindled racism, smoldering, perhaps, since the slave ships sailed years before.

November 1963. Shots ring out in Dallas. A president dies. Charges are leveled in New Orleans. A conspiracy is born. Characters abound. Character assassination flourishes. A Lewis Carroll fantasy provides fewer absurdities. Everyone involved seems to fall down a rabbit hole where truth is as elusive as the Cheshire cat, press conferences resemble Mad Hatter tea parties, the Queen of Hearts screams for a head, and the city that care forgot turns into Wonderland.

Party invitations are extended, but plans change. New party invitations go out, and the plans change again. When the party finally starts, unforeseen events interrupt. By the time the festivities begin again, no one cares. Apply to the Manuel Noriega trial in 1991, and you have a recipe for what a "trial of the century" is not. Add bad timing to the mix—at the same time, Eurasians have the disintegration of the Soviet Union as a theme, a Florida jury has William Kennedy Smith and his family's legacy to contemplate, and Iraqi soldiers have Operation Desert Storm to escape—and you have a long, strange, baffling, legal quagmire that strains everyone's attention span.

Stupidity or fear or hate—or a combination of each—causes the death of a young homosexual in Wyoming in 1998. After all, a hate crime is nothing more than an act committed out of fear forged by stupidity. And, of all the cases presented, this is perhaps the least publicized, the least prominent. But it is the case that summarizes the other nine, for at the core of each we uncover stupidity or fear or hatred—or a combination of each—one way or another.

Make no mistake; this is no esoteric study. It is colorfully written narratives about 10 crimes, the subsequent trials, the media coverage of each. It is a book about witchcraft, about religion, about slavery, about socialism. It paints portraits of a racist America, a capitalistic America, an anarchist America. It relates compelling tales of compassion, greed, stupidity, and hate beginning in seventeenth-century colonial times and ending in present-day America. One final point for you jurors: At times, and in many ways, it is the story of America.

1

THE CASE OF THE SALEM WITCH TRIALS (1692)

Lloyd Chiasson Jr.

"God knows I am innocent . . ."

Christmastime in New England. Snow covers the rocky soil the farmers so religiously toil in the springtime. Although frenetic bursts of farmwork mark late spring and summer, winter's lethargy blankets the landscape much as the snow, and residents huddle indoors, safe from the pristine, but lethal, weather.

It is a typical Christmas for the people of Salem Village, but for one propitious addition. The hamlet has a new resident, a reverend hired to minister their spiritual needs. Villagers thank God for that. Salem has been without a religious leader for nearly two years.

Nothing more than a collection of isolated farmhouses, little sets Salem Village apart from other hamlets in Massachusetts Bay Colony. Life outside of Boston is hard and unsure. The rocky New England ground makes farming particularly laborious, and the threat of both Indians and disease provides residents with a constant reminder of their precarious existence. Yet the countryside suits the somber Puritans; the rolling hills and cold, meandering waterways enhance its melancholy beauty. A finger of the Woolesfon River, known to locals as Frost Fish River, touches the village boundary line to the southeast where the waterway turns into Frost Fish Brook. To the west, near Thomas Bailey's home, lies Wilkins Pond. In the south, "the Great River" (also known as Ipswich River) skirts Bald Hill and Fairmaid's Hill. Slicing through the western and less populated section of the village, the river flows near Thomas Putnam's house, while Nichols Brook meanders through the northern part of town. Near the middle of the village runs Old Meeting Road, where Joseph Hutchinson lives. Not far away on Ipswich Road is Thomas

Preston's house. Near Bass River outside the village to the east, Dorcas Hoar resides, and just south of the village line sits the home of Giles Corey. Farther south at Proctor's Corner is the home of John Proctor, a short walk from Trask's Mill on the North River near where he soon will be hanged.[1]

It is a typical winter in Salem Village when, without warning, the stillness shatters under the weight of an inexplicable and deadly evil. For inside one house—the home of Salem's newest resident—a sacrilege, vile and abhorrent, takes place: Convulsions grip the child. She violently thrashes about the floor, gasping, moaning, screeching. Suddenly, she drops to all fours, barking and braying as she scampers beneath the furniture. Bewildered onlookers swear the girl's skin shows pin or prick marks from some unseen force, and as they pray, the child's screams drown out their words. In a final flurry of rage, the young girl grabs a Bible and throws it across the room.

Welcome to Salem Village, home of the Devil. See his handiwork, most notably innocents Betty Parris, Abigail Williams, Ann Putnam, and Mercy Lewis. And the not-so-innocent: Tituba, Sarah Osborne, Rebecca Nurse, and Sarah Good. Meet those who confront evil: Reverend Samuel Parris, Thomas Putnam, William Stoughton, John Hathorne, and Reverend Cotton Mather. Come witness a colonial witch-hunt, the accused, their confessions, their inevitable executions.

Journey back in time to 1692 and consider one of the strangest events in American history.

Although witchcraft hysteria can be traced back hundreds of years in Europe, events at Salem may have had their genesis in nearby Boston four years earlier. There, in the colonies' largest town, four children, four seemingly normal children, suddenly begin to howl at the moon, have epileptic fits, scream blasphemies that would shame the staunchest atheist. Although they have never exhibited abnormal behavior before, their bizarre episodes continue, then quickly worsen, becoming so outrageous and so public that community and church leaders intervene. Meet the God-fearing Goodwin family of Boston.

The year is 1688, and the Devil is an active member of the Massachusetts Bay Colony. Of course, Puritan residents know this, most prominently the revered Cotton Mather, one of Boston's spiritual leaders. Officious in appearance as well as temperament, Mather is not a patient man regarding witchcraft. When it comes to dealing with the Devil, he acts with swift assurance. He is an expert on the subject, having read his father's detailed account of witchcraft and demonic possession in *An Essay for the Recording of Illustrious Providences,* having written of the "demonic possession" of 16-year-old Elizabeth Knapp almost 20 years earlier and having written his own popular text on witchcraft and possession, *Memorable Providences Relating to Witchcrafts and Possessions.*[2] *Memorable Providences* is Mather's take on the Goodwin incident, which he terms a "faithful account" of "the marvellous Trouble and Releef Experienced by a pious Family in Boston, very lately and sadly molested with Evil Spirits."

In the Goodwin case, Mather's expertise leads him to Irish washerwoman Dolly Glover, also called the Witch Glover. She is judged and found guilty. Her crime? She somehow has afflicted the children, aiding and abetting their possession by the Devil. How she accomplished this is unclear. Nonetheless, she must die. Prayer is useful but no substitute for a strong rope.

Four quiet years later, the same devilish montage is revisited in nearby rural Salem Village, this time by young friends, one the minister's daughter, who howl, bray, cower in corners and under chairs, scream nonsensical utterances, contort their bodies, shriek at the sound of "The Lord's Prayer."

Having quickly exhausted any natural causes for the girls' actions, just one explanation remains, proclaim those close to the subjects. Witchcraft. The girls are bewitched, Mather and others surmise, and that leaves but one course: Find those evil persons in the community responsible for hexing these poor, afflicted innocents.

The search and ultimate disposition of those caught in this puritanical, superstitious web became known as the Salem Witch Trials. "Trials" is a misnomer, however, for what transpired was an inquisition. It engulfed that small Massachusetts hamlet and surrounding areas, and its residue claimed 24 lives, 19 hanged on Gallows Hill in Salem Town. Those hanged perhaps suffered a better fate than those who did not. Take the case of 80-year-old Giles Corey. After pleading not guilty to charges of witchcraft, he refused trial, so his accusers had him stripped naked and placed a board on his chest, putting as many stones on the board as it could stand. For two days, Corey's neighbors watched him die a slow, painful death.

The list of those condemned for witchcraft is homogeneous only by geography. Although people from outside Salem Village were charged, events began there, many of the examinations and trials were consummated there, and executions took place at nearby Gallows Hill on the outskirts of the village. Even as the hysteria spread beyond Salem Village, the afflicted area remained relatively small. About 27 percent of the accused came from nearby Andover, nearly the same amount as from Salem Village. Although everyone hanged had connections to Salem Village, Salem Town, Andover, or surrounding hamlets, they seemed marked more by differences than similarities. Men and woman, rich and poor, liked and disliked, religious and the not-so-religious. The hangman's noose had no favorites.

As Bernard Rosenthal points out in *Salem Story,* "The orgy of accusations cut across towns and villages and across gender, class, and age."[3] Rosenthal also provides an evenhanded overview of the "how" of events. "People fed all sorts of names to the accusers, either in sincere belief that a particular person was a witch, or for motives rooted in malice, greed, or the need to justify the proceedings." Rosenthal adds, however, that "no grand conspirator" hid in the background; "instead, varieties of individuals, for varying motives, responded to the open invitation of the society in which they lived to provide names to those who have been defined as the witchfinders of their day." He concludes that minus a broad conspiracy, "the context of events did 'conspire' to produce a continuous supply of fresh names for the accusers."[4]

Some victims did not even know the girls who accused them. Perhaps only one, Sarah Good, even knew why. The destitute Good, it seems, had committed the unpardonable, and very witchlike, sin of cursing neighbors and children for refusing her pleas for charity. Named as a witch by carib slave Tituba, corroborated by the afflicted girls and others, and supplemented by her four-year-old daughter (who had been imprisoned as well), Good's fate seemed preordained. Her answer to the charge was not. When, at the last moment, a local minister sought a confession from Good, she cried out from the scaffolding, "You are a lyer; I am not more a witch you are a wizard, and if you take away my life God will give you blood to drink."[5] Legend has it her curse came true when the minister, a man named Noyes, died of internal hemorrhage, bleeding profusely at the mouth.[6]

Good's response to her accusers was consistent with others charged. The vast majority proclaimed their innocence. Those who confessed did so either after facing jail, the harshness of the trial environment, coercion to confess, or intense pressure to implicate others in order to save themselves. Those who asserted their innocence faced the dilemma of proving it. Pitted against witchcraft charges, supplemented by the afflicted girls' timely fits, those persons accused had little chance for justice. The real story of the trials seems to be the inordinate amount of importance the court allocated to the accusation—and histrionics—of the "afflicted."

Take the case of Mary Easty. During her public exam for physical evidence of witch marks, Easty clenches her hands together. So does one of the afflicted girls in the room. When Easty tilts her head to hear a question, the girls scream for her to straighten her neck, claiming that as long as Easty's neck is bent, their necks are broken.[7] After two months in prison, Easty's release dismays the afflicted girls to such an extent they immediately suffer prolonged fits they claim are brought on by the apparition of, you guessed it, Mary Easty. On September 9, the court condemns Easty. Thirteen days later, she hangs.

Consider Mary Easty's 71-year-old sister, Rebecca Nurse. After 39 of Salem's prominent residents sign a petition on her behalf,[8] Nurse appears on the verge of being acquitted. At crucial moments of the trial, however, the afflicted girls suffer fits before both the magistrate and courtroom spectators, a deadly combination throughout the witch trials. In a rare moment of clarity, the court finds Nurse not guilty. An uproar from both audience and afflicted quickly follows, and after deliberating yet again, the court puts things right: It rules Nurse guilty. Nurse's story takes yet another twist when Governor William Phips grants her a reprieve. Almost immediately, her accusers have renewed fits, a sign to many residents that Nurse in fact is guilty.[9]

The final disposition of Nurse's case? Execution.

The sticking point in unraveling the "why" of this bizarre colonial tale is determining where the story begins. Clearly, village politics played a role in what transpired. The still unresolved question—how big a role?

In 1639, Salem Town acquired the legal right to settle land to the west, an area to be known as Salem Village. The village, therefore, did not exist as a separate entity from Salem Town, a point of contention for years. Twenty miles from Boston and eight miles distant from Salem Town, Salem Village was politically conflicted, primarily because about half the village (the farmers in the western portion) wanted to separate from Village Town. Those wishing to stay under the political auspices of Salem Town did so primarily because of economic ties with the thriving town.

When the village sought to hire its own minister, political bickering turned personal. One point is certain: Regarding the ministerial position, dissension in the village existed early on. In 1672, the residents hired James Bayley as the first preacher of Salem Village. Seven years later amid criticism, Bayley resigned. A year later in 1680, George Burroughs became the new preacher. Three years later he departed the village, eventually residing in Maine until trial officials abducted him from that colony, put him on trial for witchcraft, and hanged him. In 1684, Deodat Lawson succeeded Burroughs, and in 1687, a failed attempt to form a village church and ordain Lawson resulted in Lawson's departure as minister. A year later Lawson left the village, and Samuel Parris arrived. In 1689, Salem Village Church was established with Parris as the minister. Villagers divided over Parris, however, and two years after that in October 1691, Parris's opponents gained control of the Salem Village Parish Committee.[10]

Just two months later in December, Parris's 9-year-old daughter, Elizabeth, and 11-year-old niece, Abigail Williams, begin having "fits." By January 1692, accusations by the girls led to the first arrests for witchcraft. A three-step scenario from February through May proved simple and consistent: fits followed by charges, charges followed by examinations, examinations followed by imprisonment. From June to September, fourth and fifth steps were added: imprisonment followed by trials, trials followed by executions.

Since events under consideration occurred during Reverend Parris's tenure as village vicar, since almost every element from the fits to the penalties had religious underpinnings, and since events started with his daughter, niece, and servant, Parris undoubtedly played a significant role in how events unfolded.

It begins late in 1691. Several young girls meet in informal gatherings at which they apparently endeavor to use sorcery—perhaps learned from Parris's household slave, Tituba—to satiate curiosity about their futures. Tituba is a major character in the drama about to unfold. Originally from South America, she was taken to Barbados as a child and sold into slavery. At some point, she came to be owned by Parris and essentially ran his household. As the most prominent hypothesis goes, Tituba introduced the girls to native superstitions, thereby creating a "fatal spark"[11] that somehow overcame the adolescent girls. Although this is the favorite—and likely—hypothesis of many historians, it remains unproven.[12]

First to exhibit strange behavior: Elizabeth and Abigail. They scream blasphemies, endure convulsive seizures and body contortions, enter trance-like states, suffer mysterious spells. Parris has the local physician, William Griggs, examine the girls. His diagnosis? The girls may be affected by "The Evil Hand," that is, witchcraft.[13] At this point, seventeenth-century logic becomes evident. If Griggs is correct and the girls are not "diseased," it follows they are victims of witchcraft. That means a crime has been committed against them.

Parris then turns to other clergy for advice, many of whom, if not all, believe in witchcraft. Reverend John Hale, noting similarities to the Goodwin case, observed that the two girls

were bitten and pinched by invisible agents; their arms, necks, and backs turned this way and that way, and returned back again, so as it was impossible for them to do of themselves, and beyond the power of any Epilectick Fits, or natural Disease to effect. Sometimes they were dumb, their mouths stopped, their throats choaked, their limbs wracked and tormented so as might move an heart of stone, to sympathize with them.[14]

As rumors sweep about Salem Village, events take on a life of their own. In an attempt to reveal the witches responsible, Parris agrees to let Tituba and John Indian, the West Indian couple he owns, bake a witch cake—urine of the two girls mixed with rye meal—then feed it to a dog to observe its effects.[15]

The witch cake provides no answers, and when physical causes for Abigail and Betty's behavior still are not found, Parris remains fixated on spiritual causes. Within a month, however, Parris, with prominent residents and village officials, affix the cause: Satan.

By late February, Reverend Parris holds prayer services and asks for community fasting. Salem officials hold interrogations. Under pressure to identify someone as a witch, the two girls, along with newly "afflicted" Ann Putnam and Elizabeth Hubbard, name Sarah Good, Sarah Osborne, and Tituba.

On March 1, two members of the provincial legislature, Jonathan Corwin and John Hathorne, arrive in Salem to conduct public examinations of the accused. Again, events might have taken a different course if Corwin and Hathorne had been less zealous in their approach to the witchcraft examinations and trials. Hathorne's approach, in particular, differed markedly from Increase Mather's principle that "ten suspected witches should escape than that one innocent person should be condemned."[16] Hathorne, however, treats the accused as if they either conceal information or are outright liars. His approach to questioning can be summarized by his first question in the April examination of Deliverance Hobbs: "How come you to commit acts of Witchcraft?"[17]

In the first examinations conducted, Good and Osborne swear they are innocent, but Tituba, after denying any wrongdoing, confesses to practicing witchcraft, says she has seen the Devil in the form of animals—"sometimes like a hog and sometimes like a great dog"[18]—and claims a conspiracy of witches is at work in Salem. Tituba's confession is critical to the events that follow. If she had not given the magistrates—and Salem residents like Parris and others of his ilk—what they wanted to hear, the hearings may have ventured along less deadly avenues or perhaps even ended there. But that is speculation. She confessed, and events traveled a disastrous course. (Good's was a particularly tragic case. After being found guilty, she was chained and jailed. At the time, she was "either pregnant or had recently given birth, for during her imprisonment she is known to have been nursing an infant, which died in jail."[19])

About this time, several other village girls between the ages of 12 and 19 began to act similarly to the four already afflicted. Elizabeth Booth, Sarah Churchill, Rea Jemima, Mary Warren, Susannah Sheldon, Mercy Lewis, and Mary Walcott share symptoms of one form or another. Other females, some older and married, like Sarah Bibber, Bathshua Pope, and Ann Putnam, Sr., join the group over time.[20] As events run their course, however, Elizabeth Parris disappears from the picture after March, and Abigail Williams fades by July, while the older teenagers, Ann Putnam, Mercy Lewis, and Mary Walcott (all who live in the same household), continue their histrionics and are involved in the vast majority of accusations and convictions.[21]

By mid-March, other people testify to seeing strange apparitions of some community members. Accusations spread. Martha Corey is accused of witchcraft; Rebecca Nurse is denounced as a witch, as is Elizabeth Proctor and Sarah Cloyce. All endure examinations for "witch marks," signs of their witchcraft. All endure pretrial and trial questioning. All endure these before "friends" and neighbors. Those asking the questions generally assume guilt as a matter of course, and questions focus on the "how" rather than the "why."

The March 1 pretrial examination of hapless Sarah Good by Hathorne and recorded by Cotton Mather's teacher, Ezekiel Cheever, provides a model:

Hathorne: Sarah Good, what evil spirit have you familiarity with?

Good: None.

Hathorne: Have you made no contract with the devil?

(Good answers no.)

Hathorne: Why do you hurt these children?

Good: I do not hurt them. I scorn it.

Hathorne: Who do you employ, then, to do it?

Good: I employ nobody.

Hathorne: What creature do you employ then?

Good: No creature. But I am falsely accused.

Hathorne: Why did you go away muttering from Mr. Parris's house?

Good: I did not mutter, but I thanked him for what he gave my child.

Hathorne: Have you made no contract with the devil?

(At this juncture, the judge asks the afflicted girls to look at Good, who the girls name as their tormentor, then they immediately become possessed.)

Hathorne: Sarah Good, do you not see now what you have done? Why do you not tell us the truth?

Good: I do not torment them.[22]

As does Hathorne's prosecutorial questioning of Bridget Bishop, highlighted by his catch-22 question: "How do you know, you are no Witch & yet not know what a Witch is?"[23]

In part because the accused had no defense counsels, in part because they were prosecuted as much as judged, in part because spectral evidence—apparitions of their tormentors seen by accusers—left them in an indefensible position, in part because the victims and general public were allowed to participate in the examinations and trials, the accused could do little but assert their innocence. A flimsy defense but, essentially, their only defense:

William Hobbs: "I can deny it to my dying day."

Dorcas Hoar: "I will speak the truth as long as I live."

Bridget Bishop: "I am innocent . . . I know not what a witch is."

Rebecca Nurse: "I am as clear as the child unborn."

Elizabeth Howe: "If it was the last moment I was to live, God knows I am innocent . . ."

Martha Carrier: " . . . I am wronged. It is a shameful thing that you should mind these folks that are out of their wits."

George Jacobs, Sr.: " . . . I am falsely accused. I never did it."

Mary Bradbury: "I do plead not guilty. I am wholly innocent of such wickedness."

Mary Easty: " . . . if it be possible no more Innocent blood be shed. . . . I am clear of this sin."[24]

And so on.

Some of the accused—Margaret Jacobs, for example—did confess, but usually with a caveat:

Jacobs: "They told me if I would not confess I should be put down into the dungeon and would be hanged, but if I would confess I should save my life."[25]

In April, the hysteria resembles an infectious disease spreading like a wildfire across communities. By April 11, the next examinations are held in Salem Town rather than Salem Village, "and not before Hathorne and Corwin only, but before the deputy governor, six magistrates, and a 'very great assembly.' "[26] Next to be examined are Abigail Hobbs, Bridget Bishop, Giles Corey, and Mary Warren. Abigail Hobbs confesses. Soon after, Nehemiah Abbott, William and Deliverance Hobbs, Edward and Sarah Bishop, Mary Easty, Mary Black, Sarah Wildes, and Mary English are examined. Abbott is cleared of charges.

At this point, no trials have been held, the prisons are overflowing with accused witches, and charges keep coming.

By May, Sarah Morey, Lydia Dustin, Susannah Martin, and Dorcas Hoar are examined. A few days later, George Burroughs is arrested in Wells, Maine. George Jacobs, Sr. and granddaughter Margaret also are examined. Margaret testifies that her grandfather and George Burroughs are witches.

Meanwhile, Sarah Osborne dies in her Boston prison cell. Mary Easty is released, then soon arrested again. By now, about 200 people are imprisoned, primarily because of spectral evidence provided via the afflicted, who are kept quite busy by the vast covey of witches in the area.

Also in May, Governor William Phips establishes a special Court of Oyer and Terminer to try the witchcraft cases. Those appointed include Lieutenant Governor William Stoughton (the chief judge), Nathaniel Saltonstall (who resigned soon after, unhappy with the direction of the proceedings), Hathorne and Corwin, and other prominent citizens. All were from Boston or Salem, except for Saltonstall, a Haverhill resident.

Acceptable evidence admitted by the court includes intangible and spectral evidence, direct confessions, the victims' actions, and witch marks.

With the coming of June, the court decides Bridget Bishop's fate. Although she claims innocence throughout the proceedings, Bishop is hanged on June 10, the first official execution of the Salem witch trials. It would not be the last. Also in June, Rebecca Nurse, Susannah Martin, Sarah Wildes, Sarah Good, and Elizabeth Howe are condemned and executed a month later. Says Howe: "God knows I am innocent."[27]

In July, tentacles of fear continue to spread as Joseph Ballard of nearby Andover enlists the help of the young Salem victims to expose witches there. In August, George Jacobs Sr., Martha Carrier, George Burroughs, John and Elizabeth Proctor, and John Willard are condemned. All but Elizabeth Proctor are hanged a few days later on Gallows Hill.

In September, Martha Corey, Mary Easty, Alice Parker, Ann Pudeator, Dorcas Hoar, Mary Bradbury, Margaret Scott, Wilmott Redd, Samuel Wardwell, Mary Parker, Abigail Faulkner, Rebecca Eames, Mary Lacy, Ann Foster, and Abigail Hobbs are condemned. A few days later, Giles Corey is pressed to death. Dorcas Hoar, who originally pled innocent, confesses to witchcraft. About the same time, Martha Corey, Margaret Scott, Mary Easty, Alice Parker, Ann Pudeator, Wilmott Redd, Samuel Wardwell, and Mary Parker are hanged.

By now, 20 people have been executed, many more have been jailed, and more of the citizenry is questioning the entire process. Governor Phips begins to receive harsh criticism, while at the same time his wife is named as a witch. The governor then orders that spectral and intangible evidence be excluded from further proceedings. Within days, he dissolves the court. Remaining cases are heard a year later in superior courts. No one is convicted.

The witchcraft hysteria is ended.

Viewed through modern and perhaps slightly rose-colored lenses, the hysteria surrounding the witchcraft trials appears more like a gothic horror film than life in colonial America. In 1692, the fear of witchcraft reflected a common attitude among residents of the Bay Colony. What occurred that year was in some ways a reenactment of events in Europe, yet in many ways it was a unique Salem phenomenon.

According to Hans Sebald, author of *Witch-Children,* the Salem episode was characterized by a number of features uncommon to European witch trials. "The persecution came on fast, like a tornado, tore through the community, and was gone within about a year's time"[28] compared to the European witch-hunts stretching over several centuries. In addition, restitution and official declarations of regret were made to the victims or to the victims' families, people who were not lower class or disreputable citizens as was usually the case in Europe.[29] Also, the accused displayed highly individualistic personalities unlike their European counterparts.[30] Finally, and perhaps most important, when the madness in Salem ended, witchcraft no longer was viewed as "a civil deviance, a punishable crime."[31]

Bernard Rosenthal expressed the differences between Salem and other witch-hunts in even simpler terms, calling the events in Salem unique in "the annals of witchcraft trials" because they "reversed the traditional rules whereby confessing witches were executed: In Salem, only those who did not confess were executed."[32]

Features that proved consistent with previous witch-hunts included the children's hysteria, their accusations, the unquestioned creditability granted to the children's testimony,[33] the quick trials, condemnations and hangings, and the "role of neighbor's quarrels and denunciations."[34]

Still, the question beckons: What caused this tragedy? Is it possible mass hysteria could last as long as it took for the accusation, trials, and executions to take place? Surely, it was not a case of outright fraud, given the gravity of the charge and the youth of the girls. Could other factors have been at work? Yes, say some scientists who postulate that the girls suffered from ergotism, a form of fungus poisoning that could cause delirium, hallucinations, muscular contractions, and even seizures and dementia.[35] True, ergotism would cause delusions, and the winter of 1691 had been particularly wet, which may have led to the growth of ergot in the grain supply, but that answers little as to the actions of the residents, judges, and clergy. Harder to support is speculation by some physicians that the bizarre outbursts of the girls were "symptoms of 'post traumatic stress syndrome,' induced by the drudgery of daily life or perhaps by abuse from stern parents."[36]

A more narrow question, perhaps more baffling than the first, also begs to be asked: Why did the children act as they did? Why would young girls for months act in such a consistent fashion to such a deleterious effect? Sebald's answer: "When a community screams out in horror of witches, children are quick to seize the day by using accusation to transport all sorts of emotional want and distress." Adding: "[T]he plethora of emotions and motives include guilt, fear, rebellion, revenge, seeking status and praise, derring-do, the ecstasy of power, and sometimes pure malice." His simple conclusion: "[T]he suggestibility is two-sided: Children manipulate adults as much as adults manipulate them, and neither side is usually aware of it."[37]

Sebald also writes that the girls "were judged to be possessed—which included the understanding that they suffered innocently and against their will"—and that their "behavior remained unpunished and even escalated into ever greater hysteria, as they took advantage of the opportunity to rebel against the restrictions imposed by tradition and adult society." Sebald explains that only the villagers' unshakable belief in the power of the Devil explains "why they felt pity and compassion for the 'poor suffering children,' instead of punishing them for offensive behavior. In fact, the hysterical youths achieved the status of celebrities."[38]

Did Abigail and Betty read *Memorable Providences,* Mather's book about demonic possession, then act out? Quite possibly. Since Parris owned a copy, a reasonable assumption would be that the original two "afflicted" children (and perhaps Tituba) either read it or had it read to them. Past experience also may have played a role in the genesis of events at Salem. The Parris family was quite familiar with the Goodwin case since they lived in Boston at the time. In fact, "they might have seen the actual hanging, taking along, as tradition allowed, little Betty."[39]

Written accounts of witchcraft cases in England also existed in Massachusetts Bay Colony, and, as Thomas Hutchinson witnessed, "the conformity between the behavior of Goodwin's children and most of the supposed bewitched at Salem, and the behavior of those in England, is so exact, as to leave no room to doubt the stories had been read by the New England persons themselves, or had been told to them by others who had read them."[40]

In addition, the strong religious foundation of the Massachusetts Bay Colony created a perfect environment for the fermentation of superstitious fears. The essential source for interpretation of events was the Bible—as interpreted by church leaders—many of whom viewed events much like Parris, Lawson, Hale, and the Mathers and all of whom served the function of modern-day media. Long before the witch trials, the pulpit had been a forum for the dissemination and interpretation of current events.

Largely neglected from the picture painted thus far is one of the Bay Colony's best-known figures, the minister of Boston's Old North Church, Cotton Mather. Mather's influence on events should not be minimized. His writings made him an "expert" on witchcraft, thus giving him status far above the role of observer. In addition, three of the five judges were members of his church as well as friends. Mather's input, although unclear, certainly influenced the court and probably Governor Phips. Although Mather seemed distressed with court procedures at times, in a statement to the governor he recommended that "for the Detection of Witchcrafts," the "speedy and vigorous Prosecution of such as have rendered themselves obnoxious" according to the laws of God and to English statues.[41] In a sermon given August 4, Mather seemed to support the notion of spectral evidence when he said that witches "have their spectres, or Devils, commissioned by them, and representing of them."[42] Here lies the problem with interpreting Mather's position. His vagueness allowed him to be ambidextrous with the thorny issues running throughout the entire witchcraft frenzy. One definitive Mather suggestion to the court, however, was that the accused be required to recite the Lord's Prayer[43] since it was widely believed that witches could not say that prayer correctly, a contention of Mather's in the Goodwin case.

Particularly critical to the legal proceedings was the acceptance of spectral evidence since it was an accepted notion that people possessed were clairvoyant—sometimes referred to as having second sight—and could therefore see spirits. Since the Devil could not assume the appearance of an innocent person, it logically followed that any apparitions the girls saw were either devils or witches.[44]

Also, the degree to which the judges either believed the girls or were willing to ignore the obvious cannot be overstated. During proceedings against Sarah Good, one of the afflicted girls cried out she was being stabbed with a knife by the apparition of Good. When a broken knife was found on the girl, and when a man testified he had broken it the day before and some of the afflicted girls had seen him thrown it away, the court warned the girl not to lie again, then moved on as though nothing out of the ordinary had occurred. As already related, Good was found guilty and hanged.

The importance of gossip and rumor, supplemented by "scholarly tracts" about witchcraft and the supernatural, should not be underestimated. Clearly, nebulous and provocative hearsay helped form, then cement, public opinion. What media were available appear to have supported the hysteria. Increase Mather's essay on the Devil and witchcraft, *An Essay for the Recording of Illustrious Providence* (published in 1684) and Cotton's *Memorable Providences Relating to Witchcraft and Possession* (published in 1689), promoted the concept of demonic possession and had widespread circulation in the Bay Colony.[45] Other books, particularly secular books, may have had a slight dulling effect on superstitious beliefs, but witchcraft fears proliferated and were viewed as a battle between good and evil.

Just as the printing press and, later, the Internet have exponentially increased the number of information outlets and improved cross-pollination of ideas from different fields of study, they also have provided outlets for rumor and misinformation. The relatively new print culture of the colonial period proved fertile ground for this, and printed materials associated with the occult proliferated. Regarding the early effects of the printing press in fifteenth-, sixteenth-, and seventeenth-century Europe, historian Elizabeth Eisenstein writes that few "readers could discriminate between the two (fantasy and reality)"[46] and that "new forms of mystification were encouraged.[47] . . . When 'technology went to press,' so too did a vast backlog of occult lore."[48] It follows that the same applied for colonial America. The result? A growing belief in the occult by both church and lay members. Clearly, this describes the belief system in place at the Bay Colony.

No newspapers existed in the colonies at the time of the witchcraft hysteria, although two years earlier the first colonial newspaper, *Publick Occurrences, Both Foreign and Domestick,* was published in Boston. Unfortunately, it survived only one printing, and another newspaper would not be established until 1704, again in Boston. There is no evidence, however, that the existence of newspapers would have altered public opinion, particularly since newspapers existed in Europe during countless witchcraft prosecutions and executions.

It is entirely possible that the presence of newspapers would have exacerbated the witchcraft frenzy. In the mid-twentieth century, a remarkably similar tapestry to the Salem trials was woven with fear, guilt by association, and finger-pointing. In 1950, media coverage of Senator Joseph McCarthy's charges of communists in the State Department magnified his unsubstantiated, "spectral" claims; helped ruin previously spotless reputations; and assisted in laying a foundation from which the "Multiple Untruth" was tilled, sowed, and harvested.[49] As McCarthy biographer Richard Rovere writes in *Senator Joe McCarthy,* the Multiple Untruth is a technique comparable in many respects to Hitler's "Big Lie" since it need not be "a particularly large untruth but can be a long series of loosely related untruths, or a single untruth with many facts."[50] Rovere adds that the Multiple Untruth is "composed of so many parts that any one wishing to set the record straight will discover that it is utterly impossible to keep all of the falsehood in mind at the same time."[51] The Multiple Untruth certainly played well in Salem from the moment Tituba said Sarah Good was a witch and the young girls claimed they were afflicted by Sarah Good, Sarah Osborne and Tituba. Tituba then claimed Sarah Good to be the culprit. Soon after, Good's daughter Dorcas points to her mother. A recurring pattern was thus established and continued throughout the spring and summer. Afflicted accuses, accusee denies but sometimes points to a relative or a neighbor, and relative or neighbor points elsewhere. People from across the area, anxious to stay off the "witch list," point in all directions. With so many people and directions, the amount of charges escalated to the point that even the most practical person would find it hard to keep track and might believe that some truth to the charges, no matter how small, existed.

Another connection between McCarthy and the witch-hunts exists—believability based on status. McCarthy's position as a senator helped substantiate his claims with many Americans who questioned some of his facts but not his basic point that communists worked for the U.S. government. Could a U.S. senator make such authoritative claims without there being some truth to them? The answer for many was no. The claim itself provided some sort of validation. In Salem, authority figures like Parris, Cotton Mather, and other clerics; the judges and the governor; and many of the respected members of the community lent credibility to the claims of the afflicted girls that witches were at work in the heart of their community. Could men of God make such authoritative claims without there being some truth to them? The answer for many Salem residents was no. The trials themselves provided some sort of validation.

The media furthered McCarthy's self-serving goals through its unwillingness or inability to call into question the validity of the senator's charges against innocent and defenseless victims. One reason for this was unwillingness on the part of the twentieth-century media to question, then challenge, authority figures. To believe that a seventeenth-century medium would act differently lacks substance and believability.

Interestingly, Arthur Miller's *The Crucible,* a play set in 1692 Salem, illustrates the parallels between the two periods. In compelling fashion, the play reveals the symmetry among the witchcraft and communist hysterias and the witch-hunts accompanying both.

As eccentric as the Salem events appear with twenty-first-century hindsight, cases of mass hysteria no less bizarre have occurred in contemporary times. In 1938, the "War of the Worlds" radio broadcast left media analysts scrambling to explain the mass hysteria associated with a perceived threat from Mars. Common threads between events in 1692 and 1938 not only exist but are strongly compelling. First, neither hysteria was founded in fact. Second, the contemporary settings for each had a significant impact on both events.

In 1938, radio had become the primary source of news, and "on the scene" reporting was a new, welcome, and highly believable reporting technique. In addition, the "War of the Worlds" broadcast came at a stressful economic time that was worsened by the threat of a major war filling the horizon. In 1692, the witchcraft hysteria came at a stressful time when the residents of Salem Village felt conflicted over their church leadership and, perhaps more important, felt particularly vulnerable to Indian attacks.

Reactions in both 1692 and 1938 were based, in part, on religious beliefs. In the Massachusetts Bay Colony, Puritan beliefs fostered a confrontational attitude between what many viewed as outside forces—God and the Devil. As Sebald so aptly puts it, "It seems that the Puritans of New England were more Devil-fearing than God-fearing."[52]

Americans in 1938 were not so different. The definitive study of the causes of hysteria emanating from the "War of the Worlds" broadcast found that people with strong religious beliefs were likely to think that the Martian invasion was an act of God and that the end of the world was near. This sheds light on the hysteria in Salem. In 1692, the Devil no longer waited at the gates—he had entered Salem. Indecision meant death or, worse, loss of salvation. Many residents acted as they believed God-fearing people must act. In 1938, the existence of Martians challenged people to evaluate their core beliefs, forcing many to consider other worldviews.[53] With little time to incorporate new concepts and restructure belief systems, the resulting mass hysteria becomes easy to understand.

Another point: Both events were gripping because of the believability of essential information sources. In 1692, it was friends, neighbors, and, to a large degree, clergy; in 1938, it was radio.

Now a few noteworthy footnotes to this bizarre tale:

Some researchers argue that both Increase and Cotton Mather strongly opposed the use of spectral evidence in the trials, and Increase and Cotton did make such statements—until the case of George Burroughs. A former minister of the Salem flock, Burroughs had been plucked from his home in Wells, Maine, and returned to Salem, where he admitted to the court that he had not taken communion in some time, nor had he had his children baptized (except the oldest). Either Burroughs had lost his faith or he held dissident religious views. In short, Burroughs sounded much like a Baptist, and before a Puritan court, this did not bode well for the defendant.[54] The subject of baptism—and rebaptism either by the Devil or Burroughs (at times indistinguishable)—ran throughout his trial. As Bernard Rosenthal writes, "The backlash against the Baptists made him (Burroughs) an exemplary monster and appropriate metaphor for what the orthodox saw as the ungodly religious wave of the future."[55] The result? Increase and Cotton approved of the hanging of Burroughs, even though Burroughs did what Cotton had written was impossible: He recited the Lord's Prayer perfectly the day of his execution.

After hearing rumors that his wife soon would be named a witch, Increase Mather wrote *Cases of Conscience,* in which he generally debunks the use of spectral evidence but somehow manages to approve of the judicial proceedings, perhaps to avoid any conflict with son Cotton's position, which appeared much more conflicted and convoluted than his father's.[56]

Once the trials ended and the hysteria died down, Cotton Mather received the official court records and published a book of the events titled *Wonders of the Invisible World.* Whether he ever changed his opinions about the validity of spectral evidence remains unclear.

If religious beliefs played a major role in perpetuating the witch hysteria, religious leaders were no less important. Besides Samuel Parris's obvious involvement, both Increase and Cotton Mather were crucial to the flow of events. But so were others. Samuel Cheever, John Higginson, and Nicholas Noyes, all of Salem Town, took active roles as events unfolded, as did Samuel Willard of Boston, John Hale of Beverly, and Deodat Lawson of Scituate. George Burroughs's unfortunate involvement has already been documented.

One of the unfortunates charged with witchcraft but not executed was young Abigail Hobbs. After being arrested, she confessed and implicated her parents, Deliverance and William. Deliverance was arrested, and after intense questioning, she confessed, implicated her husband, and was eventually set free. Of the three, William never confessed to being a witch, although he remained in prison until December 1693. After being released, he left town.

By the spring of 1693, Governor William Phips pardoned all those imprisoned for witchcraft. Two years later, he died.

As Chief Justice of the Court of Oyer and Terminer, William Stoughton, perhaps because of both "his past theological training and lack of legal training, allowed many deviations from normal courtroom procedure during the witchcraft trials."[57] Other noteworthy aspects to the judicial process, besides the admittance of spectral evidence, included private conversations between accusers and judges, spectators interrupting the procedures with personal remarks, no defense counsel allowed for the accused, and judges acting as prosecutors.

Samuel Sewall later apologized for his role as judge on the Court of Oyer and Terminer. Sewall also achieved historical renown by writing in 1700 the first antislavery publication in the colonies, *The Selling of Joseph*.[58]

Ann Putnam, one of the Salem "afflicted," came close to admitting a fraud had been perpetuated when in 1706 she told fellow churchgoers the following:

I desire to be humbled before God for that sad and humbling providence that befell my father's family in the year about '92; that I, then being in my childhood, should, by such a providence of God, be made an instrument for the accusing of several persons of a grievous crime, whereby their lives were taken away from them, whom now I have just grounds and good reason to believe they were innocent persons; and that it was a great delusion of Satan that deceived me in that sad time, whereby I justly fear I have been instrumental, with others, though ignorantly and unwittingly, to bring upon myself and this land the guilt of innocent blood; though what was said or done by me against any person I can truly and uprightly say, before God and man, I did it not out of any anger, malice, or ill-will to any person.[59]

At age 37, Putnam died in 1716.

Although George Burroughs's reality was horrific at the end of his life, he became a hero of fiction. In *Rachel Dyer* (1828), by John Neal, he was the novel's protagonist. Burroughs also appears in Durward Grinstead's *Elva* (1929).

Embarrassed by his grandfather's (John Hathorne) role in the trials, the great American author Nathaniel Hawthorne changed the spelling of his name. One of Hawthorne's most notable works was *The House of Seven Gables,* a novel that displays elements drawn from the witch trials. As the story goes, the House of Seven Gables was built by Colonel Pyncheon, but the land was owned by Matthew Maule. When he refuses to sell the land to Pyncheon, Maule is charged with witchcraft and burned. Just before being executed, however, he utters the famous words of Sarah Good: "God will give him blood to drink."[60]

In *The House of Seven Gables,* Hawthorne's attitudes about witchcraft in general and about Salem in particular might be gleaned from the following passage:

Old Matthew Maule, in a word, was executed for the crime of witchcraft. He was one of the martyrs to that terrible delusion, which should teach us, among its other morals, that the influential classes, and those who take upon themselves to be leaders of the people, are fully liable to all the passionate error that has ever characterized the maddest mob. Clergymen, judges, states-men,—the wisest, calmest, holiest persons of their day,—stood in the inner circle round about the gallows, loudest to applaud the word of blood, latest to confess themselves miserably de-ceived.[61]

Some noteworthy writers that either based works on or made mention of the Salem witch trials include Hawthorne in *The Scarlet Letter,* Henry Wadsworth Longfellow in "Giles Corey of the Salem Farms" in *The New-England Tragedies,* Mary Wilkins Free-man in *Giles Corey, Yeoman,* J. W. DeForest in *Witching Times,* Arthur Miller in *The Crucible,* Alison Lurie in *Imaginary Friends,* and Ann Rinaldi in *A Break with Charity.* Two films, *The Crucible and Three Sovereigns for Sarah: A True Story,* tell the story cinematically.

In 1992, 300 years after the fact, the First Church of Salem voted to readmit Giles Cory and Rebecca Nurse—both had been excommunicated—to the Unitarian Church.[62]

At present, Salem (not Salem Village, which is now named Danvers) has turned itself into a tourist attraction based on the witchcraft legacy. Drive into Boston and head east, and you find a twentieth-century town juxtaposed against a seventeenth-century motif. Even today, the Salem trials live on.

Looking back through the mists of 300 years, the witch trials leave us with more questions than answers. Are we too far removed, too sophisticated, too secular, to make sense of events? Perhaps the mystery of Salem is as simple— and as complex—as the human animal. Perhaps the answer lies in the inhab-itants' belief that if they have the truth from God, no room for compromise exists. Given that real possibility, puritanical determination fueled by their fear provides us an answer.

For a few moments, leave behind twenty-first-century trappings. Turn down the television, pause the CD player, attend to the e-mail later. Journey back in time to seventeenth-century New England. Put down your looking glass and observe, not from a distance but up close. See for yourself. Feel the villagers' fear. Listen:

Evil lives here, a foul evil crawling about the minds of our young innocents. Even now, it eats away at the sanity of dear Betty Parris, her sweet cousin, Abigail, and the comely Ann Putnam.

The Evil One has invaded our village to caress the souls of his wicked paramours. How many have signed their names to his unholy book? We can but thank God for the afflicted, for without their infirmities those enemies who appear as neighbors and friends would pass undetected.

See, there across Hadlock's Bridge walks Sarah Good, wretched woman she be. Her evil muttering to the hamlet's children condemn her. Even daughter Dorcas condemns her. No one's guilt is surer than Sarah Good's.

And that trollop, Bridget Bishop. No Puritan, she. Married three times. She drinks. She laughs too loud. She dresses inappropriately. That red boddice, but one obvious example. A devil's snare.

And those horrid sisters, Rebecca Nurse and Mary Easty. Oh, how it pains my heart to admit I once called them friends, yet Nurse always gave the appearance of being a God-fearing woman. How were we to know? Yet, when that 71-year-old blaspheming witch cried out the name of God at her trial, her pitiful victims—Abigail, Ann, and the other afflicted—immediately fell into fits. In that telling moment, Nurse proved her guilt beyond doubt.

And Nurse's sister. See, there she walks, across the way by the meetinghouse. Thinking herself safe now that she be freed from jail. But just wait, Mary Easty. Your deeds will hang you. Sooner rather than later. . . . And still, one wonders about that the third sister, Sarah Cloyse.

Thank God their leader has been discovered and jailed. George Burroughs. No man of God, that. A sorcerer who tempted dear Mercy Lewis in the foulest of manners. As Mercy testified before us and before God, Burroughs brought her to a mountain so high she could see all the kingdoms of the earth, all offered up to her if she but sign his book.[63] God save us all from this scourge, Satan's disciple in Salem.

God grant us strength to stay the course, to do what we must to free ourselves from this curse that plagues the land and our sweet, sweet home. Salem.

NOTES

1. A complete map of Salem Village and the surrounding area can be found in volume 1 of Charles W. Upham's *Salem Witchcraft, with an account of Salem Village and A History of Opinions on Witchcraft and Kindred Subjects* (1867; reprint, Williamstown, Mass.: Corner House, 1971).

2. Increase Mather published *An Essay for the Recording of Illustrious Providence* in 1684. In 1689, Cotton published *Memorable Providences, Relating to Witchcrafts and Possessions* (Boston, 1689).

3. Bernard Rosenthal, *Salem Story: Reading the Witch Trials of 1692* (New York: Cambridge University Press, 1993), 192.

4. Ibid.

5. Cited in Rosenthal's *Salem Story*, 87, from Robert Calef, "More Wonders of the Invisible World" (1700), and reprinted in part in *Narratives of the Witchcraft Cases 1649–1706*, ed. George Lincoln Burr (New York: Charles Scribner's Sons, 1914), 289–394.

6. The story first appeared in Thomas Hutchinson, *The History of the Colony and Province of Massachusetts-Bay (1764)*, vol. 2, ed. Laurence Shaw Mayo (Cambridge, Mass.: Harvard University Press, 1936), 41. In *Salem Story*, Rosenthal does not say it did not happen, only that it was legend.

7. Paul Boyer and Stephen Nissenbaum, eds., *The Salem Witchcraft Papers* (New York: Da Capo Press, 1977), 361. For easy access see the complete text of the *Salem Witchcraft Papers* as edited by Boyer and Nissenbaum, http://etext.virginia.edu/salem/witchcraft/texts. This site provides the transcripts in three volumes as well as accompanying analysis. See Mary Easty, 288, ibid.

8. Upham, *Salem Witchcraft, with an Account of Salem Village and A History of Opinions on Witchcraft and Kindred Subjects,* vol. 2, 272.

9. Boyer and Nissenbaum, *The Salem Witchcraft Papers.* See Rebecca Nurse, http://www.law.umkc.edu/faculty/projects/ftrials/salem.

10. In *Salem Possessed: The Social Origins of Witchcraft* (Cambridge, Mass.: Harvard University Press, 1974), Paul Boyer and Stephen Nissenbaum continue the history of church struggles. In March 1694, Parris supporters regained control of the parish committee, and a month later an ecclesiastical council headed by Increase Mather met at Salem Village. The council recommended that Parris resign. Approximately 84 villagers favored the recommendation; 105 opposed it. In June, Salem Village Church supported Parris, who remained minister until 1699, when he resigned and was replaced by Joseph Green.

11. See Calef, "More Wonders of the Invisible World"; Burr, *Narratives of the Witchcraft Cases 1649–1706,* 342; and Rosenthal, *Salem Story,* 11.

12. Ibid.

13. See Calef, "More Wonders of the Invisible World," 342; Samuel Parris, "Meditations for Peace," Church Records, 26 November 1694; and Boyer and Nissenbaum, *Salem Possessed,* 2.

14. Rev. John Hale, "A Modest Inquiry," in *Narratives of the Witchcraft Cases 1648–1706,* ed. George Lincoln Burr (New York: Charles Scribner's Sons, 1914), 413.

15. As indicated by Boyer and Nissenbaum in *Salem Possessed,* the dog displayed no ill effects from the witch cake, and Parris subsequently publicly reprimanded the resident who originated the idea of the cake.

16. Increase Mather, *Cases of Conscience Concerning evil Spirits personating Man, Witchcrafts, infallible Proofs of Guilt in such as are accused with that Crime, All Considered according to the Scriptures, History, Experience, and the Judgment of many Learned men* (Boston, 1692), 66.

17. Boyer and Nissenbaum, *The Salem Witchcraft Papers.* See Deliverance Hobbs, http://www.law.umkc.edu/faculty/projects/ftrials/salem, 419.

18. Boyer and Nissenbaum, *The Salem Witchcraft Papers.* See Tituba, http://www.law.umkc.edu/faculty/projects/ftrials/salem, 361.

19. Kenneth Silverman, *The Life and Times of Cotton Mather* (New York: Columbia University Press, 1985), 97.

20. Rosenthal, *Salem Story,* 41.

21. Ibid.

22. Boyer and Nissenbaum, *The Salem Witchcraft Papers.* See Sarah Good, http://www.law.umkc.edu/faculty/projects/ftrials/salem, 356.

23. Ibid., 84.

24. Boyer and Nissenbaum, *The Salem Witchcraft Papers.* See http://etext.lib.virginia.edu/salem/witchcraft/texts, 426, 390, 84, 505, 434, 185, 475, 116, 304.

25. Boyer and Nissenbaum, *The Salem Witchcraft Papers.* See Margaret Jacobs, http://etext.lib.virginia.edu/salem/witchcraft/texts, 491.

26. Boyer and Nissenbaum, *Salem Possessed,* 5.

27. Boyer and Nissenbaum, *The Salem Witchcraft Papers.* See Elizabeth Howe (her name is spelled "How" in the original Salem trial documents), http://etext.lib.virginia.edu/salem/witchcraft/texts, 434.

28. Hans Sebald, *Witch-Children, from Salem Witch-Hunts to Modern Courtrooms* (Amherst, N.Y.: Prometheus Books, 1995), 67.

29. Ibid., 68.

30. Ibid.

31. Ibid.

32. Rosenthal, *Salem Story*, 28–29.

33. Sebald, *Witch-Children*, 68.

34. Ibid.

35. The original theory connecting ergotism to the hysteria appears in Linnda Caporael's "Ergotism: The Satan Loosed in Salem?" *Science* 192, no. 4234 (April 2, 1976): 25; see also *The Economist,* "The Misogyny, Ergot, or Envy? The Salem Witch-Trials," 16 May 1992. For symptoms, see Alan Woolf, "Witchcraft or Mycotoxin? The Salem Witch Trials," *Journal of Toxicology: Clinical Toxicology* 38, no. 4 (June 2000), 457–460.

36. *The Economist,* "The Misogyny, Ergot, or Envy?"

37. Sebald, *Witch-Children*, 237.

38. Ibid., 70.

39. Ibid., 69, as cited from Marion Starkey, *The Devil in Massachusetts: A Modern Enquiry into the Salem Witch Trials* (New York: Knopf, 1949), 22.

40. Lawrence Shaw Mayo, ed., *The History of the Colony and Province of Massachusetts-Bay (1764),* vol. 2 (Cambridge, Mass.: Harvard University Press, 1936), 414–15.

41. Cotton Mather letter to Governor Phips, "The Return of Several Minister," (1692). See also Silverman, *The Life and Times of Cotton Mather,* 100.

42. Silverman, *The Life and Times of Cotton Mather,* 108.

43. Rosenthal, *Salem Story,* 146.

44. Sebald, *Witch-Children,* 72.

45. See Douglas Linder, "An Account of Events in Salem" at http://www.aw.umkc.edu/faculty/projects/ftrials/salem/salem.htm. Also see Rosenthal, *Salem Story,* 2.

46. For a complete look at the impact of the invention of movable type, see Elizabeth Eisenstein, *The Printing Revolution in Early Modern Europe* (New York: Cambridge University Press, 1983). Eisenstein discusses the changes brought about by printing on society and the individual. For specifics detailing public opinion regarding fantasy and the occult, see pp. 129, 141–42.

47. Ibid.

48. Ibid.

49. Richard Rovere, *Senator Joe McCarthy* (New York: Harper Colophon, 1959), 109–10.

50. Ibid.

51. Ibid.

52. Sebald, *Witch-Children,* 67.

53. See Hadley Cantril, *The Invasion from Mars: A Study in the Psychology of Panic* (Princeton, N.J.: Princeton University Press, 1940).

54. Rosenthal, *Salem Story,* 132–35.

55. Ibid., 135.

56. Mather, *Cases of Conscience Concerning evil Spirits Personating Man.* See also Rosenthal, *Salem Story,* 134–38.

57. See the profile of Stoughton at http://www.law.umkc.edu/faculty/projects,trials/salem.

58. Samuel Sewell, *The Selling of Joseph, a Memorial* (Boston, 1700). Reprinted from an original in George H. Moore, *Notes on the History of Slavery in Massachusetts* (New York, 1866).

59. Upham, *Salem Witchcraft, with an Account of Salem Village, and A History of Opinions on Witchcraft and Kindred Subjects,* vol. 2, 510.

60. Nathaniel Hawthorne, *House of Seven Gables* (Cambridge, Mass.: Houghton Mifflin, 1924), 21.

61. Ibid., 20.

62. Sebald, *Witch-Children,* 68.

63. See Mercy Lewis testimony in Boyer and Nissenbaum, *The Salem Witchcraft Papers.* See http://etext.lib.virginia.edu/salem/witchcraft/texts; see also Rosenthal, *Salem Story,* 134.

2

THE CASE OF THE *AMISTAD* MUTINY (1839–1840)

Bernell E. Tripp

"Give us free! Give us free!"

Throughout the day, the opposing counsel detailed the case against the Africans. Wrapped in a white blanket that exposed only his head, Joseph Cinquez remained silent as he squatted on his haunches among a dozen other Africans, rousing slightly only when someone mentioned his name during the court proceedings. In the afternoon, U.S. District Attorney William S. Holabird turned to challenge Cinquez, the group-appointed leader. "Who killed the captain? Who killed the crew?" he shouted, almost too rapidly for the interpreter, James Covey, to translate the words into Mendi, Cinquez's native tongue.

As the onslaught of question after question assailed him, Cinquez finally propelled himself to his feet and tossed aside the blanket to reveal the red flannel shirt and white duck pantaloons he had worn while on the *Amistad*. At first, Covey translated Cinquez's words as rapidly as they were spoken. However, Cinquez's passionate account soon became too spirited for Covey to follow. His frenzied story related in Mendi gave way to gestures and movements that mimicked his experiences aboard ship. His hands lashed forward, sometimes grabbing his throat like a noose as he tried to justify the fight to free himself and his brethren. At other times, he demonstrated how the Spaniards had examined the Africans to ascertain if they were healthy. Finally, his voice crescendoed in Mendi before dissolving into a shriek in English.

"Give us free! Give us free!" he implored the crowd.

"I object. Take this man out of Court. He will have an unfair influence on decisions!" Holabird proclaimed, too late to prevent the effect of Cinquez's impassioned words on everyone in the room. Abolitionist Lewis Tappan bowed his head and sighed in relief.[1] He had provided the abolitionist movement with a "safe cause" in this simple pursuit of liberty as well as a new hero with which to spur both civic and political action against slavery.

Besides the pure emotional drama of the *Amistad* case, it raised numerous questions regarding slavery and racial prejudice and their relevance in determining nineteenth-century liberties. While the Africans' case failed to strike a death blow against the institution of slavery, it played a pivotal role in determining the path of the abolitionist movement during the decades leading up to the Civil War.

A story that started with the abduction of an African by the name of Sengbe Pieh, a Mende villager to become known in the United States as "Cinquez,"[2] followed a bizarre path into American history. What began with the seizure of one "insignificant" African resulted in a battle that ended with a small Spanish schooner called the *Amistad* winding its way to the top of the judicial ladder—the U.S. Supreme Court—as it made its mark on American society racially, politically, and morally.

The case of the *Amistad* began in West Africa, either in Sierra Leone or in neighboring Liberia. Sengbe Pieh was illegally "stolen" like so many other West Africans—in the open near his village home. Sengbe's enslavement was rather ordinary. He was marched with others to the mouth of the Gallinas River, where they were sold to Spanish slave traders. The slave traders housed Sengbe and the other captives in baracoons, little more than open-air pens. Chained together, the slaves awaited their next home, which sailed into the mouth of the river several weeks later. Then the prisoners were herded onto the slave ship *Tecora* to begin their "middle journey," a two-month trip to Cuba. For most, it was the first glimpse of the sea, and the fear of that endless, changing ocean was probably the most horrific of their lives.

Yet their situation would worsen. Cramped into the incredibly small holding area below deck, the prisoners found themselves in a dark, depressing hole from which they emerged only occasionally, and then only to eat rice. The rest of the time they were trapped below, and those who did not die from disease were forced to live in their own excrement.

When the *Tecora* finally reached Cuba, its cargo was quickly and quietly spirited inland under cover of darkness to avoid British patrol ships looking for slave vessels. No such clandestine operations would be needed later when the slaves were brought to Havana, where they would be auctioned off, although they had been brought into Cuba and sold by Spanish slave traders in direct contravention of the treaties between Spain and Great Britain and in violation of the laws of Spain.[3]

In any case, plantation owner Jose Ruiz purchased 49 male slaves, while his friend, Pedro Montez, bought three young girls and a boy. The men then obtained doctored passports that claimed the slaves were Cuban born and not illegally imported Africans. To further this ruse, each African was provided with a Spanish name. So it was that Sengbe Pieh became Jose Cinquez.

The complex events that centered around Cinquez and about three dozen companions began just before midnight on June 27, 1839, when the *Amistad,* the Spanish word for "friendship," left Havana harbor to deliver the slaves to plantations in nearby Puerto Principe on the island's northwest coast.

Unlike the lengthy trip aboard the larger *Tecora,* the *Amistad*'s journey was to be but a few days. The *Amistad*'s crew consisted of Captain Ramon Ferrer, Antonio, a cabin boy, a mulatto cook named Celestino, and two crew members. Ruiz and Montez and their 53 pieces of chattel made up the passenger list.

When the wind changed directions and it was clear to Ferrer that the trip would take longer than expected, he rationed the slaves' food—two potatoes and a banana per day for each slave. When some slaves drank more than their allotted cup of water, they were flogged and their wounds rubbed with gunpowder and vinegar.[4]

The third night a storm busied the crew on deck. Below in the hold, Cinque used a nail to unlock his chain collar as well as the other captives. The slaves then armed themselves with sugarcane knives, part of *Amistad*'s cargo. Just before dawn, the Africans attacked, killed Captain Ferrer and Celestino, and took possession of the vessel. They spared the lives of the two Spanish dons who had purchased them on the condition that they direct the ship toward Africa. Steering toward Africa by day and north toward the United States by night, Montez and Ruiz arrived off Long Island, New York, on August 26 and anchored within half a mile of shore. Had they docked at any one of the southern proslavery states, the story of *Armistad* and its crew surely would have turned out differently.

Geography meant little to Cinquez and the other Africans, however. More pressing was their desperate need for water and provisions. While Cinquez and some of the others went to shore to gather what they could, Lieutenant Thomas Gedney, commander of the USS *Washington,* and his crew seized control of the *Amistad* and recaptured the Africans, including those on shore. Rather than proceed to the free state of New York, Gedney transported his prize to New London, Connecticut, where slavery was legal, and filed for salvage for the vessel, the cargo, and the Africans.

Accounts of the arrival of the mysterious black schooner dominated the local newspapers. Many of the early reports were inaccurate, describing the "black pirates" who murdered the crew in cold blood and would have continued their killing spree on the shore if not for the bravery of Gedney's crew.[5] The *New Haven Daily Herald* reported,

Our information is imperfect, but this is no doubt the vessel reported sometime since to have sailed from Havana with a number of slaves on board and several white families to whom the slaves belonged. The blacks rose upon the whites and murdered them all—men, women, and children—to the number of 26 persons and took possession of the vessel and the valuable effects on board.[6]

Although southern newspapers were hesitant about providing coverage of the ship's arrival, northerners reveled in the excitement, and curiosity about the *Amistad* and its passengers spread throughout New England. Since most of newspapers did not send correspondents to New London, they relied on accounts from newspapers located near the events or from accounts by some of the correspondents for the larger New York penny papers. One sensationalized story in the *New London Gazette* focused on the Spaniards and the African leader. It read, in part,

[Pedro Montez] is the most striking instance of complacency and unalloyed delight we have ever witnessed, and it is not strange since only yesterday his sentence was pronounced by the chief of the bucanniers, and his death song chanted by the grim crew, who gathered with uplifted sabres around his devoted head, which, as well as his arms, bear the scars of several wounds inflicted at the time of the murder of the ill-fated captain and crew. He sat smoking his Havana on the deck, and to judge from the martyr-like serenity of his countenance, his emotions are such as rarely stir the heart of man. . . .

On board the brig we also saw Cinquez, the master spirit and hero of this bloody tragedy, in irons. He is about five feet eight inches in height, 25 or 26 years of age, of erect figure, well built, and very active. He is said to be a match for any two men aboard the schooner. His countenance, for a native African, is unusually intelligent, evincing uncommon decision and coolness, with a composure characteristic of true courage, and nothing to mark him a malicious man. He is a negro, who could command in New Orleans, under the hammer, at least $1500.[7]

The timing of the *Amistad*'s arrival could not have been better. Fearful of losing ground to proslavery supporters after a series of setbacks, including several incidents of anti-abolition mob violence in Pennsylvania and Illinois, abolitionist leaders were eager to find something to unify the movement.[8] Radical abolition, riding the momentum of the new reform movement, was gaining in popularity. Impatient with the subtle strategies of older abolitionists, young men and mounting numbers of women were looking for more immediate solutions to ending slavery. However, they could not agree on the best methods, the time required to reach the goal, and the social adjustments necessary to accommodate an entire race of African Americans with full citizenship rights. Many abolitionists were convinced that the only way to end slavery in the United States was to eliminate racial prejudice. Others, called "Christian abolitionists" by some, felt that people should be persuaded to abolish slavery by appealing to their sense of morality and presenting enslavement as a sin against the laws of God. Still others viewed the legal and political arena as the ideal location to confront proslavery advocates head on.

The *Amistad* case offered opportunities for all three approaches and provided a common goal for everyone. The abolitionists believed that many northerners' reluctance to take a strong antislavery stance stemmed from not having personally confronted the horrors of slavery. This was an opportunity to discover firsthand how the slaves were treated while being captured in their homeland, shipped across the ocean, and sold on the auction block. The "Christian abolitionists" who viewed slavery as a moral issue could work to prove that the Africans had an inherent faith in God and, as such, should be treated as God's children. Those who viewed the justice system as a more viable approach to ending slavery would use the courts to secure the liberty of the *Amistad* Africans as well as other slaves. The common denominators for the three groups were freeing the *Amistad* mutineers and convincing the American public that slavery should be ended once and for all.

Because of the complex nature of events in the *Amistad* case, there was a judicial hearing and two trials, one criminal and one civil. Coverage of the events would be a crucial component in garnering public support for both sides in the conflict. Already, news items about the *Amistad* and the captives were beginning to have an effect on the American public, and readers eagerly perused the pages of their daily papers, hoping to find some snippet of information about the mysterious schooner and its occupants. Long before the *Amistad*'s capture, sightings of the "long, low black schooner" cruising haphazardly along the coast had ignited a multitude of speculations and suspicion.[9]

Once seized, the schooner presented the answers to innumerable mysteries. The "murderous demons" were described in detail. The *New London Gazette* ran a series of articles to excite public opinion against the Africans and for the Spaniards. The Africans were characterized as lustful, stupid, cannibalistic savages, while the Spaniards were described as intelligent, gentlemanly, and pious.[10]

While proslavery journals followed this approach, abolitionist publications tended to take a different tack. News coverage (both positive and negative) was crucial in creating an open forum for the discussion of the issues and questions surrounding the slavery system, and many abolitionist leaders (particularly Tappan) felt that many fence-straddling individuals who had not made a definite stand for or against slavery might be swayed to the antislavery side if they could be exposed firsthand to slavery in this highly visible case. Therefore, continued coverage of the *Amistad* events was an essential part of the campaign against slavery.

Once notified of the ship's capture, the U.S. district attorney for Connecticut, William S. Holabird, ordered a judicial hearing on the *Washington* to determine whether a crime had been committed and whether U.S. courts had jurisdiction. There was also the matter of salvage rights, which were claimed by the crew of the *Washington*.[11]

On August 29, 1839, District Judge Andrew T. Judson opened a hearing on complaints of murder and piracy filed by Montez and Ruiz. Though unable to understand the words, the 39 surviving Africans attended the hearing, which included the first mate of the *Washington*, Montez, and Ruiz as the three principal witnesses. The manacled Cinquez, wearing a red flannel shirt and white duck pants, occasionally made a motion with his hand to his throat to suggest a hanging. Interestingly, in a hearing to decide their fate, the Africans were not represented or allowed to present their side of the conflict.

After listening to the testimony, Judge Judson resolved that a grand jury should settle the case, and he issued his order:

To the Marshal of the District of Connecticut—greeting.

Whereas upon the complaint and information of the United States by William S. Holabird, District Attorney of the United States for said District, against [the Amistad] for the murder of Ramon Ferrer, on the 20th day of June 1839, on the high seas, within the admiralty and maritime jurisdiction of the United States, it was ordered and adjudged by the undersigned that they against whom said information and complaint was made, stand committed to appear before the Circuit Court of the United States for the District of Connecticut, to be holden at Hartford, in said District on the 17th day of September, 1839, to answer to the said crime of murder, as set forth in said information and complaint.

You are therefore commanded to take the said persons, named as above, and charged with said crime, and them safely keep in the jail in New Haven in said District, and then have before the Circuit Court of the United States to be holden at Hartford, in said District, on the 17th day of September A.D. 1839. Hereof fail not, &c. Dated at New London. August 29, 1839.

ANDREW T. JUDSON,
Judge of the United States for the District of Connecticut.[12]

The Africans' arrival caused quite a stir across New England—both as a spectacle and as a profitable venture. A letter from Boston, dated September 2, praised the prosperity that resulted from the mutiny, especially for the newspapers. The writer boasted,

The capture of the "low, black schooner" has created a great excitement in our little quiet city.—Following the good example of your original self, 4000 copies of an extra, containing a full account of the examination, &c. were sold yesterday before 12 o'clock. Speaking of extras, it would do your heart good, causing it to leap into your mouth with joy, could you stand in our City Hall, in the entry of the boxes of the Post Office the day after the arrival at New York of a steamship from Liverpool, and see how fast the extras of the New York Morning Herald are disposed of at 6 pence apiece by the money making carriers, one of whom is quite a wit. While selling the extras containing the news by the British Queen, two rivals stood beside him, disposing or endeavoring so to do, of the New York Sun, and Boston Times extra. It was "no go" with them. After having sold more than 100 of the Herald, while his rivals arms were as full as when they took their stand, he very coolly remarked, to the amusement of the bystanders—"Oh! it's no use—you may as well go home and give your papers to the girls—the New York Herald is so well known here, that I can sell more extras at 6 cents than you can find people to take of yours for nothing"—and sure enough, he sold all his papers in a very few minutes. Come now, does not this speak well of the discernment of Bostonians? In this connection I would suggest the expediency of your sending a regular number of the Herald daily to an agent in this city, to be disposed of. A subscription list could be readily filled for it, I'll be bound. Think of this.[13]

The abolitionists lost no time in initiating assistance for the *Amistad* captives. New Haven abolitionist Dwight P. James enlisted attorney Roger Sherman Baldwin, the future governor of Connecticut, to represent the group, requesting him to do everything for them that "humanity and Justice require."[14] James also contacted the Reverend Joshua Leavitt, editor of the American Anti-Slavery Society's *Emancipator*, in New York. James charged Leavitt with two tasks: to investigate the ship's papers in New York in order to determine if the Spaniards had legal title to the Africans and to locate someone who spoke the captives' language and to dispatch him to New Haven to hear the Africans' side of the story.

In Quincy, Massachusetts, former President and current Congressman John Quincy Adams analyzed the legal questions involved in the case and framed the beginning of a speech in the Africans' behalf to be delivered from the floor of Congress.[15]

In New York, as soon as he read of the Africans' plight, abolitionist and businessman Lewis Tappan sought ways in which to aid the prisoners. Tappan called a meeting of the leading abolitionists in New York, including Simeon Jocelyn, pastor of a church for African Americans in New Haven, and William Jay, son of Vice President John Jay. They formed the Committee for the Defense of the Africans of the *Amistad,* also known as the Friends of the *Amistad,* for the sole purpose of securing defense counsel for the prisoners and ensuring their satisfactory treatment. The first order of business for the committee was to construct a defense team. They needed attorneys with abolitionist leanings, and this narrowed the field considerably. The group finally settled on Baldwin in New Haven, along with Seth P. Staples Jr. and Theodore Sedgwick of New York City.[16]

The committee also drafted a statement of purpose and an appeal for donations to fund their plans, both to appear in the *Emancipator*. Their "Appeal to the Friends of Liberty" first appeared in the paper's September 5 issue. It read,

Thirty-eight fellow-men from Africa, after having been piratically kidnapped from their native land, transported across the seas, and subjected to atrocious cruelties, have been thrown upon our shores, and are now incarcerated in jail to await their trial for crimes alleged by their oppressors to have been committed by them. They are ignorant of our language, of the usages of civilized society, and the obligations of Christianity. Under these circumstances, several friends of human rights have met to consult upon the case of these unfortunate men, and have appointed the undersigned a committee to employ interpreters and able counsel, and take all the necessary means to secure the rights of the accused. It is intended to employ three legal gentlemen of distinguished abilities, and to incur other needful expenses. The poor prisoners being destitute of clothing, and several having scarcely a rag to cover them, immediate steps will be taken to provide what may be necessary. The undersigned therefore make this appeal to the friends of humanity to contribute for the above objects. Donations may be sent to either of the Committee, who will acknowledge the same, and make a public report of all their disbursements.

SIMEON S. JOCELYN,
34 Wall Street.
JOSHUA LEAVITT,
143 Nassau Street.
LEWIS TAPPAN,
122 Pearl Street.
New York, Sept. 4, 1839

The next day, the members of the committee set about fulfilling their assigned tasks. In the office of the *New York Evening Post,* editor William Cullen Bryant proposed that Sedgwick write a series of articles discussing the legal aspects of the case. Sedgwick, who had already been contacted by Leavitt and agreed to serve as defense counsel, accepted Bryant's proposal on the condition that he could sign the articles with the pseudonym "Veto." Tappan, arriving in New Haven, approached Baldwin with a similar offer to serve as counsel, and Baldwin immediately accepted the role of chief counsel for the Africans.[17]

In the meantime, the grateful Spaniards, able to travel freely about the city, published a letter expressing gratitude to the American people for their rescue from the Africans:

NEW LONDON, AUGUST 29, 1839.

The subscribers, Don Jose Ruiz, and Don Pedro Montez, in gratitude for their most unhoped for and providential rescue from the bands of a ruthless gang of African bucaneers and an awful death, would take the means of expressing, in some slight decree, their thankfulness and obligation to Lieut. Com T. R. Gedney, and the officers and crew of the U.S. surveying brig Washington, for their decision in seizing the Amistad, and their unremitting kindness and hospitality in providing for their comfort on board their vessel, as well as the means they have taken for the protection of their property.

We also must express our indebtedness to that nation whose flag they so worthily bear, with an assurance that the act will be duly appreciated by our most gracious sovereign, her Majesty the Queen of Spain.

DON JOSE RUIZ,
DON PEDRO MONTEZ.[18]

While Ruiz and Montez enjoyed their freedom, the Africans attempted to adjust to yet another form of imprisonment. Tappan arrived at the New Haven jail with several Africans to act as interpreters in conversing with Cinquez and his comrades. However, only one man, John Ferry, knew enough Mendi to communicate with the prisoners. Most of the prisoners could understand him, although none could speak his dialect. Tappan commented, "You may imagine the joy manifested by these poor Africans, when they heard one of their own color address them in a friendly manner, and in a language they could comprehend!"[19]

Tappan and the others were also allowed to visit Cinquez, who was housed in a separate cell. He explained,

[Cinquez] is with several savage looking fellows, black and white, who are in jail on various charges. Visitors are not allowed to enter this strong hold of the jail, and the inmates can only be seen and conversed with through the aperture of the door. The jailer is fearful that some of them would escape if the door was opened in frequently. Even the other African prisoners are not permitted to hold converse with their Chief. Before they and he were deprived of this privilege, and when he occasionally came among them, they gathered around him, all talking at once, and shaking hands, as if they rejoiced to see him among them. They appeared to look up to him, I am told, with great respect.[20]

According to Tappan's account, he found a nearly naked Cinquez lying on the floor, a single blanket partly wrapped around him. Tappan said Cinquez seemed hesitant at first, unwilling to answer the interpreter's questions, until Ferry convinced him it was safe to speak. Cinquez, who pronounced his name as "Shinquau" in his native language, told his story for the first time—being captured in his homeland, taken to Havana, and placed on the schooner.[21]

Tappan provided one of the first detailed descriptions of the Africans and their behavior among the whites. It may have been an attempt to refute prejudiced accounts printed in anti-abolition papers. He pointed out,

The prisoners are in comfortable rooms.—They are well clothed in dark striped cotton trowsers, called by some of the manufacturers "hard times," and in striped cotton shirts. The girls are in calico frocks, and have made the little shawls that were given them into turbans. The prisoners eyed the clothes some time, and laughed a good deal among themselves before they put them on. Their food is brought to them in separate tin pans, and they eat it in an orderly manner. In general, they are in good health. . . . They are robust, are full of hilarity, especially the Mandingos. . . . Neither Cinquez nor any of his comrades have been manacled since they have been here. Their demeanor is altogether quiet, kind, and orderly. . . .

Cinquez is about 5 feet 8 inches high, of fine proportions, with a noble air. Indeed, the whole company, although thin in flesh, and generally of slight forms, and limbs, especially, are as good looking and intelligent a body of men as we usually meet with. All are young, and several are quite striplings. The Mandingos are described in books as being a very gentle race, cheerful in their dispositions, inquisitive, credulous, simple hearted, and much given to trading propensities. . . .

The African prisoners are orderly and peaceable among themselves. Some of them sing well, and appear to be in good spirits and grateful for the kindness shown them.[22]

Less convinced than the general population about the Africans' docile nature, the proslavery *New York Morning Herald* challenged Tappan's account of his visit in a scathing assessment of its own, using letters from editor James Gordon Bennett. The *Herald* countered,

The abolitionists are making immense exertions to get the negroes set free; they are
raising subscriptions, collecting money, clothing and feeding them; employing the
most able counsel, riding over the country, by night and day, to get interpreters who
can converse alike in their language and in English; rummaging over musty records,
old statutes, treaties and laws, in order to "get a peg to hang a doubt upon" in relation
to delivering them up. . . . The canting semi-abolition papers, like the "Journal of
Commerce" and the "American" and "Post" are all endeavoring to mis-state, misrep-
resent, and throw difficulties upon the matter in order to get the black murderers set
free. The Southern papers have articles proving the propriety of the surrender.

And

Meanwhile, the negroes are getting fat and lazy; perfectly indifferent to the disposal
to be made of them. They only do two things on the coast of Africa; that is, eat and
steal. . . . Senor Ruiz says that they are all great cowards, and had the captain killed
one on the night of the mutiny they would have been subdued instantly, and all have
run below. His impression is that they will be sent out to Havana, the ringleaders
executed, and the rest given up to him. We shall see. It is a most singular case; we
shall follow it up closely; and, unlike the "Journal of Commerce," we shall do so
accurately.[23]

    Political and racial matters also continued to magnify the case's importance.
On September 6, the Spanish minister in Washington, Angel Calderón de la
Barca, issued a series of demands to Secretary of State John Forsyth, insisting
that the American government return the *Amistad* and its cargo and return
the captives to Cuba to stand trial for mutiny and murder. Seeking to avoid
a confrontation with Spain over anything related to slavery, the Van Buren
administration set about devising a strategy that would dismiss the matter
without damaging the Democrat's reelection hopes for the presidential election of 1840.[24] Ironically, Bennett also predicted that the *Amistad* affair
might figure mightily in the upcoming presidential election. Government
involvement was evident. He prophesied,

The "Journal of Commerce" and several other abolition papers, are very busy trying
to create excitement out of the Amistad case and captured Africans. The Rev. David
Hale, with a hypocritical cast of the eye—not an honest, downright squint like mine—
is publishing the correspondence of Lewis Tappan & Co., who intend, out of this case,
to revive the dying embers of abolition in the north.

Bennett promised his reporters would be "in constant attendance," adding
that

this strange affair bids fair to excite a stronger feeling throughout the Union, than any
event that has happened in a long time. Whatever disposition be made of these Africans, the laws and treaties between nations ought to govern its course, in exclusion of
those mischievous appeals to the passions of the mob of pious or profane loafers. We
should not be surprised even, if the Amistad case entered deeply into the next election.
Every thing about it looks black enough for a squall. Get out your great coats and
umbrellas—we know not the moment the clouds will pour down, or the wind may
blow.[25]

As the conflict surrounding the Africans wore on, newspaper editors throughout the country puzzled over the circumstances of the case, pondering not only the legal questions presented by the slaves' mutiny and their capture but also the moral questions. The initial impulse to help the Africans might have come from purely humanitarian concerns, but the abolitionists quickly realized the value in the captives' cause. The human injustice of slavery could be placed against the backdrop of the constitutional processes of liberty. They also reasoned that the *Amistad* case might be God's way of manifesting the evils of slavery for all to see. Comparing the *Amistad* uprising to the American rebellion against British control, the *Herald of Freedom* declared,

Cinquez is no pirate, no murderer, no felon. His homicide is justifiable. Had a white man done it it would have been glorious. It would have immortalized him. . . . Something important, we feel may grow out of [this] to the anti-slavery cause. God may have cast this chieftain on our shore at this crisis to aid us in the deliverance of his people.[26]

Even editors previously unsympathetic to the abolitionist cause were willing to withhold judgment before pronouncing the Africans guilty. The strongly anti-abolitionist *New York Morning Herald* told its readers,

We despise the humbug doctrines of the abolitionists and the miserable fanatics who propagate them; but if men will traffic in human flesh, steal men from their homes on the coast of Africa, and sell them like cattle at Cuba, they must not murmur if some of the men stealers get murdered by the unfortunate wretches whom they have wronged and stole.[27]

Attempting to sort through the legal conundrum, the *Herald* analyzed the options for each of the parties involved and criticized the Spanish government for its attempts to regain control of the Africans. The *Herald* concluded,

It is certain that the Spanish Government, at Havana, recognizing the right to steal, buy and sell blacks, will, instantly demand the slaves of this government; it is also possible that this government will give up the men, and sell the vessel and cargo for salvage; in that case it is also certain that every one of the male blacks, who rose on the captain will be executed.

The various questions that will arise will be most curious; and the great difficulty will be that the vessel they seized was not a slaver; that they had been sold as merchandize in Cuba, and seized a merchant vessel, and killed a merchant Captain. This alone will constitute them pirates in the fullest sense of the word. Had they merely seized the vessel, without murdering any one, and tried to take her to Africa, our government would have been justified in sending them back to their native homes. Or had they rose on the Captain of the slaver that brought them from Africa, and murdered the Captain and all the crew, by the laws of God and man, the laws of nature and of nations they would have been perfectly justified. But their having been landed at Havana from a slave ship, sold there, and reshipped . . . will totally alter the aspect of their position and be the main ground of all the arguments for delivering them up and treating them as pirates. It is a hard case, for had they rose on their Captain and his crew two weeks before or been driven into Halifax or Bermuda, they would now have been free as the winds of Heaven. As it is, they will probably be hung.

Let the case be decided as it may, they in all probability, will have to suffer. It is a lamentable state of things.[28]

The first *Amistad* trial, beginning on September 19, 1839, in U.S. Circuit Court in Hartford, pertained to criminal charges of murder, mutiny, and piracy levied against the Africans. On September 14, all the Africans, with the exception of one named Burna, who was ill, were transported to Hartford, partly by canal boat. Along the way, people crowded the banks of the Connecticut River to catch a glimpse of the prisoners. The same crowds welcomed the arrival of a paddle steamboat bearing the other principal players in the courtroom drama, especially after it ran aground in a fog along the canal. The stranded men included Ruiz, Montez, and Lieutenant Gedney as well as Tappan and Sedgwick.[29]

The usually quiet town of Hartford literally bubbled with excitement, taking on a carnival sideshow atmosphere. The captives were the center of attention in the jail, providing a perverse entertainment for at least 3,000 people in three days.[30] As the time of trial approached, lawyers, reporters, and strangers from Boston to New York filled hotel rooms, roamed the public streets, and picnicked on the lawn in front of the two-story brick courthouse. Visitors filled theater houses to view *The Black Schooner, or the Pirate Slaver Amistad,* a nautical melodrama based on the Africans' journey. The play included walk-on parts for the slaves and the *Washington* crew, with "Zambra Cinques, Chief of Mutineers" as one of the main characters.[31]

Vendors hawked engravings of Cinquez (from a portrait completed by Jocelyn's brother Nathaniel) or the schooner *Amistad.* An exhibit of a gigantic painting of the mutiny, depicting Cinquez murdering the ship's cook, traveled from town to town, and engravings of the work were sold to visitors as souvenirs. Even advertisers used the high-profile case to their advantage. Using a picture of the schooner in their ad, the manufacturers of American Hygiene Pills and Tomato Pills charged a rival company with stealing their formula, declaring in a headline "PIRATES! The long low black schooner comes again."[32]

The excitement and attention surrounding the case pleased Tappan and his fellow abolitionists. As many as 4,000 people a day had paid 12 cents each to catch a glimpse of the Africans, money that would be used toward their defense and for supplies and clothing for them.[33] Although all the leading New York papers provided correspondents to give the trial extensive coverage, no paper attached more significance to the case than the *Emancipator.* Abolitionist Gerrit Smith proclaimed in the paper's trial-day issue that "God has ordered [the African to our shores] to hasten the overthrow of slavery."[34]

In a courtroom filled to capacity, Tappan sat on a bench next to the little girls from the *Amistad*. Montez had claimed them as his slaves, and the abolitionists and their lawyers had asked the Circuit Court of Connecticut for a writ of habeas corpus that would order the release of the three girls from custody. The defense team and abolitionists had chosen to limit their initial effort to the girls for two reasons: to focus attention on the girls, who played no role in the mutiny and who could be expected to generate public sympathy for the abolitionist cause, and to illustrate that the girls' young age and inability to speak Spanish proved they were most certainly Africans and a judge should have a hard time concluding that they had been sold as slaves legally. If the writ were to be granted for them, it would be strong precedent for other Africans.[35]

The scene depicted all the drama the abolitionists had hoped for. Wrapped in white blankets, the girls sobbed loudly as they sat next to Tappan, clutching his hand and that of their jailer, who tried to cheer them up with apples. The frightened young girls probably failed to understand why they were in the courtroom.[36]

Two federal judges and a grand jury were assembled in Hartford to deal with the various components of the complicated case. In addition to the habeas corpus petition of the abolitionists, the case presented issues of criminal law, property law, admiralty law, and jurisdiction. The presiding judge, Associate Justice Smith Thompson, directed a grand jury to decide whether the Africans should be indicted on the charges.

Lawyers laid out their arguments in the courtroom, while the grand jury met in another room in the courthouse to investigate the testimony related to the mutiny and murders, occasionally interrupting the main proceedings to ask the judge's assistance on their deliberations. Attorneys for the Spaniards demanded the return of the Africans as slaves lawfully purchased in a nation where slaveholding was legal. Other attorneys argued for salvage rights to the ship and its cargo, including the slaves, for the sailors who had helped apprehend the mutineers. Similarly, Holabird, the U.S. district attorney, cited a 1795 treaty as the basis for having the Africans placed under the control of President Van Buren, who would most assuredly have turned them over to the Spanish government to maintain amicable relations with his allies.[37]

Newspaper accounts varied as to the effectiveness of each attorney's legal maneuvering. In the *New York Commercial Advertiser,* Tappan's characterizations were laced with comments reflecting his abolitionist leanings. According to Tappan, the attorneys for the defense delivered powerful and eloquent arguments, while presentations by Holabird and the attorneys for the Spaniards were lame and deviously resourceful. The proslavery *Herald* concluded that the case was primarily a struggle between the government and the abolitionists for possession of the Africans, either to deliver them to the Spanish authorities or "to make saints of them." Despite obvious bias, the *Herald* did concede that the abolitionists' attorneys had made a strong showing, especially Baldwin's closing "with an effective appeal to the sympathies of the court."[38]

The cloudy outcome of the trial was not an overwhelming victory for either party. After three days of arguments, Judge Thompson accepted the grand jury's facts concerning the mutiny and on September 23 ruled that the court had no jurisdiction over the case because the alleged crimes had been committed on a Spanish ship in Spanish waters. Thus, the crimes were not punishable under U.S. law, and there could be no criminal prosecution in his courtroom. However, he refused to issue a writ ordering the Africans' immediate release, leaving their fate to be decided in district court. According to Thompson, the law also dictated that the district court had the right to keep the Africans in custody until it decided who held a claim on them as property.[39]

Although known to oppose slavery, Thompson probably would have liked to grant the Africans their freedom, but he could not allow his personal sentiments to influence his ruling. His task as judge was to decide only whether the Africans were to be held accountable under U.S. criminal law, not whether the prisoners were to be treated as human beings or as property. Even as an abolitionist, Thompson was not ready to establish a precedent that blacks were human beings with rights assigned to them under the law. It would have removed the obstacles for slaves in other countries to seek asylum in the United States or for those in the slave states to rebel, knowing that they could not be prosecuted in a U.S. court. Defense attorney Sedgwick reluctantly admitted, "It is too late or rather let us hope too early to contend in the courts of the U.S. that there can be no property in Human Beings—in Africans at least."[40]

Immediately after the decision, Judge Judson convened the district court and directed the attorneys to determine exactly where Gedney had captured the *Amistad*. In the meantime, the court would adjourn until the third Tuesday in November in Hartford, and the Africans would receive favorable incarceration in the New Haven jail.[41]

The *New York Herald* reveled in the decision, cheerfully reporting that the abolitionists would now have to "send home their darkies and disperse." The writer rejoiced that the abolitionists were "half frantic" at Thompson's refusal to release the Africans, meaning that *Liberator* editor William Lloyd Garrison would not be able to lease a cannibal to the Zoological Institute to pay the paper's debts and that Tappan would not realize his hope that intermarriage might someday turn all Americans "copper-colored."[42]

Ironically, the circuit court ruling was quite advantageous for the abolitionists. They had wanted to keep the Africans and the case before the American public. Not only had they succeeded in gaining the public's attention, but they had turned the case into one of charitable concern for the prisoners rather than a move against slavery or for racial equality. Even the most prejudiced individuals could not resist feeling paternalistic toward the hapless prisoners, who posed no threat to the white community.

In the weeks before district court was scheduled to reconvene, the abolitionists worked to strengthen their case. Tappan located an interpreter—a former Mende slave who spoke Mendi fluently—while the attorneys sued

Montez and Ruiz for assault and battery and false imprisonment on behalf of Cinquez and another prisoner.[43] Hoping to convince the court that the Africans were kidnapped from their homeland and deserved their freedom on the basis of universal God-given rights, Tappan and the *Amistad* committee selected a team of teachers to instruct the Africans in the Christian religion. The strategy seemed simple enough—facts are useful but religiosity is better. In addition, the Africans' piety would aid in convincing the public that blacks were not inferior and were quite capable of civilized behavior.

Bennett's *Herald* presented a highly slanted account of the abolitionists' activities. In the October 4 issue, the paper described,

Every kind of engine is set in motion to create a feeling of sympathy and an excitement in their favor; the parsons preach about them, the men talk about them, the ladies give tea parties and discuss their chivalry, heroism, sufferings; thews and sinews, over their souchong; pious young women get up in prayer meetings and pray for them; scouts are sent round the country to hunt up all the negroes that can speak any kind of African dialect; interpreters by dozens arrive daily at Hartford; grammars and spelling books and primers without number, in all sorts of unknown tongues, are sought for and secured.[44]

The *Herald* also did not miss the opportunity of criticizing the Africans' behavior as well as the behavior of their supporters.[45] According to the *Herald,* the animal-like prisoners basked in a carefree existence in Connecticut, while enjoying the opportunity to "eat more, drink more, chatter more, gambol [*sic*] more, and turn more somersets [somersaults] than ever," without the worry of having to work for a living. The journal also included a drawing to illustrate the public's response to Africans' celebrity status, criticizing numerous aspects of the situation—in the center, one prisoner turning a somersault before a mixed group of whites and blacks, with two prisoners in the foreground scratching themselves; on the left, Tappan and another abolitionist looking on while Cinquez kisses a young white girl held up by her "sympathetic" mother; near the mother, a phrenologist who, convinced of Cinquez's intelligence after reading the bumps on his head, is busy formulating a vocabulary of the Mendi language; and to the far right, the "fashionable, pious, learned, and gay people of Connecticut" receiving lectures and instructions in African philosophy and civilization.[46]

The civil case was tried in U.S. District Court before Judge Andrew Judson, beginning November 19, 1839, in Hartford. The United States had filed a separate libel and claim on behalf of Spain, while Antonio Vega, vice-consul of Spain, filed a claim for the slave Antonio, a 16-year-old cabin boy, on behalf of the heirs of the murdered captain, Ramón Ferrer. The Africans also filed a plea in abatement that called for dismissal of the case on jurisdictional grounds, as in the circuit court proceedings.[47]

Tappan's biggest worry concerning the trial was Judge Judson, a foe a few years earlier during the controversial trial of Prudence Crandall. The young white schoolteacher had come under fire for opening an all-black girls' academy in rural Connecticut near Judson's home. Judson rallied townspeople to pressure the state assembly to enact the "Connecticut Black Law," which required nonresident blacks to be expelled from private school. Judson prosecuted Crandall, the first defendant under the new law, and received a conviction. When Connecticut's supreme court overturned the conviction on a technicality, a mob set fire to her house, and Crandall decided to give up her school.[48]

Despite Tappan's misgivings regarding Judson, the abolitionists possessed one crucial witness who had offered his help after hearing of the *Amistad* case. Richard Madden, the British Commissioner of Liberated Africans at Havana, had verified that the blacks aboard the *Amistad* were imported from Africa, and he had come to offer his testimony despite the disapproval of his superiors. He had remained on the sidelines during the opening day's arguments, which focused on the vessel's location at the time of capture and whether the Africans were free or enslaved. After several hours of argument, however, Judson postponed the trial to January 7 because of the illness of James Covey, the African interpreter, and moved the location back to New Haven. To avoid postponing Madden's return to England, Judson permitted Madden to make a deposition in the judge's chamber on the afternoon of November 20. The deposition would be used when the trial reconvened in January.[49]

Before the group of attorneys and interested spectators, Madden described the system of fraud, collusion, and corruption that aided the slave traders in buying and selling human beings in Cuba. Madden corroborated that Spanish officials had falsified documents, illegally classifying the blacks as *ladinos* rather than *bozales*. Although such actions clearly violated Spanish law, Madden had had no authority to intervene once the Africans had been brought ashore and sanctioned by the fraudulent documents. Therefore, the Africans were free according to Spanish law at the time of the uprising, and they should not have been claimed as property.[50]

Madden's testimony generated considerable excitement because it confirmed everything the abolitionists had maintained throughout the case: that Cinquez and his fellow prisoners had been kidnapped and unlawfully enslaved. His firsthand observations had also exposed the inhumane treatment the Africans could expect if returned to Cuba. Madden's testimony had focused the primary issues of the *Amistad* case. The rest would be up to the attorneys when court reconvened.

While the two sides planned their strategies for court, the Van Buren administration secretly maneuvered to ensure a settlement to appease the Spanish government. The president ordered the Navy to dispatch the USS *Grampus* to anchor in New Haven harbor as early as January 10, ready to take charge of the prisoners as soon as Judson issued the Van Buren administration's anticipated decision—that the Africans be transported to Cuba to stand trial for murder and piracy. When the *Grampus* slipped into the harbor on January 9, Tappan viewed its arrival as a deliberate attempt to subvert the judicial process.[51]

Lawyers, interested parties, and curious spectators squeezed into every available seat in the New Haven courtroom on January 7. Students from Yale Divinity School and Yale Law School, which had dismissed classes early so students could attend the trial, refused to leave the courtroom for fear of losing their places. Women occupied most of the seats in the small court-room, while those individuals unable to acquire a seat crowded the doors and jockeyed for standing room among the spectators. Almost a dozen law-yers huddled at their desks as they prepared to represent a litany of clients— the Africans, the Spaniards, the salvage claimants, and the U.S. government. Tappan, sitting near the Africans, gazed at the remarkable scene.[52]

Judson, serious and stern, listened intently from the bench as the attorneys pleaded their case. The defense focused its arguments on the evidence that the Africans were kidnapped and illegally sold into slavery, a violation of their most basic of rights. The government attorneys countered that the United States had no jurisdiction in the case and that, as such, the ship and the cargo should be returned to Cuba. The other attorneys dealt exclusively with the salvage claims of their clients.[53]

Many of the spectators in the crowded courtroom had come to hear the testimony of Cinquez, who had become a hero during the months of his incarceration. Earlier that day, Roger Baldwin received loud cheers from the mostly pro-African audience as he eloquently argued for the prisoners' right to liberty. Then a parade of abolitionist witnesses offered evidence of the Negroes' African origins, including Cinquez. Courtroom spectators listened attentively as he told the story of his kidnapping on a road near the home of his wife and three children, his journey on the *Amistad,* and his arrival in the United States. Cinquez even sat on the courtroom floor to show how he was manacled, hands and feet together, on the Middle Passage voyage.[54]

After days of debate, Judson announced his multifaceted decision. Con-cerning the salvage claims, one-third of the value of the ship and its nonhu-man cargo was awarded to Gedney and the remaining two-thirds to the Spanish government. Antonio, the cabin boy, was to be returned to his owner as determined by the Spanish authorities. Judson ruled that the Africans could not be part of the salvage claim. They were never slaves and, therefore, never the property of Spanish subjects. Thus, they would not be returned to Cuba to stand trial as accused murderers and pirates. Judson also ordered that the Africans be placed under the control of the president and returned to Africa.[55]

Unfortunately for the abolitionists and the Africans, the case did not end with Judson's ruling. Appeals before the U.S. Circuit Court and finally the U.S. Supreme Court, including a nine-hour argument from John Quincy Adams, prolonged the Africans' incarceration until 1841. Following the Su-preme Court's decision affirming the Africans' freedom, Cinquez and his comrades concluded that it was time to go home. Homesickness had begun to plague most of the former prisoners, and they were eager to make the long voyage back to Africa and their families.[56]

Though not completely satisfied with the legal approach, Tappan saw Judson's decision as a compromise the abolitionists could live with. No one should have expected Judson to issue a decision repudiating the institution of slavery or declaring that blacks were human beings who enjoyed the same rights as whites. Although the decision was a small victory, it was a decisive step forward in the struggle to abolish slavery.

The *Amistad* mutiny case thrust the issues of slavery and racial equality into the public arena, providing a platform to discuss the morality of slavery. The possibility of using legal and political avenues to hasten slavery's demise was more closely studied. However, the case not only increased interest in whether a human being could be declared property but also permitted the abolitionists to demonstrate that a key argument by supporters of slavery was fatally flawed—that Africans were neither intelligent nor civilized.

The case also increased support for the abolitionist cause, especially among northerners who had previously been hesitant about taking a firm stand against slavery. By putting a face to the enslaved, a wave of enthusiasm resulted at a time when the abolitionist movement had been weakened by its inability to function as a unit. A smaller dividend was the abolitionists' willingness to put aside their own personal differences long enough to take on a common foe.

It is perhaps fitting that the debate over the intricacies of the *Amistad* mutiny incident continued until the advent of the Civil War. The case raised questions that politicians, journalists, and the American public had avoided discussing for years. With the key issues in the forefront of the antislavery struggle, leaders could no longer evade addressing the situation. Slavery would eventually meet its demise, and the *Amistad* trials had provided the momentum to nudge the country toward that end.

Meanwhile, back in Africa, 35 of the original 53 *Amistad* abductees arrived home almost exactly three years after they were kidnapped. One, Sengbe Pieh, was informed that for many Mende, war already had come and gone. During his absence, his village, along with much of his family, had been wiped out by the slaving wars. There is no record that Sengbe was ever reunited with his wife and children.[57]

In America, the coming war would answer the question of slavery. In Africa, answers proved more elusive.

NOTES

1. *New York Journal of Commerce,* 10 and 11 January 1840; John W. Barber, *A History of the Amistad Captives* (New Haven, Conn.: E. L. & J. W. Barber, 1840), 19–21; "Testimony of Cinque, 8 January 1840, U.S. District Court Records for Connecticut," reprinted at http://amistad.mysticseaport.org/library/court/district/1840.1.8.cinquetest.html. Accessed 14 December 2001.

2. There is little consistency in the spelling of several names. "Cinquez" is spelled "Cinque" in some histories. The same is true for Pedro "Montez," also spelled "Montes" in some newspaper reports and various historical renderings. In addition, the name of the tribe has been written as "Mende" and "Mendi." For this chapter, "Mende" is used for the tribe, "Mendi" for the language of the tribe.

3. Barber, *A History of the Amistad Captives,* 6–8; Mary Cable, *Black Odyssey: The Case of the Slave Ship Amistad* (New York: Penguin Books, 1977), 3–16; Howard Jones, *Mutiny on the Amistad* (New York: Oxford University Press, 1839), 14–30. *Charleston Courier,* 5 September 1839; *New York Journal of Commerce,* 28 August 1839; *New York Morning Herald,* 2 and 9 September 1839.

4. http://amistad.mysticseaport.org/library/court/district/1840.1.8.cinquetest .html. Accessed 20 December 2001.

5. *Morning Courier* & *New York Enquirer,* 30 August 1839; *New York Morning Herald,* 28 August 1839; *New York Evening Star,* 4 September 1839.

6. *New Haven Daily Herald,* reprinted in Cable, *Black Odyssey,* 9.

7. *New London Gazette,* 26 August 1839; see also Barber, *A History of the Amistad Captives,* 4–5.

8. Abolitionist editor Elijah P. Lovejoy was murdered in Alton, Illinois, in 1837, and Philadelphia's Pennsylvania Hall, where abolitionist meetings were held, was destroyed. The Philadelphia mob continued its rampage throughout the city, terrorizing African American neighborhoods.

9. See *Norfolk Beacon,* 24 August 1839, reprinted in the *New York American,* 27 August 1839; *New York Advertiser & Express,* 28 August 1839; and *New York Commercial Advertiser,* 26 and 27 August 1839.

10. See, for example, *New London Gazette,* 26 August 1839.

11. Some estimates placed the value of the *Amistad*'s cargo of wine, saddles, gold, and silk at $40,000 in 1839 dollars, and the slaves had a market value of at least half that much. See *Charleston Courier,* 5 September 1839.

12. Transcript of the trial. Reprinted at http://amistad.mysticseaport.org.

13. *New York Morning Herald,* 4 September 1839; *New York Advertiser & Express,* 7 September 1839.

14. Dwight P. James to Roger Sherman Baldwin, New London, 30 August 1839, reprinted in B. Edward Martin, *All We Want Is Make Us Free: La Amistad and the Reform Abolitionists* (Lanham, Md.: University Press of America, 1986), 10.

15. Jones, *Mutiny on the Amistad,* 35–42; Cable, *Black Odyssey,* 17–23; William A. Owens, *Black Mutiny: A Revolt on the Schooner Amistad* (Baltimore: Black Classic Press, 1997), 147–55.

16. Ibid.

17. Ibid.

18. Barber, *A History of the Amistad Captives,* 8.

19. Letter to the *New York Evening Post,* reprinted in the *Emancipator,* 19 September 1839. See also http://www.law.umkc.edu/faculty/projects/ftrial/amistad/AMI_ LTR.HTM. Accessed 7 December 2001.

20. Ibid.

21. Ibid.

22. Ibid.

23. *New York Morning Herald,* 9 September 1839.

24. *New York Morning Herald,* 10 September 1839. Calderón to Forsyth, 6 September 1839, U.S. Department of State, Notes from the Spanish Legation in the U.S.

to the Department of State, 1790–1906. Information reprinted in Jones, *Mutiny on the Amistad*, 50–52. See also Document No. 185, Amistad case evidence. Reprinted in Barber, *A History of the Amistad Captives*, 31–32.

25. *New York Morning Herald*, 13 September 1839.

26. *Herald of Freedom*, reprinted in the *New York Colored American*, 28 September 1839.

27. *New York Morning Herald*, 2 September 1839.

28. Ibid.

29. Cable, *Black Odyssey*, 36.

30. Ibid., 36–37.

31. Ibid. The drama played to packed houses throughout the North, taking in $1,650 in the first week.

32. Ibid.

33. Jones, *Mutiny on the Amistad*, 65.

34. *Emancipator*, 19 September 1839.

35. Barber, *A History of the Amistad Captives*, 16–18; Jones, *Mutiny on the Amistad*, 64–74; Owens, *Black Mutiny*, 175–88.

36. Ibid.

37. *New York Morning Herald*, 20 September 1839.

38. Ibid., 23 September 1839.

39. *New York Morning Herald*, 25 September 1839; *New York Colored American*, 28 September 1839; *Richmond Enquirer*, 25 September 1839.

40. Sedgwick to Tappan, 12 October 1839, reprinted in Jones, *Mutiny on the Amistad*, 78.

41. Jones, *Mutiny on the Amistad*, 78. The prisoners received favorable treatment in the jail. They were permitted almost unrestricted visitation privileges, religious instruction from Yale University faculty members, and exercise periods on the green.

42. *New York Morning Herald*, 1 October 1839.

43. See Barber, *A History of the Amistad Captives*, 17; Martin, *All We Want Is Make Us Free*, 17; *New York Morning Herald*, 18 and 24 October 1839; and *Richmond Enquirer*, 25 October and 1 November 1839. In addition to keeping the case before the public, the suits were intended to force the courts to solidify the status of the blacks, either as people having legal rights or as slaves not entitled to sue their masters. With the prisoners claiming $3,000 in damages, Montez and Ruiz were arrested, and bail was set at $1,000 each. Montez was released on his own recognizance and fled back to Cuba, while bail for Ruiz was reduced to $250. Ruiz made bail in February 1840 and fled to Cuba also. Proslavery editorialists fumed at what they variously called a ruse, while southern editors feared that slaves throughout the country might attempt similar suits.

44. *New York Morning Herald*, 4 October 1839.

45. The *Herald* editors had taken great pleasure in attacking the abolitionists and the Africans throughout the entire incident. See, for example, *New York Morning Herald*, 17 September and 29 and 31 October 1839.

46. *New York Morning Herald*, 4 October 1839.

47. Ibid., 20 and 21 November 1839.

48. Jones, *Mutiny*, 96–99.

49. *New York Morning Herald*, 21 and 22 November 1839; *Richmond Enquirer*, 26 November 1839; *Charleston Courier*, 26 November 1839.

50. *New York Morning Herald*, 21 November 1839.

51. Some historians maintain that Tappan developed a secret plan of his own. Several rumors circulated that he and other abolitionists had also procured a schooner to be used to transport the Africans to Canada, should things go against the prisoners. See Jones, *Mutiny on the Amistad*, 114.

52. *New York Journal of Commerce*, 10 January 1840; Barber, *A History of the Amistad Captives*, 19–21.

53. Ibid.

54. Ibid.

55. *New York Journal of Commerce*, 13 and 15 January 1840; Barber, *A History of the Amistad Captives*, 23–25.

56. After several more months of waiting while the *Amistad* committee raised funds to send them home, the 35 Mende survivors left New York aboard the *Gentleman* in November 1841. They were accompanied by members of the "Mende Mission" committee, abolitionists traveling to Africa to establish a mission for ministering to the religious needs of the country's inhabitants.

57. http://amistad.mysticseaport.org/library/court/district/1840.1.8.cinquetest.html. Accessed 1 January 2002.

3

THE CASE OF THE SIOUX UPRISINGS (1862)

Joseph P. McKerns

"Let them eat grass."

It was a Sunday like so many other Sundays. Like any other Sunday in western Minnesota since the "white man" came. Nothing remarkable; life was peaceful, pastoral.

The white settlers of the sparsely populated area attended church services as they did every Sunday. Many of the farmers paused after services to shake their minister's hand and exchange a few friendly words. The Sioux living near the settlements also attended church services, including Little Crow, chief of the Mdewakanton Sioux, who made his usual appearance at the Episcopal church near the Lower Sioux Agency along the Minnesota River above New Ulm. He, too, paused after services to share a few friendly words with his pastor. Everything seemed peaceful enough, but on that day, August 17, 1862, a spark was struck that would ignite a firestorm of Sioux rage and fury and consume the Minnesota frontier in the bloodiest conflict between Native Americans and Euro-Americans in the history of the West.[1]

It started like so many other Sundays. It ended as most bloodbaths—hell on earth.

The war, and the sensational news coverage it received, created an indelible image of the Sioux as treacherous savages who should never be trusted no matter how friendly they seemed. From this time forward, to the collective consciousness of white Americans, the Sioux were bloody brutes who deserved no rights or favorable considerations.[2]

At the heart of this conflagration resided the most improbable of characters. Little Crow seemed the least likely of Indians to lead the Sioux in a war against whites. About 52 years old at the time, he was recognized as the titular head of all the Santee Sioux. His father, Big Thunder, had been head chief of the Mdewakanton Sioux. Little Crow was known to his people as Taoya-teduta (His Red Nation). He had become a "cut-hair," a Sioux who cut his long hair short, took up farming or some trade, and adopted the white set-tlers' ways. He lived in a two-story house and wore white men's clothes. He had accommodated himself to the white man and owed his status and power to the whites' greater power as much as to his own tribe. Although he was considered assiduous in negotiating with the federal government, some of his people accused him of accepting bribes in return for trading away Indian lands and threatened to kill him.[3] Despite appearances, Little Crow, described as an "individual rife with contradictions and torn by cultural confusion," would become responsible for the greatest calamity involving white civilians on the American frontier in the nineteenth century.[4]

It started with an argument over eggs.

Four male Mdewakantons in their 20s were returning from a hunting trip 40 miles northeast of the Rice Creek village of the Lower Sioux Agency on August 17, 1862, when they came upon eggs in a hen's nest near a split-rail fence marking the property of Robinson Jones, a farmer. The hunt was un-successful, and the young men—Brown Wing, Breaking Up, Killing Ghost, and Run Against Someone When Crawling—were hungry. They began to argue about whether to take the eggs and risk incurring the white man's anger. Posturing and dares followed, and soon the eggs were "hurled down and war splattered from the broken shells."[5] That's the popular, uncompli-cated explanation for a war in which more than 400 white settlers, 113 federal soldiers, and approximately 200 Sioux lost their lives.[6] The story of the smashed eggs may explain what sparked the Sioux rage of August 18 and 19, 1862, but the reasons why the rage ignited are complex.

The Santee, who were the eastern division of the Sioux Nation, were com-prised of four tribes: Mdewakanton ("people of the sacred or spirit lake"), Wahpekute ("people who shoot in the leaves, or hunt in the timber), Wah-peton ("people of the leaf, or people who live in the timber), and Sisseton ("people who live in the swamp").[7] Minnesotans did not see the Sioux as necessarily warlike or threatening before 1862. They knew many of the Sioux, especially those who had become "cut-hairs," and considered them friendly. Of course, most people had heard the stories of the Spirit Lake Massacre of 1857, when a small band of Santee Sioux led by Inkpaduta murdered 30 settlers in northwestern Iowa. Inkpaduta and his band became enraged when they found that whites had built homes and fences along the sacred Okoboji Lakes (the Spirit Lakes). But everyone knew those Sioux were renegades, outcasts from their tribes. Their leader, Inkpaduta, a Wahpekute, was a violent man, described as a hot-tempered, hateful person. He was, and is, recognized as a military leader of considerable talent but is remembered by history as an "incorrigible killer without equal in the long story of the Sioux people."[8]

Minnesotans may have believed that Inkpaduta and his band were atypical of the Sioux they knew, but what they misunderstood or failed to see altogether was what lay beneath Inkpaduta's fury. The Santee harbored a deep resentment against whites that stemmed from broken treaties, broken promises, dishonesty, disrespect for Sioux traditions, and abuse, especially of Sioux women. The once-vast Santee lands were eroded by treaties in 1851 and 1858. By 1862, the Santee lands were reduced to a sliver, 10 miles wide and 150 miles long, following the flow of the Minnesota River, northwest to southeast, from Big Stone Lake near the Dakota border to the settlement of New Ulm. Two Indian agencies served the area: an "Upper Sioux Agency" near Yellow Medicine River and, to the southeast, a "Lower Sioux Agency" near Redwood.[9] Sioux Indian agent Thomas J. Galbraith said the agencies were part of the government's policy to transform the Santee into farmers:

The theory . . . was to break up the communal system among the Sioux; weaken and destroy their tribal religion; individualize them by giving each a separate home, and having them subsist by industry—the sweat of their brows; till the soil; make labor honorable and idleness dishonorable; or, as it was expressed in short, "make white men of them."[10]

An argument over eggs may have been the spark, but it was the mistreatment by traders and agents the Santee were forced to endure that provided the tinder that fueled their rage. According to Chief Big Eagle, the list of grievances was long:

- Unscrupulous traders who appropriated much of the annuity goods intended for the Sioux.
- Dishonest Indian agents who substituted goods for the money to be paid Indians.
- The treaties of 1851 and 1858, which promised the Sioux annual annuities of gold and provisions in return for their land, but often the Sioux never received the payments, which instead went to pay debts to traders and agents.
- Delayed disbursements of food provisions during 1862 even though the agencies' stocks were full. One local tradesman, Andrew Myrick, said, "If they're hungry, let them eat grass." When the Sioux were forced to make bread with grass, it sickened and weakened them.
- Cultural differences between the whites and the Sioux, which included whites' arrogance toward the Sioux and disdain for Sioux beliefs and customs.
- White men's frequent abuse of Sioux women.[11]

After smashing the eggs, the four young Mdewakanton males went up to Robinson Jones's house and demanded food. Jones refused. When Jones and a friend named Webster walked to the house of Howard Baker, where Mrs. Jones was, the four Santee followed. The young males proposed a game of target shooting to which Jones agreed, but after a few rounds they turned on Jones and fatally shot him. Webster, Mrs. Jones, and most of the other whites were also killed, including Jones's 15-year-old adopted daughter. After they left Baker's farm, one of the young males stopped at Jones's house and shot the girl as she waited on the porch for her parents.

The young men had committed an act the Santee leaders knew would incur the wrath of whites. All Santee would be punished for the young men's rash act, they believed, so it was better to fight and die than to wait for the white man's vengeance.[12] At first, Little Crow tried to dissuade the Santee from going to war, saying, "Kill one, two, ten and ten times ten will come to kill you."[13] However, he finally relented and agreed to lead them. A decision was made to attack the Lower Agency on the morning of the next day, August 18, 1862.

Originally the chiefs planned the attack to be aimed only at the soldiers, the forts, and the agencies, but the smoldering resentment of the Santee over their condition burst into a rage and fury, and the "peaceful Santee farmers of Sunday reverted to the painted Santee warriors of Monday." Following the attack on the agency, the Santee returned to the Sioux way of war—warriors breaking off into small independent bands that raided across the area. It also meant the merciless killing of whatever enemy crossed their path—men, women, children. In short, everyone.[14]

When the attacks began, there were four Army garrisons in the region around the Santee Reservation: Fort Abercrombie, Fort Ripley, Fort Ridgely, and Fort Randall. Frontier forts at the time were not constructed as popular culture and the mass media portray them today; that is, they were not "stockades." The forts were usually build without walls or barriers, typically a collection of buildings surrounding a central parade or drill area. The total command at the four forts numbered 600 volunteers. There had been 900 regular Army troops garrisoned there in 1860–61, but with the start of the Civil War, the regulars were transferred east to join the main Union Army. These volunteer troops were matched against 800 to 1,500 Santee warriors. There was a total white population of 175,000 in the region.

At the Lower Agency, Andrew Myrick was among the first killed, "with the grass he'd have the Sioux eat stuffed in his mouth."[15] More than 20 other whites at the agency were also killed. One white who survived began to spread the warning that the Santee were attacking the agency. A detachment of 46 soldiers sent to investigate were attacked. Half were killed, including their commander, Captain John Marsh. In a 23-county area on that first day, more than 400 white civilians died.

On August 20, a large body of Santee, under the leadership of Little Crow, attacked Fort Ridgely. Although nearly two dozen soldiers were killed, the attack failed because the fort had advance warning about the attack on the Lower Sioux Agency. On August 22–23, the Sioux attacked New Ulm, a German–Scandinavian settlement near the southern end of the Santee Reservation. The townspeople were prepared for the attack and had constructed barricades and earthworks. Attacks during the two days were repulsed, but

36 people were killed. The settlement was evacuated on August 25, and a number of buildings were burned by the Sioux. Fear spread over a four-state area as rumors spread that the Chippewa and other tribes would join the Santee and the other Sioux tribes in a massive attack. But the rumors were unfounded—the Santee were alone. The Chippewa were their enemies and even offered to fight them. However, news reports that the rumors were false were buried beneath a wail of sensational news accounts of atrocities, massive Indian armies, and Confederate agents instigating and orchestrating the fighting.[16]

Minnesota Governor Alexander Ramsey sent an urgent message to the Union Army's general-in-chief, Henry Halleck, asking that reinforcements be sent to the Minnesota frontier. Halleck refused to do so, but with rumors of Confederate influence in the Santee uprising bubbling, Ramsey was able to convince Secretary of War Edwin M. Stanton to appeal to President Abraham Lincoln because Minnesota was as much in danger of being lost to the United States as were the southern states. Lincoln responded by creating a Military Department of the Northwest on September 6, 1862, composed of Minnesota, Wisconsin, and the Dakota Territory. General John Pope, who had commanded the Union Army in its demoralizing defeat at Second Bull Run in July, was given the command.

Former Governor Henry Hastings Sibley, who many considered sympathetic to the Sioux plight before August 18, was appointed to command a regiment of 1,500 troops to pursue Little Crow and the Santee. The setbacks suffered by the Santee at Fort Ridgely and New Ulm demoralized many of Little Crow's followers, and soon the Sioux chiefs from the Upper Agency began to waver and abandon Little Crow because they thought the fight was hopeless. Sibley's forces relentlessly pursued Little Crow and inflicted defeats in several battles. At Wood Lake, on September 22, rather than wait to be attacked by Sibley, Little Crow decided to attack first. The Santee held the upper hand at first, but the battle turned against them, and they broke off. That night the remaining chiefs and Little Crow argued about what to do next—give up, flee, or fight. Most favored staying and surrendering, hoping that by releasing their white hostages they would gain some favorable considerations. However, Little Crow and many of the other leaders escaped with a band of 200 men, women, and children. They evaded capture for some time, but in the end they were captured or killed or returned to the reservation. On September 23, Sibley planned to assault the Santee camp, but the Sioux who remained surrendered. More than 2,000 Sioux were arrested during the next two weeks.[17]

The perception of Sioux held by white Americans as a result of the war was due as much to images created by newspaper accounts of the war as it was to the atrocities committed. Suddenly, the West seemed to be a particularly dangerous place to live. To many easterners, the West became a place of sudden, violent death—at least so it seemed to those who regularly read the newspapers. Sometimes the only news of the West was "bad" news—violence, bloodshed, death. Historian John Coward has said that as a result of the way journalists wrote about the West, and especially about Native Americans, Indians in the press seemed more threatening and violent than real-life Native Americans, an observation made by many western travelers of the time.[18] At times, the Indian was portrayed in the press as a sensitive and proud child of the forest, but in news stories of Indian attacks, the dominant image was of a sneaky, treacherous, cruel, and barbaric "cutthroat"—a race of naturally violent and warlike people.[19] The news was almost always couched in sensational and graphic detail:

Mr. Porter . . . saw four wounded persons, . . . in the agonies of death. They were cut with hatchets in the head, arms, &c. One little girl was cut across the face, breast and side; a little boy was dreadfully cut up, also, a middle-aged woman. . . . In an adjoining room . . . a child with its head cut off, and sixteen other gashes upon its person, and eleven others similarly mutilated.[20]

Separating truth from falsehood, rational account from overwrought imagination, and rumor from fact in the news about the West was as difficult then as it is now. The manner in which newspapers reported western news, especially news of war, death, and Indians, may account for the prevalence of rumor and exaggeration amid a wealth of heinous acts committed by both sides during the history of Plains warfare. Many newspapers seemed to publish every report, every rumor, every "eyewitness" account that came their way, with little attempt to verify the stories. Of course, if the only information reaching the newspapers was exaggeration and rumor, then it would have been especially difficult to verify anything to the contrary. However, the problem was not just the sources of information; it was as much the perception of information and the expectations of journalists and readers about the events at hand that shaped the news. Communication scholar James W. Carey has said of news that "nothing new is learned, but . . . a particular view of the world is portrayed and confirmed."[21]

The Sioux may have seemed friendly before 1862, but the overall perception of Native Americans held by white Americans for a long time had been skewed toward two extremes—the romantic "noble savage" image of James Fenimore Cooper's "Leatherstocking Tales" and Henry Wadsworth Longfellow's "Hiawatha" or the fiendish and cruel "devils in human shapes" of every white person's nightmare.[22] In wars with Native Americans, the worst was expected and usually affirmed. John Nicolay, Abraham Lincoln's secretary, visited Minnesota after the Sioux war and wrote an article for the *Continental Monthly* magazine in 1863 describing his reaction to what he had seen and heard about the furious Santee attacks. His reaction may be taken as representative of the reaction of many Euro-Americans in the East who had never seen the frontier but knew about it only through what they read in the newspapers and magazines:

We were beginning to regard the poetry of the palisades as a thing of the past, when, suddenly, our ears were startled by the echo of the war-whoop, and the crack of the rifle, and our hearts appalled by the gleam of the tomahawk and the scalping knife, as they descended in indiscriminate and remorseless slaughter, on defenseless women and children on our border.[23]

If one were to group the newspaper accounts of the 1862 war into categories or themes, it would become clear that most stories focused on a small set of themes, all of which seemed to play off or up to whites' fears of Indians. Many of the stories portrayed the Santee as wild beasts on the hunt, excited by the smell of blood. The Sioux were reduced to being less than human.

Another theme that emerges out of the news stories sees the Santee as an accomplished, disciplined fighting force, such as European armies of the time, when in fact the Sioux traditionally waged war by attacking and raiding in small bands and seldom as a large group. The words used to describe the Santee were of the kind often used in describing formal European-style warfare in which large bodies of trained soldiers were maneuvered about a battlefield under a clear set of tactical and strategic commands.

A third theme in the reporting focused on the possibilities (usually said to be confirmed fact) that the Santee were conspiring with their old enemies, such as the Pawnee and the Chippewa, and with all the other Sioux tribes throughout the West to mass together into a war of unprecedented scope and ferocity. Or another aspect of this conspiracy theme was that at the root of the war lie meddling southern agents who were inciting the otherwise peaceful Santee to war. Even the most flimsy hearsay evidence of either of these two "conspiracies" was likely to be accepted as true if it came from a source the press considered reliable, which was usually anyone who was not a Native American. The following are some examples of these themes:

INDIAN AS BEAST

Stories of this type portrayed the Sioux as if they were wild beasts and predators excited by the scent of blood and compelled to slaughter their prey. For example, one participant in the war described what happened when the Sioux first heard of the killings following the argument over eggs:

The fact that they were *Indians,* intensely hating the whites, and possessed of the inclinations and revengeful impulses of *Indians,* and educated to the propriety of the indiscriminate butchery of their opponents, would raise the moral certainty that, as soon as the first murder were committed, all the young men were impelled by the sight of blood and plunder—by the contagion of example."[24]

The *Janesville Daily Gazette,* a Wisconsin newspaper, reported an account given by a Mr. Frencer,[25] who said he visited the site of the first attack and found it to be "a habitation of death" with "the former occupants lying dead, some on the doorsteps, some inside, others scattered in yards."[26] On August 25, the *New York Times* carried its first story on the attacks with this headline:

THE INDIAN MASSACRE

Terrible Scenes of Death and Misery in Minnesota—Five Hundred Whites Supposed to be Murdered—The Sioux Bands United Against the Whites—Fort Ridgely in Danger[27]

The *Times* also carried a lengthy report on August 27, based on a letter received from a Mr. Van Warren, with this headline: "TERRIBLE BARBARITIES PRACTICED BY THE SAVAGES." In the story, Van Warren described how the roads between the Lower Agency and New Ulm "are lined with murdered men, women, and children." He told of how children were forced to watch their parents being murdered or burned alive. "Every species of torture and barbarity the imagination can picture, seems everywhere to have been resorted to."[28]

INDIAN AS MILITARISTIC FOE

These types of stories reported accounts that exaggerated the number and cohesiveness of the Sioux involved in the attacks, thus playing into whites' fears of their civilization being swept away by "barbaric hordes" in the manner of the Huns and the Mongols of Old World history. A source no less than Henry Sibley himself believed at first that there were 4,000 to 5,000 warriors involved.[29] Perhaps he had heard the report of Major Galbraith, one of the Indian agents, who said he was told "by one of the Indians" that 10,000 Sioux and other tribes from northern Missouri were in arms.[30]

Often, the Sioux's movements were described in terms and phrases usually used in explaining the maneuvers of a trained and disciplined military force, such as the Union and Confederate armies then fighting in Virginia. The Sioux were said to present "a formidable array"[31] and that they were "advancing on Mankato."[32] They were a well-equipped army, "with new muskets, having bayonets, and all the modern improved small arms."[33] Attacks by the Sioux were described much as one would expect Civil War battles to be described: "The enemy is now advancing in force from the north, and the cannon and howitzers are playing upon them."[34]

The *New York Times,* like many eastern newspapers, relied on the *St. Paul Pioneer* for most of its reports. In its August 25 edition, the *Times* reported information received, either by telegraph or through newspaper exchanges, from the *Pioneer* of August 21, which said that the Sioux were "marching" on Shasta, Minnesota, and that the towns of St. Peter, Henderson, and Glencoe have been burned. The situation of the Army garrison at Fort Ridgely was described as desperate when it reported a request for reinforcements given to Governor Ramsey: "we cannot hold out much longer. Our little band is exhausted and decimated."[35]

It was noted that even though General Sibley could not reach the fort with his 1,200 troops until the next day, "a day of reckoning for the Indians will be at hand."

INDIAN AS CONSPIRATOR

Throughout the conflict, stories reported that the Sioux attacks were instigated by Confederate agents. For example, the *New York Times* reported on August 25 that is generally believed that the Sioux were incited by Indians from Missouri as well as secessionists from that state. It went on to say that according to a letter from St. Paul, dated August 20, "the general opinion among the best informed . . . is that these Indians troubles originated with" southern agents.[36]

Another line of reporting was that the Sioux had made peace with their traditional enemies, the Pawnee and the Chippewa, who would unite with them to kill whites, or that the theater of war was extended far beyond Minnesota's borders. As evidence the *New York Times* pointed to the attack on Fort Ridgely as "unprecedented in Indian history," which was instigated by white men, probably southern provocateurs, who were seen among the Sioux before the attack.[37] Stories of this type seemed to arouse similar fears among whites, as did reports of slave rebellions instigated by abolitionists, such as John Brown's raid on Harper's Ferry in 1859, did among southern whites prior to the Civil War.

Stories that raised doubts about the rumors and exaggerations in the news were few and often undercut their own credibility. On August 31, the *New York Times* reported that news of thousands of Sioux warriors being involved in the attacks was highly unlikely since the number exceeded what was possible given the government's tallies of the total Sioux population in Minnesota. Also, the *Times* wrote that earlier reports out of Iowa that Sioux were massing there were exaggerations as well. In the end, however, the story actually reaffirmed whites' perceptions of Native Americans when it commented that the greater danger was not in the number of Sioux but in their "subtle and skulking mode of warfare."[38]

The trials of the Sioux accused of committing crimes during the war were quick and neat. Nearly 400 Sioux and mixed-bloods were charged; of these, 307 were convicted and sentenced to be hanged. Sixteen others were sentenced to prison. General Sibley convened the first trials at Camp Release, near Wood Lake, where the Sioux surrendered September 28. He then moved his army and the prisoners to the Lower Sioux Agency, where the trials resumed on October 25. The Sioux were tried before a military court-martial composed of five officers. Evidence against the accused was gathered by the Reverend Stephen R. Riggs, who, along with a mixed-blood, Antoine Frenier, acted as an interpreter. The prosecution's approach was simple. After it gathered detailed information about the attacks, murders, and other incidents, it was enough just to place an accused at the scene in order to convict him. Often, the Sioux admitted to being at a particular battle or incident, and this was sufficient for a finding of guilt. Having the wrong name or a name similar to someone else might be enough for a death sentence, as happened to one Santee who was hanged for a crime he probably did not commit despite testimony that he saved a white woman's life.[39]

The evidence may have been flimsy, but the desire for vengeance was not. Isaac V. D. Heard, the court reporter, described the proceedings in a matter-of-fact manner:

The trials were elaborately conducted until the commission became acquainted with the details of the different outrages and battles, and then, the only point being the connection of the prisoner with them, five minutes would dispose of a case.

If witnesses testified, or the prisoner admitted, that he was a participant, sufficient [cause] was established. As many as forty were sometimes tried in a day. Those convicted of plundering were condemned to imprisonment; those engaged in individual massacres and in battles, to death."[40]

The few news reports published about the trials described in graphic detail the acts committed by the Sioux. The *Janesville Daily Gazette* reported testimony that three young girls were taken captive and raped. One of the girls, aged 14, was raped by 17 "of the wretches"; another, a wounded girl, was raped and died from subsequent injuries the same day. In another instance, a girl was struck and believed dead. When a Sioux tried to rape her, she tried to stop him but was struck with a hatchet that "dashed her brains out—a blessed fate in comparison with that which otherwise was designed for her."[41] The newspaper commented that the "people of Minnesota, to a man, are in favor of their immediate execution."

The trials were expedited by the testimony of Joseph Godfrey, an African American known to the Sioux as Otakle—"He Who Kills Many." He was among the first to be tried, and the evidence against him was among the strongest presented. At first he was convicted and condemned to death, but when he volunteered to testify against the others, he won the sympathy of the court, and his sentence was commuted to 10 years in prison. His recall of incidents was articulate, detailed, and often corroborated by other witnesses. One newspaper called him "a providence, specially designated as an instrument of justice."[42] A graphic example follows:

They asked me why I didn't have a gun, or knife, or some weapon. I told them I had no gun—the old man had taken it away. One Indian had a spear, a gun, and a little hatchet. He told me to take the hatchet, and that I must fight with the Indians, and do the same they did, or I would be killed. We started down the road. We saw two wagons with people in them coming toward us.

Later in the story,

There was an old man, a boy and two young woman at the house—Dutch people. The family's name was something like "Masseybush." The boy and two girls stood outside, near the kitchen door. Half of the Indians went to the house, half remained in the road. The Indians told me to tell the whites that there were Chippeways about, and that they (the Indians) were after them. I did not say any thing. The Indians asked for some water. The girls went into the house, and the Indians followed and talked in Sioux. One said to me, "Here is a gun for you." Dinner was on the table, and the Indians said, "After we kill, them we will have dinner." They told me to watch the road, and when the teams came up to tell them. I turned to look, and just then I heard the Indians shoot; I looked, and two girls fell just outside the door. I did not go in the house; I started to go round the house. We were on the back side of it, when I heard the Indians on the road hallooing and shouting. They called me, and I went to the road and saw them killing white men. My brother-in-law told me that I must take care of a team that he was holding; that it was his. I saw two men killed that were with this wagon. I did not see who were killed in the other wagon. I saw one Indian stick his knife in the side of a man that was not yet dead; he cut his side open, and then cut him all to pieces. His name was Wakantonka (great spirit).

Godfrey continued,

There were about ten Indians at the house, and about the same number in the road. I got into the wagon and the Indians all got in. We turned and went toward New Ulm. When we got near to a house the Indians all got out and ran ahead of the wagons, and two or three went to each house, and in that way they killed all the people along the road. I staid in the wagon, and did not see the people killed. They killed the people of six or eight houses—all until we got to the "Travelers' Home." There were other Indians killing people all through the settlement. We could see them and hear them all around. I was standing in the wagon, and could see three, or four, or five Indians at every house.

When we got near the "Travelers' Home" they told me to stop. I saw an old woman with two children—one in each hand—run away across the yard. One Indian, Maza-bom-doo, who was convicted, shot the old woman, and jumped over and kicked the children down with his feet. The old woman fell down as if dead. I turned away my head, and did not see whether the children were killed.

Godfrey then described how the Indians found a jug of whiskey in the wagon and started drinking, how they came upon another house and murdered the whites living there, how they saw another wagon and became afraid, backtracking past the "Travelers' Home" and then hiding from the white men in the wagon. Then

they sounded the bugle and started to cross the bridge, running their horses. The foremost wagon had one horse, of a gray color; three men were in it, and had the flag. Just as they came across the bridge, the Indians raised up and shot. The three men fell out, and the team went on. The Indians ran and caught it. The other wagon had not got across the bridge. I heard them shoot at the men in it, but I did not see them.

After the Indians brought the second wagon across the bridge, three Indians got in the wagon. After that all of them talked together, and said that it was late (the sun was nearly down), and that they must look after their wives and children that had started to go to Red-Wood. Many of these Indians lived on the lower end of the reservation. The two horse team that they had just taken was very much frightened, and they could not hold them.

They told me I must take and hold them, and drive them. I took the team, and they all got in. We then had four teams. We started from there, and went on up. When we got to where the first people were killed, the Indians told me to drive up to the house. The two girls were lying dead. I saw one girl with her head cut off; the head was gone. One Indian, an old man, asked who cut the head off; he said it was too bad. The other Indians said they did not know. The girls' clothes were turned up. The old man put them down. He is now in prison; his name is Wazakoota; he is a good old man. While we stood there one wagon went to another house, and I heard a gun go off.[43]

In some ways, Godfrey's testimony is reminiscent of that given by the infamous Kato Kaitlan in the O. J. Simpson trial. Godfrey claimed that he was minding his own business, farming in the fields when the fighting broke out, and that he was forced to join:

The first time I heard of the trouble I was mowing hay. About noon an Indian was making hay near me. I went to help him, to change work; he was to lend me his oxen. I helped him lead some hay, and as we took it to his place we heard hallooing, and saw a man on horseback with a gun across his legs before him. When he saw me he drew his gun up and cocked it. The Indian with me asked him "What's the matter?" He looked strange. He wore a new hat—a soft gray hat—and had a new white leather ox or mule whip. He said all the white people had been killed at the agency. The Indian with me asked who did it, and he replied the Indians, and that they would soon be down that way to kill the settlers toward New Ulm. He asked me which side I would take. He said I would have to go home and take off my clothes, and put on a breech-clout. I was afraid, because he held his gun as if he would kill me.

Godfrey then relates how he went to his wife and told her they would escape downriver but that her uncle interceded:

I found my squaw's uncle at the house. He scolded my wife and her mother for trying to get away; he said all the Indians had gone to the agency, and that they must go there. He said we would be killed if we went toward the white folks; that we would only be safe to go on and join the Indians. I still had my pants off and put on the breech-clout. I did so. The uncle said we must take a rope and catch a horse.

I started with him toward New Ulm, and we met a lot of Indians at the creek, about a mile from my house. They were all painted, and said I must be painted. They then painted me. I was afraid to refuse.[44]

Of the 307 condemned to death, all but 39 had their sentences reduced to time in prison after President Lincoln reviewed the decisions. Of that 39, one more was reprieved before the day of execution, December 26, 1862. On that unusually warm day after Christmas, more than 4,000 citizens jammed the town square and the surrounding buildings of Mankato, while 1,419 armed troops, bayonets fixed, faced the crowd as they stood between them and the gallows.

At approximately 10 A.M., the 38 condemned Sioux were brought in a orderly fashion to the gallows. They were positioned over the large trap door, their hands bound and their faces covered with a white hood. They chanted their death songs as the nooses were placed around their necks. A lone drummer slowly tapped three times on a drum. The square fell silent. On the third strike the executioner cut a rope, releasing the trapdoor, and all 38 men were hanged simultaneously in the largest mass execution in American history.[45]

While the news stories about the attacks were filled with graphic details of heinous acts, the story published in the *St. Paul Pioneer* was somber, eerily reverential:

On Wednesday [December 24, 1862] each Indian set apart for execution was permitted to send for two or three of his relatives or friends confined in the same prison for the purpose of bidding them a final adieu, and to carry such messages to absent relatives as each person might be disposed to send. . . . Each Indian had some word to send to his parents or family. When speaking of their wives and children almost every one was affected to tears.

Good counsel was sent to the children. They were in many cases exhorted to an adoption of Christianity and the life of good feeling toward the whites. Most of them spoke confidently of their hopes of salvation. . . .

There is a ruling passion with many Indians, and Tazoo could not refrain from its enjoyment even in this sad hour. Ta-ti-mi-ma was sending word to his relatives not to mourn for his loss. He said he was old, and could not hope to live long under any circumstances, and his execution would not shorten his days a great deal, and dying as he did, innocent of any white man's blood, he hoped would give him a better chance to be saved; therefore he hoped his friends would consider his death but as a removal from this to a better world. "I have every hope," said he, "of going direct to the abode of the Great Spirit, where I shall always be happy."

And later in the story,

Several of the prisoners were completely overcome during the leave-taking, and were compelled to abandon conversation. Others again (and Tazoo was one) affected to disregard the dangers of their position, and laughed and joked apparently as unconcerned as if they were sitting around a camp-fire in perfect freedom.

On Thursday, the women who were employed as cooks for the prisoners, all of whom had relations among the condemned, were admitted to the prison. This interview was less sad, but still interesting. Locks of hair, blankets, coats, and almost every other article in possession of the prisoners, were given in trust for some relative or friend who had been forgotten or overlooked during the interview of the previous day. The idea of allowing women to witness their weakness is repugnant to an Indian, and will account for this.

The reporter then describes his visit to the doomed Indians later in the day:

They were all fastened to the floor by chains, two by two. Some were sitting up, smoking and conversing, while others were reclining, covered with blankets and apparently asleep. The three half-breeds and one or two others, only, were dressed in citizens' clothes. The rest all wore the breech-clout, leggins, and blankets, and not a few were adorned with paint. The majority of them were young men, though several were quite old and gray-headed, ranging perhaps toward seventy. One was quite a youth, not over sixteen. They all appeared cheerful and contented, and scarcely to reflect on the certain doom which awaited them. To the gazers, the recollection of how short a time since they had been engaged in the diabolical work of murdering indiscriminately both old and young sparing neither sex nor condition, sent a thrill of horror through the veins. Now they were perfectly harmless, and looked as innocent as children. They smiled at your entrance, and held out their hands to be shaken, which yet appeared to be gory with the blood of babes. Oh treachery, thy name is Dakota.

The reporter also described how several of the Indians received communion and were baptized by Father Ravoux. Then he related what transpired the next morning, execution day:

The doomed ones wished it to be known among their friends, and particularly their wives and children, how cheerful and happy they all had died, exhibiting no fear of this dread event. To the skeptical it appeared not as an evidence of Christian faith, but as a steadfast adherence to their heathen superstitions.

They shook hands with the officers who came in among them, bidding them good-by as if they were going on a long and pleasant journey. They had added some fresh streaks of vermilion and ultramarine to their countenances, as their fancy suggested, evidently intending to fix themselves off as gay as possible for the coming exhibition. They commenced singing their death-song, Tazoo leading, and nearly all joining. It was wonderfully exciting. . . .

After all were properly fastened, they stood up in a row around the room, and another exciting death-song was sung. They then sat down very quietly and commenced smoking again. Father Ravoux came in, and after addressing them a few moments, knelt in prayer, reading from a Prayer-book in the Dakota language, which a portion of the condemned repeated after him. During this ceremony nearly all paid the most strict attention, and several were affected even to tears. . . . The caps were then put upon their heads. These were made of white muslin taken from the Indians when their camps were captured, and which had formed part of the spoils they had taken from the murdered traders. They were made long, and looked like a meal sack, but, being rolled up, only came down to the forehead, and allowed their painted faces yet to be seen.

They received these evidences of their near approach to death with evident dislike. When it had been adjusted on one or two, they looked around on the others who had not yet received it with an appearance of shame. Chains and cords had not moved them—their wear was not considered dishonorable—but this covering of the head with a white cap was humiliating. There was no more singing, and but little conversation and smoking now. All sat around the room, most of them in a crouched position, awaiting their doom in silence, or listening to the remarks of Father Ravoux, who still addressed them. . . . The three half-breeds were the most affected, and their dejection of countenance was truly pitiful to behold.

The reporter then describes how, at 10 A.M., the condemned were led into the street, then to the scaffold:

They went eagerly and cheerfully, even crowding and jostling each other to be ahead, just like a lot of hungry boarders rushing to dinner in a hotel. The soldiers who were on guard in their quarters stacked arms and followed them, and they in turn, were followed by the clergy, reporters, etc.

As they commenced the ascent of the scaffold the death song was again startled, and when they had all got up, the noise they made was truly hideous. It seemed as if Pandemonium had broken loose. It had a wonderful effect in keeping up their courage. One young fellow, who had been given a cigar by one of the reporters just before marching from their quarters, was smoking it on the stand, puffing away very coolly during the intervals of the hideous "Hi-yi-yi," "Hi-yi-yi," and even after the cap was drawn over his face he managed to get it up over his mouth and smoke. Another was smoking his pipe. The noose having been promptly adjusted over the necks of each by Captain Libby, all was ready for the fatal signal.

The solemnity of the scene was here disturbed by an incident which, if it were not intensely disgusting, might be cited as a remarkable evidence of the contempt of death which is the traditional characteristic of the Indian. One of the Indians, in the rhapsody of his death-song, conceived an insult to the spectators which it required an Indian to conceive, and a dirty dog of an Indian to execute.

The refrain of his song was to the effect that if a body was found near New Ulm with his head cut off, and placed in a certain indelicate part of the body, he did it. "It is I," he sung, "it is I"; and suited the action to the word by an indecent exposure of his person, in hideous mockery of the triumph of that justice whose sword was already falling on his head.

At this dramatic point, the reporter wrote how a "painful and breathless suspense held the vast crowd":

Three slow, measured, and distinct beats on the drum by Major Brown, who had been announced as signal officer, and the rope was cut by Mr. Duly (the same who killed Lean Bear, and whose family were attacked)—the scaffold fell, and thirty-seven lifeless bodies were left dangling between heaven and earth. One of the ropes was broken, and the body of Rattling Runner fell to the ground. The neck had probably been broken, as but little signs of life were observed; but he was immediately hung up again. While the signal-beat was being given, numbers were seen to clasp the hands of their neighbors, which in several instances continued to be clasped till the bodies were cut down.

As the platform fell, there was one, not loud, but prolonged cheer from the soldiery and citizens who were spectators, and then all were quiet and earnest witnesses of the scene. For so many, there was but little suffering; the necks of all, or nearly all, were evidently dislocated by the fall, and the after struggling was slight. The scaffold fell at a quarter past ten o'clock, and in twenty minutes the bodies had all been examined by Surgeons Le Boutillier, Sheardown, Finch, Clark, and others, and life pronounced extinct.

The bodies were then cut down, placed in four army wagons, and, attended by Company K as a burial-party, and under the command of Lieutenant Colonel Marshall, were taken to the grave prepared for them among the willows on the sand-bar nearly in front of the town. They were all deposited in one grave, thirty feet in length by twelve in width, and four feet deep, being laid on the bottom in two rows with their feet together, and their heads to the outside. They were simply covered with their blankets, and the earth thrown over them. The other condemned Indians were kept close in the quarters, where they were chained, and not permitted to witness the executions.[46]

This lengthy story was the exception. Overall, the trials and executions received little attention from the press. The stories were spotty and few in number. The manner in which the trials were conducted mitigated against lengthy, graphic news reports as was typical of stories about the war. The trials were quickly and expeditiously handled. There was no drama, certainly nothing of the kind the press fed on in reporting the war. Lacking drama, there was no story except to report the outcome. Nevertheless, the war and its aftermath forever altered the relationship between the Sioux and the U.S. government and fixed in the American public's mind an image of the Sioux and of all the Plains Indians as "devils in human shape."

It was an image that persisted in popular culture well into the twentieth century. It did not begin to change until a vigorous movement for civil rights and human dignity by African Americans in the 1950s and 1960s forced the American public and its media to reconsider past images and beliefs about all people.

And that reconsideration continues.

NOTES

1. Rex Alan Smith, *The Moon of Popping Trees* (New York: Reader's Digest Press, 1975), 34.

2. Ibid., 35.

3. Michael Clodfelter, *The Dakota War: The United States Army versus the Sioux, 1862–1865* (Jefferson, N.C.: McFarland & Company, 1998), 20–21; Charles M. Oehler, *The Great Sioux Uprising* (New York: Oxford University Press, 1959), 17.

4. Gary C. Anderson, *Little Crow: Spokesman for the Sioux* (St. Paul: Minnesota Historical Society Press, 1986), 4, 39.

5. Clodfelter, *The Dakota War,* 35.

6. Ibid., 66–67.

7. Ibid., 18.

8. Clodfelter, *The Dakota War,* 23–27; Joseph Wall, *Iowa: A Bicentennial History* (New York: Norton, 1978), 62–62; Doane Robinson, *A History of the Dakota or Sioux Indians* (Minneapolis: Ross & Haines, 1956), 342–44.

9. Clodfelter, *The Dakota War,* 37 ff.; William W. Folwell, *A History of Minnesota,* vol. 1 (St. Paul: Minnesota Historical Society Press, 1924), 266–304, 352–54.

10. Clodfelter, *The Dakota War,* 38; Roy W. Meyer, *History of the Santee Sioux: United States Indian Policy on Trial* (Lincoln: University of Nebraska Press, 1980), 109–10.

11. Kenneth Carley, ed., "Chief Big Eagle's Story," *Minnesota History* 38, no. 3 (September 1862): 3, 130; Folwell, *A History of Minnesota,* vol. 2, 232.

12. Gary C. Anderson and Alan R. Woolworth, eds., *Through Dakota Eyes: Narrative Accounts of the Minnesota Indian War of 1862* (St. Paul: Minnesota Historical Society Press, 1988), 39; Folwell, *A History of Minnesota,* vol. 2, 415–16.

13. Clodfelter, *The Dakota War,* 37; Willoughby M. Babcock, "Minnesota's Indian War," *Minnesota History* 38, no. 3 (September 1962): 115.

14. Smith, *The Moon of Popping Trees,* 35.

15. Clodfelter, *The Dakota War,* 40 ff.

16. Ibid.

17. Ibid.; Nathaniel West, *The Ancestry, Life, and Times of Henry Hastings Sibley* (St. Paul, Minn., 1889), 224; See also, generally, Joint Committee on the Conduct of War, "Report of Maj. General John Pope," *Supplemental Report of the Joint Committee on the Conduct of War,* vol. 2, 1865 (Washington, D.C.: Goverment Printing Office, 1885); Robert H. Jones, *The Civil War in the Northwest* (Norman: University of Oklahoma Press, 1960).

18. John M. Coward, *The Newspaper Indian: Native American Identity in the Press, 1820–1890* (Urbana: University of Illinois Press, 1999), 5, 13.

19. Ibid., 7.

20. *New York Times,* 27 August 1862.

21. Coward, *Newspaper Indian,* 9–10; James W. Carey, "A Cultural Approach to Communication," *Communication* 2 (1975): 8.

22. *Janesville Daily Gazette,* 24 September 1862.

23. Theodore C. Blegen, *Lincoln's Secretary Goes West: Two Reports by John G. Nicolay on Frontier Indian Troubles 1862* (La Crosse, Wis.: Sumac Press, 1965), 45.

24. Isaac V. D. Heard, *History of the Sioux War and Massacres of 1862 and 1863* (New York: Harper and Bros., 1863), 257.

25. The name Frencer, Frenier, and Feniere appear often in the news stories of several newspapers and may actually have been the same person whose name endured numerous permutations in the hands of journalists.

26. *Janesville Daily Gazette,* 23 August 1862.

27. *New York Times,* 25 August 1862.

28. Ibid., 27 August 1862.

29. Ibid.

30. *New York Times,* 25 August 1862.

31. *Janesville Daily Gazette,* 23 August 1862.

32. Ibid.

33. *Janesville Daily Gazette,* 29 August 1862.

34. *New York Times,* 27 August 1862.

35. Ibid., 25 August 1862.

36. Ibid.

37. *Janesville Daily Gazette,* 11 and 13 September 1862; *New York Times,* 27 August 1862; Clodfelter, *The Dakota War,* 39; Joint Committee on the Conduct of War, vol. 2, 198.

38. *New York Times,* 31 August 1862.

39. Kenneth Carley, *The Sioux Uprising of 1862* (St. Paul: Minnesota Historical Society Press, 1976), 68–69.

40. Heard, *History of the Sioux War and Massacres of 1862 and 1863,* 254–55.

41. *Janesville Daily Gazette,* 22 November 1862.

42. *Janesville Daily Gazette,* 22 November 1862; Carley, *The Sioux Uprising of 1862,* 68; Clodfelter, *The Dakota War,* 57–58.

43. Much of the trial testimony is available on the Web in the form of Isaac Heard's record. See http://www.law.umkc.edu/faculty/projects/ftrials/dakota/Godfrey.html.

44. Ibid.

45. Clodfelter, *The Dakota War,* 58–59; Duane Schultz, *Over the Earth I Come: The Great Sioux Uprising of 1862* (New York: St. Martin's Press, 1992), 2–3; Charles

S. Bryant, *A History of the Great Massacre by the Sioux Indians in Minnesota, Including the Personal Narratives of Many Who Escaped* (Cincinnati: Rickey & Carroll, 1864), 477; Heard, *History of the Sioux War,* 275.

46. For the full text of the story, see http://www.law.umkc.edu/faculty/projects/ftrials/dakota/Trials_of_Prisoners.html#Execution.

4

THE CASE OF ED JOHNSON (1906)

Kittrell Rushing

"I am an innocent man."

Walking down Rowe Road from Ridgeside to the old cemetery takes about seven minutes and a hundred years. The trek from an affluent, predominantly white neighborhood to the abandoned Negro cemetery is quiet, almost lazy, but one not without ghosts. The time and distance down that path to the old cemetery reflect huge and dramatic changes, an evolution in culture, in law, and in attitudes.

The journey, however, does not begin in a white neighborhood or in a black cemetery. It begins with a black man named Ed Johnson.

Johnson was accused of the 1906 bludgeoning and rape of a white teenager, the 18-year-old daughter of the custodian of Forest Hills Cemetery. The evidence against the illiterate saloon sweeper was circumstantial, but public outrage against the suspect could not be contained. The community demanded vengeance. Proclaiming to his last breath, "I am an innocent man," Johnson was yanked from a Hamilton County jail cell to the nearby Tennessee River bridge, dragged by the neck over a bridge support, shot until the rope broke, and blasted and bludgeoned repeatedly as he died on the bridge's plank flooring.

A hundred years later, Johnson's grave is difficult to locate. The old cemetery is unkempt, neglected, and overgrown. Johnson's gravestone is missing. A 1999 book about the case engendered interest in the lynching, and now even the stone marker is gone—removed to a local African American history museum. Standing near where the old grave is supposed to be, visitors can only wonder at the tragedy that preceded Ed Johnson's burial. Today's world differs markedly from Johnson's. Some of the changes date back to that day in 1906 when a mob, in conscious defiance of orders from the Supreme Court of the United States, pulled Johnson from his jail cell and brutally murdered him on that river bridge.

Whether the 18-year-old shop clerk saw the face of the man who raped her that January evening 100 years ago will never be known. What is known is that the victim, Nevada Taylor, was walking from the St. Elmo streetcar stop to her home at the foot of Lookout Mountain. Taylor lived with her father, the cemetery's caretaker, in the cottage of Chattanooga's Forest Hills Cemetery. In the failing daylight, she bundled against the winter cold. Suddenly, a man attacked her from behind. He wrapped a leather strap around her neck and dragged the girl into a shrubbery-secluded spot near the cemetery entrance.[1]

Taylor lost consciousness during the attack. When she awakened, she mustered strength enough to reach home. Her father immediately summoned the sheriff and a doctor. The doctor's examination confirmed their worst fears; she had been sexually assaulted. Taylor later told Hamilton County Sheriff Joseph Shipp that she could remember little of what happened. One essential element of the crime remained etched in Taylor's memory. A black man had attacked her. Other than that, she just did not know.[2]

Since Sheriff Shipp's role in the long, winding, tortuous Ed Johnson case proved critical and since Sheriff Shipp ultimately became the prominent figure in its aftermath, let us take a moment to describe the man. Originally from Jasper County, Georgia, Shipp joined the Confederate Army, spent much of the war in Virginia, and even witnessed the famous duel between the *Monitor* and the *Merrimac,* the war's two most historic vessels. After the war, Shipp returned to Georgia. In 1874, he moved to Chattanooga and had success as a furniture manufacturer. By all standards of the day, Shipp had become a wealthy man by the turn of the century.

Known for his bravery and coolness in critical situations—he had been promoted to the rank of captain for bravery—Shipp was elected Hamilton County sheriff in 1904. Like many former Civil War officers, locals called him "captain," as befitted his Civil War rank. Physically, Shipp could very well have been the model for what is now seen as the stereotypical image of the southern politician. White-haired with neatly trimmed mustache and Van Dyke goatee, Shipp had the appearance of a man strength and substance. Indeed, he looked like a "captain."

Now, the sequence of events:

After hearing Nevada Taylor's description of the attack, Shipp immediately calls for a posse and bloodhounds to search the area. The dogs apparently pick up a scent but lose the trail at the nearby streetcar line.[3]

The morning after the attack, Shipp arrests James Broaden on suspicion of assaulting Taylor. The sheriff and his posse of deputies pick up Broaden because he works in the neighborhood and fits the general physical description of the assailant and is, of course, black. The captain arrests a second suspect, Ed Johnson, after 22-year-old Will Hixson contacts Shipp and identifies Johnson as the man Hixson had seen holding a leather strap near the victim's St. Elmo streetcar stop the night of the attack.

By all accounts, Johnson is illiterate. According to newspaper reports, he lives with his father, "Skinbone" Johnson, and stepmother in a small house in Red Row, a black neighborhood between Chattanooga and St. Elmo.[4] The younger Johnson scrapes by doing odd jobs, never holding anything on a regular basis. He runs errands, cleans stables, sweeps saloons. Newspapers report that Johnson frequently works in the Last Chance Saloon near the Chattanooga rail yards performing menial jobs. Saloon patrons describe Johnson as an easygoing, quiet man. Evidence of his personality, his friends, his likes and dislikes are now, nearly 100 years later, impossible to determine from remaining records. Newspaper stories describe Johnson as a "very dark brown negro" with bloodshot eyes.[5] One newspaper wrote he had a "peculiar method of walking," and when he speaks, his eyes "seem to say that he is thinking of something foreign to the conversation."[6]

The young white man who identifies Johnson as the possible rapist comes forward after newspapers announce a $375 reward. Chattanooga's newspapers leave little doubt that they believe Hixson and that the "fiend" responsible for the crime is Johnson. The newspapers call for speedy justice. News stories in Chattanooga's two dailies express fears that if the court system does not act rapidly, the community will bypass the legal system and act on its own. Fearing for Johnson's safety, Shipp transfers both suspects, Johnson and Broaden, to a jail in Nashville. Johnson will not be returned to the city until the morning of his trial two weeks after the arrest.[7]

The sheriff's concerns proved well founded. The evening after the captain spirited Johnson and Broaden from Chattanooga in a closed buggy, a mob surrounds the jail and demands that Johnson and two other blacks charged with capital crimes be turned over. One has been charged with breaking into Chattanooga's Vine Street orphanage to rape an orphan. The other is being held in the Christmas Eve shooting death of a Hamilton County deputy sheriff. The city's evening newspaper reports,

There were several factions in the mob, one desiring most the death of Westfield, the negro murder [sic], another desiring above all things the death of the rapist (Ed Johnson) and others crying for the life of Ed Smith, who entered the Vine street orphanage. . . . [T]he jail doors were broken from their fastenings and cast, splintered to the floor.[8]

Jail guards on duty summon reinforcements from Troop B of the state militia, which quickly take stations in the jail. Shots are fired from the crowd, and the mob continues its demands for the three prisoners. The crisis is defused only after several Chattanooga business and community leaders, including *Chattanooga Times* newspaper executive Milton Ochs, hurry to the jail from a nearby Chamber of Commerce meeting. The businessmen attempt to persuade the mob that Sheriff Shipp has taken Johnson to another part of the state. The businessmen plead with the mob to disperse.

Businessman and Civil War veteran T. C. Thompson formally places himself under the command of the militia's senior officer, dons a webbed cartridge belt, takes up a carbine, and joins the ranks of the soldiers between the mob and the jail cells. Meanwhile, Chamber committee spokesman Colonel W. J. Bass finally gets the attention of the mob's leaders and elicits an agreement to disperse. Representatives of the crowd are permitted to walk through the jail to see that Johnson is not there. After that, the crowd breaks up, and the street in front of the jail finally empties. The state militia posts guards and sets up outposts at several intersections nearby. The guards remain until dawn the next morning.[9]

Two weeks later, the city's afternoon newspaper, the *Chattanooga Times,* asserts that the passions of the mob did not reflect the will or mood of the city's general population. On the day Johnson's trial begins, the newspaper writes,

The mob that attempted to get at this negro when he was first arrested meant business to be sure. Had they succeeded in laying hands on him at the time, he would have been lynched. However, they were acting under the excitement of that time—when the whole community was stirred by the enormity of the crime. Two or three days was [*sic*] sufficient to cool the passions of that hour and allow the people to regain composure. The chances are that a majority of the men who were in the mob that tried to storm the jail, would now oppose mob violence were it proposed. So in its last analysis the mob is simply intense excitement, and uncontrolled anger. . . . If the negro is guilty he will be hanged by the law; if innocent it will be established and he will be liberated. The good sense of the people has triumphed over hasty and ill-considered action, and the majesty of the law will be preserved.[10]

Shipp then brings Nevada Taylor to Nashville to observe both Johnson and Broaden and, it is hoped, to identify the man responsible for the attack. She tells Shipp that, as best as she can recall, Ed Johnson looks like the man who assaulted her.

Johnson has no need to concern himself with the slow machinations of the judiciary. He is rushed to trial. The presiding criminal court judge, S. D. McReynolds, appoints three local lawyers to represent him. Two have no criminal trial experience, and all three are white, as is the hastily impaneled jury. No effort is made to find black legal representation for Johnson, although several black attorneys practice law in Chattanooga. No effort is made to call blacks for the jury panel. To be fair, none of this is unusual for the times. Black jurors are not considered for such high-profile cases, particularly black on white crimes. The all-white jury, however, becomes an issue later when two black Chattanooga attorneys, Styles Hutchins and Noah Parden, step forward and attempt to appeal Johnson's conviction to the federal district court.[11]

On the first day of the trial, uniformed policemen patrol in and around the county courthouse, and only the judge, court officers, law officers, members of the jury, lawyers, and newspaper reporters are allowed to enter the court-room. The police return Johnson from Nashville early in the morning. According to newspaper descriptions, he arrives in a police wagon pulled by galloping horses and surrounded by a mounted platoon of deputies.[12] The morning session of the trial's first day begins with Judge McReynolds ruling against a defense motion for a continuance, then ordering jury selection to begin.

A panel of 36 prospective jurors has been summoned, and 32 of those appear for the selection process. The *Chattanooga News* reporter lists in his description of the first day's trial the names of each of the men called, whether they are accepted to serve, and, if a man is rejected, the reason why. For a time, it appears as if a jury might never be seated. The first person called from the jury pool is W. C. Ferguson. The prosecution rejects Ferguson, according to the newspaper, because he has "conscientious scruples against capital punishment."[13] The court declares the next man, J. R. Stanfield, incompetent because he is not a freeholder (a property owner).[14] The defense challenges C. P. Mankin. The court then excuses C. B. French because he admits he already has framed an opinion about Johnson's guilt. The state challenges N. G. Taggart, and the defense rejects J. L. Walker. Charles Hall says he had an opinion about Johnson's guilt but tells the court he could lay aside his opinion. Both the state and the defense accept Hall as the first juror, and Judge McReynolds orders Hall to take a seat in the jury box.[15] After this, jury selection continues rapidly throughout the morning, and within a few hours a jury has been impaneled. The lack of diversity among the jurors would seem inappropriate today, but in 1906 Chattanooga and mostly everywhere else, such a jury is the norm—all white, all male, all property owners.

The prosecution wastes no time as it steamrolls to the heart of the case. As its first witness, the prosecution calls the 18-year-old victim, Nevada Taylor. Taylor takes her seat in the witness chair before a hushed courtroom. She then describes events, how she had been attacked from behind, how the assault had rendered her insensible. In dramatic testimony, Taylor explains,

Before he choked me with his hand he waited a minute as if he were listening to find out if anybody were coming. Then he told me in a kind, gentle voice that if I screamed again he would cut my throat. I saw him face to face by the dim light cast by the block signal box on the poles owned by the Rapid Transit company, and it is from this light that I got my best view of him.[16]

And later,

No one came by that I know of at the time. I reached home after coming to myself about 6:45 o'clock, my home being about one and a half to two blocks from the scene of the crime. My father, two brothers and three sisters were at home when I got there and I told them what had happened. They telephoned Sheriff Shipp and Dr. H. B. Wilson was summoned to attend me.[17]

According to the *Chattanooga News,* the most dramatic moment in the morning's proceedings comes when the prosecutor asks Taylor if she would recognize the man if she sees him again. "Miss Taylor turned to the negro Johnson and after looking at him turned to the jury and said: 'I believe he is the man.' "[18]

The rape victim continues to tell her story for several minutes. The prosecutor then asks how she came to identify the man accused of assaulting her. She responds,

I went to Nashville with Sheriff Ship and saw two negroes[19] brought out in the sheriff's office where I could see them. I sat in the obscurity and they were in the light. Sheriff Shipp talked to them, and one of them, from his voice, his size, his face, and everything combined I thought was the negro who assaulted me. He at first had the same soft voice he used in talking to me, and later he changed it to make it deeper. I looked at the negroes and listened to them. Though this negro tried to change his voice I believe that I recognized it. His hat, the one he had on the night of the assault, and the one he had on at the Nashville jail was a soft, dark hat. The brim looked like it had been rolled at one time and had become straightened out. There is no trouble in my mind about this negro being the right man. I want the guilty man punished and I don't want an innocent man punished.[20]

After Taylor leaves the witness stand, the young man who originally identified Ed Johnson as the possible rapist is called. The newspaper describes Will Hixson as a 22-year-old white man employed by the Chattanooga Medicine Company. Hixson tells the court that about 10 minutes to six on the night of the assault, he saw the defendant holding a leather strap near the spot where Nevada Taylor was attacked. Hixson testifies that he knows the man's face from when they worked on the Rock Church, a notable Chattanooga structure at the time. Hixson says that he saw the man and could not be mistaken in his identification:

This defendant here is the negro I saw. The negro looked me full in the face for a minute and then turned away and walked up toward the cemetery gate. I saw him before on Monday morning for he asked me for a match. I looked at the negro good for I had heard that on the night before a purse had been snatched from a lady's hand in Mountain Junction . . . I helped find Johnson, for I remembered seeing the negro with the strap on the night of the crime. I hunted for him from Wednesday morning at 10 o'clock until Thursday at 1 or 2 o'clock. I hunted over Mountain Junction, Alton Park, St. Elmo, Whiteside street, East and West Ninth streets and finally saw him at the rock church talking to a negro.[21]

After spotting Johnson, Hixson says that he telephoned Sheriff Shipp. The sheriff and several deputies arrived shortly afterward. They traced Johnson to the Red Row neighborhood, where they arrested him.

Defense attorneys attempt to undermine Hixson's testimony by pointing out that the young man has come forward only after a $375 reward had been announced. Hixson remains firm that he began hunting for Johnson before he knew of the reward.

During the morning of the trial's second day, the clocks in the Last Chance Saloon become an issue. Trying to place Johnson in the saloon at the time of the crime, defense attorneys call a number of witnesses who testify that they had seen Johnson in the saloon near or at the hour of the crime. The witnesses, the *Chattanooga News* reported, are all "colored, and habitués of the Last Chance saloon" who base their stories on a clock that hangs on the saloon's rear wall. A second, older clock in the saloon hangs on the building's south wall. This second clock, according to most of the witnesses, has not operated for quite some time. The majority of defense witnesses say they base their knowledge of when they saw Ed Johnson in the saloon on the time given by the newer, rear-wall clock. Controversy develops about the clocks when one defense witness contradicts the testimony of other witnesses when he says that on the night of the attack, no clock hung from the rear wall.[22]

The next day's edition of the *Chattanooga News* reports under large headlines,

Dramatic Incidents at Johnson's Trial

Clock Man Testifies He Put Important Time

Piece In Saloon Two Days After the Crime

An employee of a business supply company is placed on the stand and testifies that he installed the working clock on the rear wall of the Last Chance Saloon on January 25, two days after the assault on Nevada Taylor. The prosecution then points out that defense witnesses' testimony placing Johnson in the bar at the time of the attack is based on a nonexistent timepiece. The prosecution's clear implication is that the witnesses have concocted stories to provide an alibi for the defendant.

Shortly after the clock testimony, one of those bizarre moments in a bizarre trial takes place. A juror, C. E. Bearden, suddenly throws up his hands and shouts, "I can't stand it. I can't stand it." As people in the courtroom attend to Bearden, he sits in the jury box, tears streaming down his face. The judge orders a recess until the juror can regain composure.

When the jury returns, the defense requests that Nevada Taylor be brought to the front of the courtroom. Then arrives another bizarre moment as juror J. N. Wrenn requests that Ed Johnson be made to stand with Taylor before the jury. Wrenn then asks, "Miss Taylor, can you state positively that this negro is the one who assaulted you?" Taylor's response: "I will not swear that he is the man, but I believe he is the negro who assaulted me."

At this point, Bearden, the juror who has broken down just minutes before and for whom the recess has been called, begins to weep uncontrollably and cries out, "Miss Taylor, as God sees you, can you say that this is the negro, the right negro?"

Taylor answers in a strong voice. "Listen to me. I would not take the life of an innocent man, but I believe that is the man."

Ordered to stand before Taylor, Johnson puts on his hat, and the three people—Johnson, Taylor, and Bearden—stand in the center of the court-room. The *Chattanooga News* reports the following sequence of events:

Every eye was fastened on the three central figures in this strange group, the weeping juryman, the accused rapist and the victim of the terrible outrage. Back of the jury the judge sat, while to right and left the attorneys for the defense and prosecution leaned forward or stood in their places, watching this scene, which in their memory had never had a precedent in the criminal court room of Hamilton county. At 11:05 o'clock the state closed and it was probably fifteen minutes later when this dramatic scene, which had in it for the spectators all that interest which could center about a scene from some powerful drama played out on a smaller stage for the edification of play-goers, occurred.[23]

Despite what later would be considered significant errors, no moves are made by the defense counsel or the judge for that matter to challenge the judicial proceedings that allow such active jury participation.[24]

The next morning, Friday, February 9, two weeks after the attack, the jury announces the verdict. Ed Johnson is guilty of raping Nevada Taylor. Judge McReynolds orders Johnson to be put to death by hanging. The execution is scheduled 32 days from sentencing—Tuesday, March 13, 1906.

After the verdict, Johnson's lawyers consult with several other prominent Chattanooga attorneys. Their conclusion? No appeal. An appeal, reasons Johnson's court-appointed defenders, would only prolong the inevitable and further inflame the community. Perhaps another point receives considera-tion—that the defense attorneys' safety might be at risk if they attempt to delay the execution. As one bluntly puts it,

We discussed the recent mob uprising and the state of unrest in the community. It was the judgment of all present that the life of the defendant, even if the wrong man, could not be saved; that an appeal would so inflame the public that the jail would be attacked and perhaps other prisoners executed by violence. In the opinion of all of us a case was presented where the defendant, now that he had been convicted by a jury, must die by the judgment of the law, or else, if his case were appealed, he would die by the act of the uprising of the people.

In view of all the conditions, it was the unanimous vote that the law ought to be allowed to take its course if Judge McReynolds were satisfied with the verdict, and if he were to approve it and pass judgment of death on it.[25]

Like so much else in this trial, however, that decision will not stand.

On Monday morning, February 12, three days after the Friday verdict and the apparent abandonment of Johnson by his court-appointed defense team, black Chattanooga attorneys Noah Parden and Styles Hutchins stand before Judge McReynolds and ask permission to appeal the case to the Tennessee Supreme Court. McReynolds tells the men to file a formal motion. The next day, Hutchins and Parden again face McReynolds, this time to request a new trial. The judge denies the motion on a technicality—the motion for an appeal comes one day after the three-day statutory limit for such filings.

In the face of McReynolds's denial, the only option open to Hutchins and Parden is to appeal directly to the Tennessee Supreme Court without the trial judge's sanction. The state court quickly denies the motion. On March 3, 10 days before the scheduled execution, Tennessee's high court explains in catch-22 language that since the original trial judge did not favorably entertain the motion, the high court will not review the case.

The same day that the Tennessee Supreme Court rejects Johnson's plea for review, Parden files a petition for a writ of habeas corpus[26] in the U.S. Circuit Court sitting in Knoxville. The petition alleges that Johnson has been deprived of rights guaranteed by the U.S. Constitution in the conduct of the state criminal trial. Parden's appeal of a state criminal court verdict to the federal court is highly unusual. Many defendant rights that have evolved in the years since 1906 did not then exist. In 1906, no recognition of the right to effective representation existed. In 1906, no clear recognition of a right against self-incrimination existed at the state level. And, finally, in 1906, the applicability of the then 38-year-old's 14th Amendment guarantee of due process was in its early stages of evolution.

Ed Johnson's appeal pushes the federal courts into new territory. The appeal could open the door for federal intervention into the actions of state criminal proceedings. Johnson's lawyers base the appeal on the Habeas Corpus Act of 1867 since the 14th Amendment's guarantee of due process remains an embryonic concept. Ed Johnson's lawyers seek from federal courts what they cannot obtain from the state courts—a new trial—and prevailing opinion and tradition echo the same depressing message: Federal courts have no jurisdiction in state criminal proceedings.

March 10, three days before the scheduled execution. Knoxville's District Court Judge C. D. Clark dismisses Johnson's petition, ruling the district court does not have jurisdiction. Johnson then is turned over to Sheriff Shipp to be hanged. Although Judge Clark denies the petition for habeas corpus, his ruling suggests that Judge McReynolds petition the Tennessee governor to grant a 10-day stay of execution to permit an appeal of the district court's decision.

Judge McReynolds's response, as printed by the *Chattanooga News:*

We do not concede that Judge Clark has a right to grant a stay of execution in Johnson's case, or that he did do it in fact. His order was practically this: "Johnson is given into the hands of the sheriff of Hamilton county to be kept for ten days." The only step now open to the lawyers for Johnson is to take the case to the supreme court and apply for a writ of error.[27]

A survey of Chattanooga lawyers by the *News* reveals that virtually all believe no power can stop or even delay the execution.[28]

On the petition of Judge McReynolds, Tennessee's governor changes the execution date from March 13 to March 20. Parden immediately takes a train to Washington, where he requests an audience with U.S. Supreme Court

Justice John Marshall Harlan. Harlan is the circuit justice of the Sixth Circuit, Tennessee's circuit. If observers consider Johnson's appeal of a state criminal court conviction to a federal district court an unusual tactic, the decision to take the case to the U.S. Supreme Court must appear nothing short of remarkable.

Parden meets with Justice Harlan on Saturday, March 17. Persuaded by Parden's argument, Harlen agrees to hear the appeal of the circuit court's decision. Two days later, one day before Johnson's scheduled execution, the U.S. Supreme Court orders a stay. That order gives the justices time to review Johnson's appeal. Immediately following the issuance of the stay, Sheriff Joseph Shipp receives a telegram informing him that Johnson has become a federal prisoner and that, pending review, Johnson is not to be put to death.[29]

Chattanooga receives the news with consternation. The *Chattanooga News* publishes a lengthy account of the order,[30] quoting state officials that the federal courts have no jurisdiction in state criminal proceedings. The newspaper comments,

The general impression among lawyers is that the Supreme Court will uphold Judge Clark. If it does it will be thirty or sixty days before Johnson can be legally executed, as we understand the case. All of this delay is aggravating to the community. The people of Chattanooga believe that Johnson is guilty, and that he ought to suffer the penalty of the law as speedily as possible. If by legal technicality the case is prolonged and the culprit finally escapes, there will be no use to plead with a mob here if another such crime is committed. Such delays are largely responsible for mob violence all over the country.[31]

The afternoon before the Supreme Court agrees to hear the Johnson petition, a large number of Chattanooga's St. James Baptist Church members visit Johnson in the county jail.[32] The group holds a church service during which Johnson professes his belief in Christ before being baptized in the jailhouse bathtub.

Outside the jail, frustration with the court-ordered delays grow. The belief that the federal courts have no right to interfere with the actions of local courts and local communities proliferate. The county prosecutor says he believes that Judge Clark's dismissal of the petition for a writ of habeas corpus will be upheld. Nevertheless, rumors circulate that citizen action will be taken that evening, and late in the afternoon, men begin to gather outside the county jail.

Sheriff Shipp later claims he had no idea that anyone in the city seriously considered a second attempt against the life of his prisoner. He is so unaware of any danger, Shipp later testifies, that he sends the jail's normal contingent of deputies home; and afterward, he goes home, leaving the responsibility for the jail and its prisoners in the hands of a single jailer, Jeremiah Gibson.

Shortly after the sheriff and his deputies depart for the evening, the crowd outside the jail, now quite large, begins chanting for Ed Johnson. Soon, the emboldened crowd surges into the jailhouse, again splintering the doors only recently repaired from the mob assault a month before. The attackers demand the prisoner and experience no resistance until confronted with the large iron door separating the jail cells from the administrative section of the building. Someone produces a hammer and begins whacking at the locked door.

At this point, the mob demands Jeremiah Gibson's keys. The jailer quickly assents. However, the pounding on the lock has damaged the tumblers. Gibson's key no longer works. The infuriated throng calls for larger and heavier hammers, and the assault continues with sledgehammers. For more than two hours, the enraged mob hammers at the iron doors, uninterrupted by any official.

The men take turns pounding the hinges and door casing. Vibrations from the hammering shake the building. Finally, someone summons Shipp. The sheriff walks from his home to the jail, pushes his way through the crowd, and confronts the mob's leaders. Shipp's presence has no effect, and angry members of the mob push the sheriff into a bathroom. Shipp later claims he attempted to persuade the men to leave, but Shipp also admits he made no effort to seek help from the Chattanooga police, the militia, or his own deputies.

After hours of hammering, the weakened iron hinges of the cell-block door gives way, and the mass surges through. When the attackers reach Johnson on the jail's upper floor, they jerk him from the cell. Johnson stumbles through the wrecked doors and into the street—into the waiting crowd. Witnesses claim Johnson appears stoic and resigned. Johnson pleads to the crowd, asserting his innocence, but witnesses say he remains outwardly calm and brave, apparently determined to remain strong to the end.

According to later testimony, Johnson is dragged, half walking, half running the three blocks to the river. The crowd surges onto the bridge. At this point, the hangmen realize the rope they have tied around Johnson's neck is too short to reach the bridge girders. At the far end of the span, members of the mob stop a trolley and strip the streetcar's bell ropes. As the trolley cords slip over his head and around his neck, the vigilantes drag Johnson under the second span of the bridge. His last words, according to witnesses: "God bless you all."[33]

The doomed man's words inflame the crowd. The noose tightened, and several men heave on the rope, jerking the struggling man high above the shouting throng. People in the mob pull guns and shoot the writhing figure. Johnson is struck several times, and so is the rope. It parts, and the mortally wounded Johnson drops to the bridge floor. One man walks over, points his gun at Johnson, and fires several shots, the body jerking as each bullet hits.[34] The crowd mills about for some time. Photographs are taken, souvenirs one must suppose. If any photographs survive, they have not been located.

Chattanooga newspapers detail the horror of the lynching. The morning paper, in a noticeable change of tone, decries the lawlessness represented by the mob's action:

Chattanooga suffers the shame sent upon her by the red hands of rioters and in humiliation confesses the sin of the wicked wreakers of vengeance who numbered less than fifty out of a community's population of over 70,000. But Chattanooga's good citizenship is dominant and resents with vigor and vehemence the great wrong perpetrated by the unlawful and unruly who are incident to every prosperous and progressive city.

It adds,

Yesterday's news in The Times reporting the tragic ending of Ed Johnson proved a shocking surprise to the great mass of the entire community. The work of Monday's mob was so quickly effected and so little anticipated that the entire public was astounded. As the day advanced there was manifest a disposition on the part of excitable people to magnify reports and rumors of further trouble. Fortunately the situation was taken in hand promptly by the authorities and with the cooperation of conservative men both white and colored the day passed without conflict or unusual incident.[35]

Despite the newspaper's assertion that the day after Johnson's murder passed quietly, the black community reacts. Outraged by the lynching, large numbers of blacks participate in a work stoppage. The strike is almost universal. Chattanooga's larger factories report few blacks come to work the day after the murder, and of those who do, most leave by midmorning.[36]

More than 2,000 people attend Johnson's funeral on Wednesday afternoon. To avoid further mob action, this time from the black community, Sheriff Shipp swears in extra deputies to patrol Chattanooga's streets. The town remains quiet. The day after the funeral, Chattanooga's black population returns to work. Normalcy seems to return to the Tennessee city. Life moves on, but not without consequences.[37]

In the weeks after Johnson's death, Chattanooga newspapers editorialize about the lynching. Stories express regret that mob violence resulted in Johnson's death. However, the papers also emphasize one popular viewpoint in the white community—blame also rests on the shoulders of those who interfered with local law and local rule. The day after the lynching, the *Chattanooga News* writes,

The lynching is a direct result of the ill advised effort to save the negro from the just penalty of the laws of Tennessee. Had not that effort been made, the negro would have been legally executed today at the county jail. He was tried in the criminal court of Hamilton county and convicted of the crime with which he was charged. There was not a scintilla of doubt in the minds of the jury that he was guilty. He had able counsel to defend him; was given every opportunity to establish his innocence, and he failed. His attorneys examined the record carefully; other lawyers were called in as advisory counsel, and together they examined the record. Their unanimous verdict was that the negro had been fairly tried and that an appeal to the Supreme Court of the State was useless. They communicated their conclusion to the negro, and he expressed himself as satisfied with the trial. He waived his right of appeal and expressed his readiness to meet his fate.

It concludes,

Following this action, a couple of colored lawyers took up the case at the request, they assert, of the family of the man. By filing a petition with the judge of the Federal Court of this district for a write of habeas corpus, the case was transferred from the State to the Federal courts. Judge Clark dismissed the application for the write of habeas corpus. Then an appeal was taken to the Supreme Court of the United States. Monday that court granted the appeal, and the mob followed. . . . It was the appeal to the Federal courts that revived the mob spirit and resulted in the lynching. This fact should be a lesson in the future.[38]

To describe the Supreme Court justices as mildly displeased with events in Chattanooga would be to characterize the Civil War as a minor disturbance. The reality has to be a hard one for the justices. Johnson died at the hands of a lynch mob. The clear message from Chattanooga, written in the blood of Ed Johnson: Here's what we think of your stay order!

With Johnson's death, no reason exists for the court to review the petition for a new trial. Whether the trial has been fair or not no longer matters—at least not to a dead man. To the Supreme Court, what matters is that a Chattanooga lynch mob circumvented the court's authority. The high court immediately sends its own investigator to Chattanooga to determine what happened and who was responsible. After that, the Court will determine its course of action.

On December 24, 1906, the Court acts. Flagrant disregard for its orders will not be tolerated. In *United States v. John F. Shipp et al.*,[39] the justices order that the Hamilton County sheriff, several deputy sheriffs, and about a half dozen men identified as being a part of the lynch mob be tried for contempt. In the final and perhaps most bizarre event of all, the case of Ed Johnson has mutated into the case of Sheriff Joseph Shipp.

Three years later, on May 24, 1909, the Court rules in *U.S. v. Shipp*[40] that

the Sheriff committed other acts and did other things evincing a disposition on his part to make it less difficult and less dangerous for the expected mob to lynch Johnson; that about 9 o'clock in the evening of said March 19 (1906) defendants and others conspired to break into the jail, dragged Johnson from his jail cell and lynched him. . . .

By doing so they intended to show their contempt and disregard for this court, and prevent from hearing the Johnson's appeal; that Gibson was the only officer at the jail when the mob broke in, and that, while the mob was in possession of the jail, Sheriff Shipp arrived, but made no effort to prevent the mob from taking Johnson from the jail; that defendants Shipp and Gibson were in sympathy with the mob while pretending to perform their official duty of protecting Johnson, and that they aided and abetted the mob in prosecution and performance of the lynching; that all of these acts were committed by defendants with the intent upon their part to utterly disregard the orders of this court, and to prevent the court from hearing Johnson's appeal.[41]

Sheriff Shipp is sentenced to 90 days in the Washington, D.C., jail. Three of the other defendants, including Gibson (the jailer who gave his jail keys to the mob), are sentenced to 60 days' imprisonment.

In a way, the high court's decision to hold Captain Shipp and the others in contempt validated both the federal courts' and the U.S. Constitution's supremacy over conflicting decisions from the state courts. The decision also signaled that rights guaranteed by the Constitution would be supported and enforced, even in state courts. The decision was another loss for states' rights in the ongoing nineteenth-century battle over supremacy and authority. Ultimately, that battle would explode in the civil rights upheavals of the 1960s and 1970s.

At least one chronicler of the lynching and the subsequent Supreme Court action observed that the episode instigated a major shift in the Court's direction in the twentieth century. That may be overstatement, but there is little doubt that the contempt convictions against the Chattanooga lawmen reflected ongoing changes in U.S. legal philosophy—changes that certainly date from the earliest days of the Republic.

The philosophy and legal decisions surrounding the Ed Johnson lynching continued the transition from near-sovereign state control of legal matters to a broader application of the federal constitution. The change from state sovereignty to federal review can be traced from Chief Justice John Marshall's 1803 decision in *Marbury v. Madison,*[42] through the Nullification Crisis of the 1850s, into the Civil War and the South's defeat, to the adoption of the13th and 14th Amendments, to the Civil Rights Act of 1964, and to the Supreme Court's interpretation and application of the 14th Amendment.

The Shipp decision came during a time in which the concept and power of the 14th Amendment were developing and being used increasingly by the high court to reach into matters once held to be strictly under the purview of the states. The Shipp decision reflected a new willingness to apply federal protections to citizens in what had previously been considered state issues.

One hundred years after Ed Johnson died on a Chattanooga bridge—in part *because* Ed Johnson died on that Chattanooga bridge—virtually all criminal courts look to the U.S. Constitution for guidance.

Ed Johnson's overgrown grave on the side of historical Missionary Ridge represents many things: hate and intolerance to some, due process for all citizens to others. That hidden grave in the Chattanooga underbrush, that grave nearly forgotten by history, also bears witness to the belief in the rule of law over that of the mob.

Who would have thought Ed Johnson's long, winding road would end at the doorstep of the 14th Amendment?

NOTES

1. *Chattanooga Daily Times,* 24 January 1906.

2. Mark Curriden and Leroy Phillips, Jr., *Contempt of Court: The Turn-of-the-Century Lynching That Launched a Hundred Years of Federalism* (New York: Faber and Faber, 1999), 3. *Chattanooga News,* 7 February 1906.

3. *Chattanooga News*, 7 February 1906.

4. Ibid., 8 March 1906.

5. Curriden and Phillips, *Contempt of Court*.

6. *Chattanooga News*, 7 February 1906.

7. *Chattanooga News*, 6 February 1906.

8. Ibid., 26 January 1906.

9. Ibid.

10. Ibid., 7 February 1906.

11. Curriden and Phillips, *Contempt of Court*.

12. *Chattanooga News*, 6 February 1906.

13. Ibid.

14. A freeholder is a property owner with unconditional rights over his or her property, including the right to grant leases and to take out mortgages. At the time of Johnson's trial, many states required that jurors be property owners, that is, "freeholders."

15. *Chattanooga News*, 6 February 1906.

16. Ibid.

17. Ibid.

18. Ibid.

19. Later in the proceedings, Sheriff Shipp revealed that both suspects, Johnson and Broaden, were paraded before Nevada Taylor. The men were asked to speak, to remove their hats, and to stand before the rape victim.

20. *Chattanooga News*, 6 February 1906.

21. Ibid.

22. *Chattanooga News*, 7 February 1906.

23. *Chattanooga News*, 8 February 1906.

24. Curriden and Phillips, *Contempt of Court*.

25. *U.S. v. Shipp*, 214 U.S. 386.

26. A writ of habeas corpus is an order to bring someone who is being held into court, usually for a court review on whether the detention is lawful.

27. *Chattanooga News*, 12 March 1906.

28. Ibid.

29. *U.S. v. Shipp*, 214 U.S. 386.

30. *Chattanooga News*, 19 March 1906.

31. Ibid.

32. Ibid.

33. *Chattanooga News*, 20 March 1906.

34. Ibid.

35. *Chattanooga Daily Times*, 20 and 21 March 1906.

36. Ibid., 21 March 1906.

37. Ibid., 22 March 1906.

38. Ibid., 20 March 1906.

39. 203 U.S. 563 (1906).

40. 214 U.S. 386 (1909).

41. *U.S. v. Shipp*, 214 U.S. 386 (1909).

42. 5 U.S. 137 (1803).

5

THE CASE OF "BIG BILL" HAYWOOD (1907)

David R. Spencer

"Why is it that they are so anxious to 'get' Haywood?"

To the north, the slim mountainous finger touches the Canadian border. To the west and the east lie the rain-soaked mountains of Washington and the mining country of Montana, respectively. Squeezed in-between is an L-shaped state, one of the most beautiful and pristine of the original 48. Its rolling tree-clad hills come in waves, leaving visitors with a sense of tranquillity.

That is Idaho today, but our tale begins on a snowy night in 1905, a night when that tranquillity shattered and the spirit of America was put to the test.

We start with Frank Steunenberg, a descendant of hard-working Dutch immigrants and governor of Idaho during some of its most troubling times. By 1905, tiring of the constant warfare between miners and mine owners, Steunenberg had been away from political conflict for five years. Nonetheless, folks in Caldwell, Idaho, where the Steunenberg family lived, still referred to him as "the governor."[1]

Caldwell hardly qualified as a typical western backwater. No swinging saloon doors, no painted ladies, no hard-as-nails pistoleros riding up and down the main street with six-guns strapped to their sides. Instead, Caldwell was a showcase for the modern West. Automobiles rolled down paved streets past homes and businesses with electricity. And many of Caldwell's citizens, as well as others across Idaho, thanked Frank Steunenberg for the modern amenities and prosperity of towns like Caldwell. Not blessed with the fertile prairie lands of the states to the south and east, Idaho was building an economy by extracting the rich veins of the numerous minerals that lay below those rolling hills. As the last decade of the nineteenth century dawned on Idaho, the men who toiled in the mines were dependent on large, faceless corporations, many in the financial corridors of the Northeast.

While miners barely earned a living wage, huge profits were gleaned from the Bitterroot ranges and promptly shipped to boardrooms and banks in New York City to fatten the purses of absentee capitalists. The rampant and determined exploitation of the miners was bound to lead to a confrontation that would eventually spill south to Caldwell and cost the "governor" his life.

The Philadelphia-based Knights of Labor had succeeded in organizing ore miners in the region between 1888 and 1890.[2] Mining companies decided to fight this "curse," as they saw it, knowing that they would have to band together as the miners had done. Consequently, the Mine Owners' Protective Association of the Coeur d'Alene (or M.O.A., as it came to be known) was founded in 1891.

Essentially, what followed was a battle played out across America during the Progressive Era: Big Business takes on Small Labor. The result: Big Business always wins. Well, almost always.

With the dawn of 1892, the M.O.A. announced a new wage scale for member mines that would, in effect, eliminate any past union victories. The miners saw this for what it was—an attack on their institutions, an assault that threatened their existence. The unions refused to accept the wage cut, and the M.O.A. retaliated by locking out the miners with the promise that never again would union labor toil in the area. Armed with a court injunction forbidding unionists from interfering with activities in the mines, the employers decided to import nonunion workers.

Unionized miners fought back by confronting the trainloads of scabs as they disembarked at railway stations in towns bordering the mines. On July 11, 1892, strikers and Pinkerton agents faced each other in the M.O.A's Frisco mines. The miners filled a railcar with explosives, sending it down a track leading to the mouth of the mine. The ensuing inferno demolished the mine and forced nonunion workers to depart hastily in fear for their lives.

Frantic mine owners called on Republican Governor Norman B. Willey to declare a state of emergency. He complied, convinced that a state of insurrection existed. Strikebreakers were guaranteed their safety, and more than 600 miners were rounded up and placed into internment camps that the detainees irreverently referred to as bullpens. Originally, every miner incarcerated was to face the wrath of the American justice system,[3] but when the sun set on the issue, only nine miners went to prison, all on contempt charges arising from ignoring injunctions.

While in the Ada County Jail, the imprisoned nine created the concepts that led to the formation of the Western Federation of Miners (WFM) and, following their release, formalized its structure and objectives in a four-day meeting in 1892.[4] Its leaders would eventually be ridiculed and mocked by no less than the president of the United States, Theodore Roosevelt, who set off a storm of working-class protest shortly after the trio was apprehended by referring to the unionists as undesirable citizens. The verbal assault was vintage Roosevelt, a man known to take on detractors with the use of such words as "low," "selfish," and, of course, "undesirable."[5] Stung by these remarks, many of the working class took to the streets. In New York, Chicago, and Boston, huge marches organized by unionists and socialists drew immense coverage from the socialist press. As New York's *The Comrade* noted,

He [the president] has discovered that political action is frequently dictated by selfish motives in the working class, instead of by that fine and lofty disinterestedness which marks his own political conduct and that of the class of which he is the expression.[6]

The president's remarks contained merit, however. The WFM and its offshoot, the Wobblies—inherently Marxist in political stance, internationalist in perspective, and pragmatically syndicalist—threatened the established order throughout North America.[7]

As governor, Frank Steunenberg had been caught up in the Coeur d'Alene turmoil and, in his opinion, blamed unfairly for mishandling the violence that plagued the region during his only term. Sensing that he could not win re-election, he unwisely decided to run for the U.S. Senate in 1900, hoping to deflect what many in the state had regarded a local issue. Steunenberg failed in the primary. Bearing the Democratic Party standard was Fred T. DuBois, who shifted loyalties from the Republican Party when voter sentiment moved in the same direction in early twentieth-century Idaho. Steunenberg returned to Caldwell to work with his family, most notably on the construction of office suites known as the Steunenberg Block.[8]

Perhaps it was the driving snow and whistling winds that deterred Frank Steunenberg from wanting to step out into the world on the last day of his life. However, he had agreed to meet a representative from the New York Life Insurance Company who had traveled from Boise to renew the governor's life insurance policy of $4,500. Late that Saturday afternoon, Steunenberg visited a downtown bank to sign the insurance papers and present proof he was in good health. His business finalized, Steunenberg walked home. As he arrived at his front yard, he opened the fence-gate latch leading to the side door of the house. Stepping into the yard, he placed the wooden barrier back into its slot when a massive explosion ripped through the cold, night air. His wife, Belle, thought the family's potbellied stove had exploded. His daughter, however, saw the horrible truth. Waiting for her father at the window, Frances Steunenberg witnessed the flash of light from the gatepost and saw her father's body hurled 10 feet through the air. Within seconds, both wife and daughter stood over the mortally wounded Steunenberg.[9]

In a feature article published Sunday, April 21, 1907, the *New York Times* reported that Steunenberg had been killed instantly and that his head had been found a block away from his house.[10] This report was inaccurate on two counts. The governor did not die instantly. In minutes, people in the vicinity arrived on the scene along with the Caldwell fire brigade. The blood-soaked body was carried into the house, where three of the town's physicians frantically attempted what they soon realized was a useless task. With his brother Will attempting to determine if the governor had seen his assailant, Steunenberg gasped and passed into eternity. It was 7:10 in the evening.[11]

Years later, "Big Bill" Haywood, secretary-treasurer of the WFM and the man who would become the focal point of the Steunenberg assassination, related his version of what took place in the weeks following Steunenberg's untimely demise. According to Haywood, a man named Hynes suddenly began to visit the WFM offices in Denver, in particular the editorial rooms of the union's communications center. Haywood said he was suspicious of the man's intentions, although it was not uncommon for miners not personally acquainted with the secretary-treasurer to drop by the office to ask for favors. Haywood observed the man's movements but did nothing until Hynes made the unusual request to see the union's financial statements.

According to Haywood, when Hynes indicated he was leaving the building, Haywood approached the janitor for a favor. "There's a man in my office, a fat fellow. When he leaves, I want you to follow him and see where he goes."[12] Haywood later wrote that Hynes had been tracked to Denver's Tabor Block, home to the notoriously anti-union Pinkerton Detective Agency and its chief investigator, James McParland, a man who had secured his reputation as a friend of big-mining capital by hanging several miners in Pennsylvania a few years earlier.

The next issue of *Mine's Magazine* carried an article about Hynes along with his photograph. The ever-defiant Haywood sent the article and the photograph as a Valentine's Day card to the Pinkerton office. He confided to his staff, "There must be more of these skunks around, they probably do not work on one shift." One redheaded "skunk" was observed lounging across from the WFM office. When Haywood and union President Charles Moyer went to a cattle show, the agent boarded the same streetcar. The next morning Moyer noticed a man leaning against a stone wall a short distance from his home.[13] Like Haywood, Moyer was concerned about the inordinate amount of attention the union seemed to be receiving from the Pinkertons.

Late on the night of February 17, 1906, knocking at his door awakened Haywood. He asked who was there. A voice responded, "I want to see you Bill." Peeking out the partly closed door, Haywood recognized the deputy sheriff. At approximately the same time, Charles Moyer was picked up at the local train station. He had been on his way to visit the Smelterman's Union at Iola, Kansas. Agents also arrested George Pettibone, a former WFM executive. All three were held in the federal wing of the county jail. There they learned that Idaho's Governor Frank Gooding had requested their detention (a request honored by the Colorado governor) and that they were suspects in the Steunenberg killing. At five in the morning, the three were spirited to the railway station, where a specially commissioned train awaited to take them to Idaho.[14] All this was accomplished without benefit of warrants or extradition papers and without the accused having access to legal counsel. Naturally, serious concerns about their respective fates were expressed. Charged with murder, the three faced the possibility of hanging.

When little Henrietta Haywood wanted to know what was about to happen to her father, President Roosevelt was slow to respond. The press was not. When news of the arrests broke, it had worldwide implications at a time when global communications systems was still in its infancy.

What followed was a groundswell of confrontations that framed the Steunenberg murder and subsequent trial: capital pitted against labor, owners against miners, haves versus have-nots, mainstream press versus the socialist/labor press. Regarding this last confrontation, three men stood out and are discussed at length later: Melville Stone, the manager of the Associated Press; Julius Wayland, the publisher of the socialist journal *Appeal to Reason;* and Gaylord Wilshire, the publisher of the similar-minded *Wilshire's Magazine*.

It is hardly surprising that the first alarm about the "kidnapping" of the three labor leaders was sounded in the socialist press. On February 24, 1906, *Appeal to Reason* (Girard, Kansas) placed the story prominently on its front page under a bold headline, "Officers of Western Federation Kidnapped." The story began as a straightforward, unemotional account of the arrest of the three suspects and their extradition to Idaho. But, in a rhetorical lashing characteristic of the *Appeal's* involvement in the legal proceedings to follow, editor Fred Warren pointed a finger at those whom he deemed criminally responsible for the illegal actions taking place:

Buckley Wells [*sic*] gained notoriety last year by his horrible and cowardly treatment of A. H. Floaten in Telluride. He is a prominent mine owner of Colorado. No sane person in the state believes that Moyer and Haywood had any hand in the murder of Steunenberg. But they are in a perilous position and subject to mob violence and perjured evidence is certain. Colorado is a second Russia and no person is safe who opposes the rule of the capitalist.[15]

The *Appeal* had spoken, and more than any other journal, it tried to prevent what many thought inevitable—that Haywood, Moyer, and Pettibone mount the gallows in Boise, Idaho.[16]

At the turn of the century, *Appeal to Reason* perhaps was the dominant voice of American counterculture. During this tumultuous period, it was obvious to anyone with eyes and ears that a significant disparity existed in the way America distributed the vast wealth being created by its capitalist enterprises. The moral of the story for many workers could be summarized in three simple words: capitalism gone bad.

Adam Smith's free marketplace had become more an ideal than a reality. Approximately one-eighth of the American people owned seven-eighths of the property. One percent of the population owned more than half the national wealth, and that 12 percent owned nine-tenths of it.[17] Just as economically debilitating was the source of the wealth. It came not from the land but from "exploitation of the natural resources, manufacturing, banking, and speculation."[18] In short, the rich got richer and the poor poorer. Capitalists like Andrew Carnegie, John Rockefeller, and J. P. Morgan had become financial oligarchs unencumbered by moral, ethical, or political controls.

Vast wealth controlled by the few was one America. The other America was populated by the have-nots, by immigrants, by exploited workers, by children in the workplace, by the abandoned, and by the homeless. This was the America captured on film by writer and photographer Jacob Riis, who shocked late nineteenth-century polite society with his graphic studies of the dispossessed, the sick, the homeless, the starving, and the dying.[19]

So it was not surprising that many working-class folks were convinced that through the sweat of their labors mansions rose on Park Avenue. To them, the inequity was clear. *Appeal to Reason* was there to provide sympathy and offer solutions.

By far, *Appeal to Reason* was the country's most successful socialist journal. In 1912, a statistician calculated that if all issues of the *Appeal* were opened and placed end to end, they would make a road two feet wide and 110,000 miles long.[20] Special editions often reached up to four million in circulation. On a normal week, the *Appeal* reached every state with circulation slightly under one million, nearly half the circulation of other socialist journals combined.[21] The journal was also delivered to homes in Canada and other English-speaking nations.[22]

Real estate tycoon Julius Augustus Wayland founded the journal in 1895, naming it in honor of Thomas Paine's famous work.[23] A repentant capitalist, Wayland established *Appeal to Reason* as a means to cleanse himself of the sin of profiteering at someone else's expense. He first launched the newspaper in Kansas City. The Kansas City sojourn lasted only two years, during which he complained of being hounded by admiring readers eager to discuss his views on the state of the world. He moved the newspaper south to the small town of Girard, ostensibly for the peace and quiet.[24]

While Wayland's journal touched the hearts of America's dispossessed, it also managed to irritate the highest echelons of the nation's ruling elites. Its detractors called it "The Squeal for Treason." President Roosevelt declared it a "vituperative organ of pornography, anarchy and bloodshed."[25] Despite its declared mission of "violently exposing and attacking capitalism and constructively upbuilding the ideals and practical framework of the Coming State," *Appeal to Reason* was hardly a doctrinaire voice for the radical left.[26] That honor belonged to *The People,* mouthpiece of the Socialist Labor Party of Daniel De Leon.

Wayland and *Appeal* editor Fred Warren were content to frame the issues of the day in a way their readers could understand. Sensationalism superseded philosophical and theoretical discussion. Thus, in the case of the three captured leaders, the reporting perspective was quite simple: The trio faced death because they dared challenge the status quo. No other crime had been committed.

While the *Appeal* was based on Thomas Paine's writings, another, similar journal was based on the writing of socialist Edward Bellamy. *Wilshire's Magazine,* established and edited by Gaylord Wilshire, was first published soon after Wilshire read the most popular socialist tract of the day, Bellamy's futuristic novel *Looking Backward 2000–1887*. In the novel, Bellamy praises communism as much as George Orwell would condemn it in *1984* 40 years later.

Like many other Bellamy converts, Wilshire's infatuation with socialism grew as rapidly as the unbridled capitalistic system around him. Before turning to socialism, however, Wilshire proved to be as capable a capitalist as Wayland had been. In the chaotic climate of late 1880s Los Angeles, Wilshire left his mark on the city by designing what became MacArthur Park and by laying out the beginnings of the famous roadway that now bears his name. When the economic boom fell apart, however, he turned to other ventures to keep afloat, eventually founding *Wilshire's Magazine*.

With Bellamy's social agenda firmly planted in his mind, Wilshire actively sought to establish Nationalist clubs to promote his new ideology. In 1890, he ran for the House of Representatives on the Nationalist ticket, an adventure that ended in a humbling defeat. By 1891, he abandoned Los Angeles for the more hospitable socialist climate, or so he thought, of New York City. There he made the acquaintance of Daniel De Leon and joined the Socialist Labor Party. In 1900 he returned to Los Angeles and launched *The Challenge,* the first of his socialist publications. Los Angeles proved to be a reluctant market for socialist ideas, however, and in 1901 he returned to New York, renaming the journal *Wilshire's Magazine*.[27]

Although both *Wilshire's Magazine* and *Appeal to Reason* covered the trial, they were not the only journals determined to counter what they believed would be the slanted, procapitalist stance of the major daily newspapers and the Associated Press. Eager to promote the socialist cause as well as defend Haywood and company were the *Daily People,* the *Montana News,* and *The Socialist*.[28]

Wayland desperately wanted Eugene Debs, the best-known socialist in the United States, to cover the trial for *Appeal to Reason*. Debs had the labor credentials that would have ensured his overwhelming sympathy for the accused. He had been involved in a number of labor disputes, including the Pullman strike of 1894 that successfully closed down most of the railways in the West. President Grover Cleveland, who then charged Debs and several of his cohorts with murder, broke the strike. Although those charges were dropped, Debs was eventually sentenced to six months for contempt of court. In prison, he was introduced to the writings of Karl Marx and became a devoted follower. In 1900, he ran for president on the Socialist ticket, the first of five appearances in presidential campaigns.

However, Clarence Darrow and Edmund Richardson—the head of the defense team—desperately wanted the provocative former unionist kept in

Girard. Debs had a legendary volatile nature that they felt might explode in Boise, further endangering the already small chance of acquittal for the accused. Indeed, they may have been right. Debs had written a highly inflammatory front-page editorial under the headline "Arouse Ye Slaves" in the March 10 edition of the *Appeal*. At his excited best, Debs addressed the mine owners and their accomplices in government. "These gory beaked vultures are to pluck out the heart of resistance to their tyranny and robbery, that labor may be stark naked at their mercy."[29]

Debs taunted the accusers boldly, declaring that if they were to hang Haywood, Moyer, and Pettibone, they would have to hang him as well, adding that "if they attempt to murder Moyer, Haywood and their brothers, a million revolutionists at least will meet them with guns"[30]—a highly provocative comment but no idle threat, as both Darrow and Richardson knew. After all, guns, bombs, riots, and murder had plagued late nineteenth-century America in the Haymarket riots, the Pullman strike, the Molly Maguires, and the Homestead workers and miners in the coal fields of Pennsylvania.

Philosophies normally foreign to American soil—social democracy, anarchism, and Marxism—had taken root. Eugene Debs was not the only threat. So was Emma Goldman, who echoed Debs's call to arms. "There is but one way to secure justice for Moyer, Haywood and Pettibone—The General Strike. The rank and file of organized labor," she wrote, "must take the initiative; let the leaders follow."[31]

On March 1, 1906, Gaylord Wilshire sent a letter of support to Haywood in the Ada County Jail. Big Bill responded on March 18, 1906:

Dear Comrade—Among the many letters of encouragement and support while in the penitentiary is your valued one of March 1st. Owing to rigid restrictions imposed upon us, I had no opportunity offered to acknowledge your letter until today. I am particularly anxious to get the next issue of Wilshire's. We are advised that Comrade Wanhope is now in Denver, the requested photographs can be secured from our folks there. In all probability you are now in possession of all the facts connected with our arrest, extradition and incarceration. The method employed clearly demonstrates the truth that capitalism will at all times condone public evils for private gain.

Fraternally yours, Wm. D. Haywood.[32]

The trio would need all the emotional support they could muster while awaiting trial. When they arrived at the prison in Boise, a sign over the gate read "Admittance Twenty-Five Cents." They did not have to pay. Since they were being accused of orchestrating a particularly foul crime, they were housed in the murderers' row. Inmates to Haywood's left and right were under the sentence of death. Since none of the unionists had yet to be tried, Haywood regarded their accommodations on death row as part of a campaign to convince the public they were guilty as charged before a single shred of evidence was presented.[33]

The April 1906 edition of *Wilshire's Magazine* did not quite meet the standard of hyperbole set by Debs the previous month, but it did not miss by much. Although Joseph Wanhope, Wilshire's flamboyant reporter, wrote extensively on the WFM issue, he was impeded by the fact that the magazine published only monthly. Wilshire, however, devoted considerable time, energy, and space to the issue in a determined bid to free the trio. He published a complete transcript of a speech made by his correspondent Wanhope in front of 4,000 screaming unionists and socialists in Denver's Coliseum on March 12, 1906. Wanhope was at the support meeting by a quirk of fate. Debs had been ticketed to fire up the crowd but had to back off at the last minute because of a sore throat and laryngitis. Wanhope pressed all the right buttons, arguing that the application of justice was never blind. Why, he demanded, was not the system on trial instead of Haywood, Moyer, and Pettibone?

Had they poisoned ten thousand of their countrymen with embalmed beef, sweated the labor of helpless women and little children with starvation wages, grabbed the assets of insurance companies and swindled widows and orphans of the workers, cornered the food supply of the country, corrupted legislatures, bribed judges and debauched the public life of the community, what heights of respectable infamy might they not have attained to, what pinnacles of sanctimonious scoundrelism might they not have reached?[34]

The April 1906 edition of *Wilshire's Magazine* began its extensive coverage of the affair by publishing a lengthy analysis of the case from William Randolph Hearst's *New York Journal*. Of all the major urban daily newspapers and news agencies that sent reporters to cover the trial, only the *Journal* expressed sympathy for the unionists' plight.

As much as the socialist press wrote with gusto, the *Journal*'s view of the case was almost clinical, carefully parsing the judicial misdemeanors committed by numerous actors:

The Governor of Idaho, having got these men in his power by illegal means, now disgraces himself and his State by declaring them guilty of murder in advance of any trial. It is known to what extent the mine owners own him. And it is known how deeply those mine owners desire the conviction and the hanging of labor leaders whom they have not been able to conquer in manly fashion. If by any chance the men are guilty—and we do not for one moment believe that they are—this newspaper will be the first to announce the fact, upon presentation of evidence and to demand their punishment by hanging. For the man who would injure the cause of labor by cowardly murder should be put out of the world. He is the vilest most dangerous criminal.[35]

Although the trial did not begin for another year, the socialist organs (unlike the mainstream press) kept up a steady drumbeat to sway public opinion as well as tap resources to pay what would prove to be extensive legal fees.

When the trial date finally neared, however, Wilshire released a so-called investigative journalism booklet called *The Pinkerton Labor Spy*. The book's author, Morris Friedman, claimed that he had been McParland's stenographer in Pinkerton's Denver office before suffering from a crisis of conscience that compelled him to leave the company. Friedman claimed to have access to the agency's private papers that clearly indicated the affair was a massive frame-up orchestrated by the mine owners. Robert Pinkerton countered that assertion when he told a *New York Times* reporter that Friedman was never employed by the agency in any capacity.[36]

By now, the coming trial had reached a rarified status as both a media event and a defining historical moment. No less than famed muckraker Upton Sinclair wrote on the importance of the trial in *Appeal to Reason,* calling it "the test upon which the right and left wings were dividing."[37] More than left and right divided, however. As time wore on, even journalists—like almost everyone else—chose sides.

It did not take long before the story of the three unionists spread overseas, thanks in part to Eugene Debs, who contacted sympathetic journals in Britain. The Social Democratic newspaper *Justice* issued a stern warning to those who were intending to prosecute Haywood, Moyer, and Pettibone:

The lawless capitalist class of America seemed determined upon hanging our comrades, Moyer, Haywood and Pettibone. But let them take warning to make apparent the fixed resolution of the working class. Our eloquent comrade Debs puts this resolution into words when he says that if our comrades die it will sound the crack of doom for capitalism.[38]

The Socialist, the organ for Scotland's Socialist Labor Party, bristled as it declared "the capitalist class is without scruple in its hatred of the militant working class. A recent act of outrageous lawlessness in America should so far prove this to workers in all countries."[39]

Finally, on May 9, 1907, the most famous worker in the world was escorted into the courtroom in Boise to begin what many felt would be the last days of his life. Across the room from Big Bill Haywood sat Senator William E. Borah, special prosecutor for the case. James Hawley, the renowned Idaho attorney who had defended the nine founders of the WFM, assisted him.

Hawley, a Democrat, had served as mayor of Boise. Borah had been born and raised in Illinois and, unlike Hawley, was a dedicated and practicing Republican. As the defendants were acutely aware, this high-powered legal talent sat across the chamber from two relatively green and unknown lawyers, WFM legal counsel Edmund Richardson and a young novice from Ohio named Clarence Darrow.[40] The presiding judge was veteran jurist Fremont Wood.

The press came from virtually every crevice of the nation. Newspapers unable to send their own reporters depended on America's most influential news-gathering operation, the Associated Press, to deliver a blow-by-blow account of the trial. The wire agency fed information to no less than 800 journals reaching approximately 25 million daily readers. Wherever the Associated Press had a member newspaper, it carefully reflected the views of that member, and in nearly every case, the press and the local power structure were inseparable.

It is important to note that the autocratic Melville E. Stone managed the most influential news organization covering the trial. Stone liked to be seen in the company of the rich and powerful, many of whom shared Stone's suspicion of anyone unlike himself.[41] It was highly unlikely that Haywood, Moyer, and Pettibone would get much sympathy from Melville Stone. Stone did not need to send reminders about "correct" reporting—the aura around him did the job. It is somewhat ironic that in the history of the Associated Press, its much-vaunted coverage of the trial takes a backseat to the speed with which the news of the birth of an heir to the Spanish throne had been transmitted from Madrid to Chicago. The Haywood affair did not merit a single sentence.[42] Stone's memoirs ignored it completely.[43]

Stone was a close friend of Robert Pinkerton, founder of the "infamous" detective agency. In a letter dated April 19, 1907, Stone advised Pinkerton that the seriousness of the proceedings warranted coverage by three of his best reporters. On their way to Boise were John Russell Kennedy, chief of the agency's New York division; Martin Egan, former chief of the Tokyo and London branches; and Robert Small, who months earlier had covered the first "trial of the century," the murder trial of Harry K. Thaw, the erratic and unstable Pittsburgh millionaire who had shot renowned New York architect Stanford White in a jealous rage over the affections of the young model Evelyn Nesbitt.[44]

Meanwhile, in Washington, D.C., a reporter who was to prove pivotal to the case received a telephone call from his managing editor asking him if he wanted to cover the Haywood trial. Oscar King Davis of the *New York Times* accepted the challenging assignment. Before he agreed, however, Davis knew that the *Times* editorial staff had little use for the WFM. On the train west, he sat with another New York reporter, Albert E. Thomas of the *New York Sun*. Like Davis, Thomas worked for a newspaper that followed a decidedly conservative slant. The trio about to be marched before the courts in Boise were hardly the types to receive positive profiles either on the front page or in the Sunday features sections.[45]

Like their Associated Press colleagues, Davis and Thomas were experienced, hard-nosed reporters who no doubt understood the culture of the early twentieth-century press. In a world of fierce competition, truth sometimes took a backseat to a good tale. Stunt journalism was the order of the day as reporters like Nelly Bly turned an around-the-world trip into a form of legalized gambling. At the same time, readers lapped up the latest love tryst in the yellow press. In this climate, the mission of the populist and scandalous *New York World* and its dynamic owner, Joseph Pulitzer, to fund a school of journalism at Columbia to legitimize the press as a pillar of democracy and freedom seemed almost laughable.

Standing against what seemed to be a wall of information destined to shape public opinion against the defendants were *Wilshire's Magazine* and *Appeal to Reason*. *Wilshire*'s Joseph Wanhope had journeyed to Boise and to Caldwell following his successful oratorical experience in Denver to make contact with the region's socialist clubs. Both a journalist and a party organizer, Wanhope was aware that if the accused had any hope at all, local support from sympathizers would be critical.[46]

Appeal to Reason's George Shoaf, a convert to the socialism of Eugene Debs,[47] was a reporter who never let conflicting facts interfere with a good story. Not surprisingly, he felt he had detected a political agenda on the part of the prosecution and its supporters:

> The heads of the capitalist hierarchy knew that the fundamental and challenging purpose of the Federation leaders was the organization and inauguration of a social, political and economic order from which exploitation of man by man would be banned and in which only those who performed useful and productive work would be permitted to eat and enjoy the good things of life. Under the new order as envisaged by the Federation leaders, social responsibility would replace irresponsible speculation and the worth of the worker would liquidate the gambler. Such as prospect ran chills of horror down the spines of every exploiter, every banker and financial swindler, every bunco steerer and common thief in the country, and automatically they ganged up with Wall Street to prevent the Federation objective by judicially lynching the federation leaders.[48]

Throughout the country, socialist and labor newspapers echoed this point of view. On March 16, 1907, before the trial began, the lead editorial in a journal published by Haywood's friends in the Industrial Workers of World posed what was to them a vital question:

> Why is it that they are so anxious to "get" Haywood? The reason is obvious. It was Haywood who systematically worked for what might be called the "higher education" in economics within the ranks of the Western Federation. It was Haywood among all the officers of that organization who first grasped the philosophy of Socialism and through him that the revolt against the capitalist system as a whole was largely augmented.[49]

Although the prosecution's key witness would be one of many witnesses to take the stand after the arduous chore of selecting a jury had been completed, former WFM miner Harry Orchard knew that the fate of Haywood, Moyer, and Pettibone would depend entirely on his ability to convince the jurors he was telling the truth. The prosecution team and Detective McParland, who was determined to repeat his past successes against miners, carefully coached him. Orchard's importance to the case was not lost on New York political writer Max Baginski, who correctly noted in Emma Goldman's *Mother Earth* that "Orchard is the rock on which the state wants to found its kingdom of justice."[50] Richardson and Darrow knew their task would be to cast doubt on the self-confessed killer's testimony.

Orchard became something of a celebrity in media circles. Reporters wanted access to the man who had confessed to building and placing the bomb that detached Frank Steunenberg from his mortal coil. Governor Gooding and McParland successfully resisted the pressure until S. S. McClure reminded the pair that extensive and positive coverage in his magazine was dependent on a promise that they made to allow George Kibbee Turner, a veteran reporter who had worked extensively with McClure, to interview Orchard. The pair complied but managed to squeeze a concession out of McClure: Other reporters could interview the state's key witness, except, of course, members of the socialist and labor press.[51]

There is little doubt that Harry Orchard (born Alfred Horsely and also known as Thomas Hogan) would present a significant challenge for the prosecution. To say the least, he would be a tainted witness with a checkered past. Although no one knew for sure, Orchard was believed to have assassinated about 18 men at the behest of the WFM leadership. But Harry Orchard did not look like the cold-blooded murderer for hire he claimed to be.

When Oscar King Davis of the *New York Times* interviewed him on Thursday May 16, 1907, Orchard seemed more Boy Scout leader than paid assassin:

The fact is that Harry Orchard now in the penitentiary is a very different man from the one arrested in Caldwell. The quiet, regular life he has led since then had made a considerable difference in him physically, but it has given him opportunity for a far greater change mentally. The man I saw this morning is one who has squared accounts with himself, has laid down a definite course of action and means to carry it out thoroughly and faithfully to the end, whatever that end may be or whatever it may cost him.[52]

George Kibbee Turner did little to destroy the vision of converted sainthood that emerged as a common theme in much of the reporting from the mainstream press:

It is difficult to believe in a transformation of this kind. The men who saw Orchard most—the professional handlers of criminals—declined at first to do so. Gradually they have become convinced. No promise of clemency has been made to the man. He refuses absolutely to favor himself in the smallest detail of his story. His judgement of the men whom he accuses is much more lenient than that of the any other person connected with the prosecution. He has turned to the task of assisting the state with the same unhesitating direction which made him the surest murderer of the generation. And every one who has seen him closely is now absolutely convinced of his sincerity.[53]

Maybe because Max Baginski and his socialist, labor, and anarchist friends were denied access to Harry Orchard, they remained steadfastly unappreciative of the reformation of the soul that this efficient killer had experienced. Baginski wrote,

Orchard, coached and drilled by the State, is trotted out as the savior of social order. He, the many time murderer, thief, counterfeiter and all around scoundrel, is in miniature what—according to Tolstoy and Kropotkin—the State is on a larger scale.[54]

Appeal to Reason, after running story after story about the criminality of capitalism, finally turned its attention to Orchard on April 20, 1907. Shoaf reversed the trend of condemnation articulated by Babinski by attempting to portray Orchard as victim rather than perpetrator. Shoaf claimed that at the time of a major strike in 1899, Orchard had been the part owner of the Hercules mine at Burke, Idaho. His investment amounted to a little more than $500. According to Shoaf, small investors had no place in the larger plans by the M.O.A. This was clearly stated at the point of a gun, wrote Shoaf, a point that convinced Orchard to sell his shares. Tired, sick, and broke, Orchard thirsted for revenge after he discovered that the shares he had sold were worth $5 million in 1905 values.[55] Shoaf concluded that Orchard's vengeance was aimed at Frank Steunenberg, friend and confidant of the M.O.A.

Outright murder or dutiful revenge? What would a jury decide? Perhaps more important, who would be on the jury? And selection of that jury was the first order of business on May 9, 1907. That area of Idaho was thinly populated, but most residents subscribed to newspapers. Clarence Darrow believed this would make jury selection difficult even though he observed that Boise citizens seemed disinterested in ongoing events.[56] Meanwhile, Shoaf and his friends at *Appeal to Reason,* along with their socialist brothers at the *Idaho Unionist,* made sure that any potential juror received free copies of their newspapers. That the socialist perspective somehow received prominent display on the front pages was considered insightful agenda setting, not propaganda.[57]

One by one, prospective jurors came and went. As the days dragged into early June and the summer heat took its toll on the patience and stamina of the participants, it seemed that 12 honest, impartial men might never be found. Haywood saw the exercise as a broad education in the class struggle, noting that "all the bankers of the county had been called as jurymen, but Darrow disposed of these in short order."[58]

By the third week in May, a jury list of 100 prospective candidates had been exhausted, and the jury had yet to be completed. A further 60 names were drawn from the local tax rolls. Finally, on Tuesday, June 4, Oscar King Davis advised his readers that evidence would soon be given. And who would hear this evidence?

It was in fact a jury of farmers. Ten of the twelve gave that as their present occupation and each of the other two had been farmers not very long ago. The average age is 56 and only one of the twelve is under 50. They are all men of family; most of them own their own homes. They are hard headed, square jawed, clear eyed lot of men, who will take the lot of convincing before they vote to take away a man's life, but when they are convinced will render their verdict without fear or favor.[59]

As he wrote those words, Davis undoubtedly had no idea how prophetic they would be. *Appeal to Reason* noted that eight of the jurors were registered Republicans, three were Democrats, and one was a Prohibitionist.[60]

Of course, everyone anxiously awaited the words of the prosecution's main witness and, as events would show, its only legitimate witness. But first, jurors, participants, and spectators had to endure the oratorical wizardry of James Hawley and the brief testimony of witnesses who were present shortly after the bomb went off at Frank Steunenberg's home. When Hawley arose to make his opening statement, Darrow, who made a series of objections, frequently interrupted it. These had little impact on Judge Wood, who heard little he cared to sustain. Hawley's take on the case contained no surprises:

We will prove that at the very outset of this conspiracy, it was planned not merely to perpetuate the power of the inner circle but to control governmental matters in the different sections of the mining country by employing desperate criminals to commit murders and other atrocious crimes against those who in official position refused to be influenced by their wishes and those who in private life ran counter to their interests.[61]

Finally, on the morning of June 5, 1907, Harry Orchard entered the courtroom. In his memoirs, Big Bill Haywood remembered him as a man "neatly dressed in a gray suit of the warden's, was clean shaven, with his hair combed smoothly over a head as round as a billiard ball."[62]

John E. Nevins of the Scripps-McRae News Service, however, contrasted Orchard the criminal—badly dressed and unshaven with "a life of indulgence and intimacy with crime [which] had left its unmistakable impression upon the sodden face"—with Orchard the witness as someone "carefully attired—collar, cuffs, scarf, even to the quietly displayed watch chain which lies across his benevolent breast."[63]

It was one thing to look dapper in the courtroom but an entirely different matter to convince the jury he was credible. As Haywood noticed from his front-row seat, Orchard "related a blood curdling tale commencing with his life in Canada where he had left a wife and child in Ontario after burning down a cheese factory there."[64] Given his situation, Big Bill's description of Orchard's testimony was surprisingly restrained.

For the most part, Orchard repeated much of the information he had related to George Kibbee Turner. It was a trail of blood and carnage and a litany of confessions the likes of which had rarely been heard in any court. He confessed to attempting to blow up the Vindicator Mine at Cripple Creek, Colorado, leaving two persons dead. He confessed to trying to blow up a mill operated by the Sullivan and Bunker Hill Mine in Coeur d'Alene. He confessed to attempting to hang the superintendent there. He confessed to the unsuccessful assassination attempt of Governor Peabody of Colorado (Peabody would later look quite colorless when told of Orchard's plans for him). He confessed to shooting and killing a deputy sheriff named Lyle Gregory in Denver. He confessed to killing 14 people when he planted a bomb at the railway station in Independence, Colorado. He confessed to placing strychnine in a home-delivered bottle of milk to one Fred Bradley in San Francisco, manager of the California-based Bunker Hill mine and a vicious opponent of miners' unions. When Bradley refused to die on cue, Orchard confessed to wiring a bomb to the man's door. As Bradley opened the door the next morning, he was blown into the street but lived to tell the tale.

Finally, Orchard even confessed to losing patience with the WFM when it was late paying him. So he created mayhem when he blew up the Florence and Cripple Creek Railway.[65]

Orchard's performance cut no ice with George Shoaf. In the June 15 edition of *Appeal to Reason,* Shoaf wrote that

Orchard during the day testified that he was a professional gambler, an ore thief, a bigamist and a general liar. Richardson is subjecting him to a very rigid examination and were it not for the continual objecting he receives at the hands of Borah, backed by words of encouragement given him between examination by Detective McPartland [*sic*] he would soon break down. The prosecution is playing a powerful hand and they are stopping at nothing to win their game.[66]

Wilshire's Magazine referred to Orchard's testimony as an "Arabian Night's tale that he had spent a year conning" and echoed *Appeal to Reason*'s highly reasonable assertions that Orchard was "a liar, a bigamist, a gambler, a firebug, an ore thief, a powder thief, a paid spy of the Mine Owners."[67] Although the WFM was hardly one of the most loved organizations in Idaho, its riots, strikes, and various other confrontations with the M.O.A. seemed tame compared to the activities of Harry Orchard. In the end, Orchard's testimony reflected more on his behavior than that of the WFM and "the big three"— Haywood, Moyer, and Pettibone.

In the final analysis, it was Judge Fremont Wood's observation that although Orchard's testimony was believable, it could not be corroborated. The result? A serious doubt was cast over the state's prime witness.

The jury listened carefully as Wood outlined the legal ramifications of the case following the closing remarks by the defense and prosecution. And then, after nearly 24 hours of deliberation, it returned with a verdict—Big Bill would leave Boise a free citizen of the United States. Haywood reluctantly left his autograph on an American flag owned by one of the jurymen, a man named Gilbert. Unfortunately, the prosecution refused to drop the cases against Moyer and Pettibone, destining both for trial at a later date.

The verdict shocked members of the press on both the left and the right. The left had been convinced that no representative of the working class could get a fair hearing in a court operated and paid for by governments funded by capitalists. On the other hand, the right never once believed the court would not reflect its conviction that Haywood and his pals were a serious impediment to social tranquillity.

Emma Goldman's leftist *Mother Earth* declared,

The conduct of the trial by the prosecution was a dismal failure from the beginning. The methods employed to manufacture evidence were worthy of the worst possible police and juristic ruffianism—the Pinkertons, the Borahs and Hawleys did not seem to credit the jury with much common sense; they evidently thought that the most barefaced inventions were good enough testimony for a jury of farmers.[68]

In the *New York Times,* Oscar King Davis wrote that Haywood was

one of the undesirable citizens [who] has received his vindication, not from his peers, for there was not a man in the jury box the equal of Bill Haywood in the courage of his convictions, and that is not said in disparagement of the jurors or to intimate that any of them failed to do his duty as he saw it, but in praise of that quality of manly assertion of his own principles and stout persistence in them which is the most conspicuous trait of Haywood's character.[69]

For his part, Harry Orchard was devastated by the verdict. He told Davis that he was content to await his fate. It would not be the noose. Orchard spent his remaining years in prison. Moyer and Pettibone were eventually freed.

Needless to say, folks in Girard, Kansas, were ecstatic. Wayland broke his routine and issued an extra of *Appeal to Reason* on August 3. In large, bold type, the front page exclaimed, "Not Guilty: The Verdict After 21 Hours Deliberation." It carried a letter on the front page that Haywood had sent to Warren and Wayland before the verdict was announced. Expecting a guilty verdict, he exhorted the journalists to carry on the war against wage slavery.

The timing of the verdict was a blessing in disguise for Wilshire since it allowed him to print the news in the monthly's early August edition. Wilshire congratulated Haywood on his acquittal but railed at the dailies that "sincerely hoped that Haywood would be able to substantiate his innocence do not show much satisfaction over the outcome. The '*Sun*' and the '*Times*' especially indulged in a display of impotent venom, which will be read with complacent interest by all Socialists and union men."[70]

Word of the verdict quickly spread to circles beyond those involved in the events in Idaho. The Philadelphia Italian-language labor journal *Il Proletario* announced simply on the front page of its August 4 edition, "Haywood Assolto!"[71] The British Social Democratic newspaper *Justice* called the verdict "a victory for the Proletariat," declaring that "capitalism—all powerful, ruthless and merciless—has been fought by the workers of the United States and the workers have won."[72]

Daniel De Leon's *The Socialist* credited the verdict to the importance of the socialist and labor journals and the work of his correspondent Wade R. Parks, who in his words "kept the workers alive to each move of the enemy, and informed them of each victory scored by the counsels for the defence."[73]

Perhaps it is appropriate to give the final word to Fred Warren, the dedicated editor of *Appeal to Reason,* in which Debs's *Arouse Ye Slaves* appeared:

Capitalism had gone down to its first acknowledged defeat, while the instigators of the dastardly outrage had skulked in their slime to temporary cover. Monster jubilee meetings were held all over the nation, while the Appeal calmly cleared the decks for the big fight into which it had become involved because of its loyal activity in the one just over.[74]

As Warren knew then and as we know now, Boise would not be the end.

NOTES

1. J. Anthony Lukas, *Big Trouble* (New York: Touchstone Books–Simon and Schuster, 1997), 1.

2. Philip Foner, *History of the Labor Movement in The United States,* vol. 2 (New York: International Publishers, 1975), 230–31.

3. Ibid., 230–33.

4. Ibid., 234.

5. Lukas, *Big Trouble,* 395.

6. *The Comrade* (New York), January 1905. In all fairness to Roosevelt and the journal, the incident was a dispute involving the president and rural letter carriers that became involved in attempting to unseat a member of the House who refused to back wage demands. However, the tone—that of Roosevelt being in the hands of vested interests—is a common theme in working-class and socialist papers.

7. Ross McCormack, "The Industrial Workers of the World in Western Canada, 1905–1914," in *Canadian Working Class History,* eds. Laurel Sefton MacDowell and Ian Radforth (Toronto: Canadian Scholars Press, 1992), 289.

8. Lukas, *Big Trouble,* 40.

9. Ibid., 17, 35, 51.

10. *New York Times,* 21 April 1907.

11. Lukas, *Big Trouble,* 53.

12. William D. Haywood, *Bill Haywood's Book* (New York: International Publishers, 1929), 191.

13. Ibid., 191–92.

14. Ibid., 192–93.

15. *Appeal to Reason,* 24 February 1906.

16. Telluride was a tough mining town in Colorado where labor strife hit the mines in 1903. Wells, owner and manager of the Smuggler-Union mine there, formed his own version of the National Guard to defend the mine owners' interests, and in 1904 he was commissioned by the governor and given the rank of captain. Both Haywood and Moyer had been implicated in the strike and the violence that followed it. Wells's first name was Bulkeley, not Buckley, as *Appeal to Reason* continued to spell it.

17. Samuel Eliot Morison, Henry Steele Commager, and William E. Leuchtenburg, *Growth of the American Republic,* 6th ed. (New York: Oxford University Press, 1969), 272.

18. Ibid.

19. Michael L. Carlebach, *American Photojournalism Comes of Age* (Washington, D.C.: Smithsonian Institution Press, 1997), 109–17.

20. George Milburn, "The *Appeal to Reason,*" *American Mercury* 23 (1931): 359.

21. W. J. Ghent, *The* Appeal *and Its Influence* in *the Charity Organization Society* (New York, 1 April 1911), 25.

22. Milburn, "The *Appeal to Reason,*" 359.

23. Paul M. Buhle, "The *Appeal to Reason* and *The New Appeal,*" in *The American Radical Press,* vol. 1, ed. Joseph R. Conlin (Westport, Conn.: Greenwood Press, 1974), 51.

24. J. A. Wayland, *Leaves of Life* (1912; repr., Westport, Conn.: Hyperion Press, 1975), 31.

25. David Paul Nord, "The *Appeal to Reason* and American Socialism, 1901–1920," *Kansas History* 1, no. 2 (summer 1978): 75.

26. Milburn, "The *Appeal to Reason*," 360.

27. Howard H. Quint, "The Challenge and Wilshire's Magazine," in *The American Radical Press*, vol. 1, ed. Joseph R. Conlin (Westport, Conn.: Greenwood Press, 1974), 72–76.

28. Socialist papers that covered the trial include Daniel DeLeons's *Daily People*, which sent the robust Wade Parks and his colleague Olive Johnson to cover the trial. Other significant socialists on the scene included George Shoaf, Joseph Wanhope, and Ida Crouch-Hazlett. Crouch-Hazlett reported for two newspapers, the *Montana News* and the *Social Democratic Herald* of Milwaukee, and often shared copy with Shoaf in particular. Ryan Walker, Wayland's cartoonist, drew sketches of the trial. W. Herman Barber, a local socialist, fed copy to a union newspaper, *The Leader* (Pittsburgh). Both Upton Sinclair and Jack London backed out before the trial began. Shoaf quickly assumed the role as the spokesperson for this group. The reporters met regularly at the cigar store of Eugene Francis Gary, a socialist sympathizer, to share stories and compare perspectives on the trial. As you might suspect with the exception of Wayland and Wilshire, both of whom were independently well off, most of the socialist, labor, and anarchist papers lived on the margins. The *Appeal* gave wholesale permission for any newspaper agreeing with its politics to use any materials from the paper. It could well afford to do so, as its circulation was high and it was profitable. As the British papers noted, their knowledge of the trial came from what Eugene Debs sent them from the pages of the *Appeal*. Finally, the list of socialist journals is much smaller than the lineup of dailies headed by the Associated Press.

29. *Appeal to Reason*, 10 March 1906.

30. Ibid.

31. *Mother Earth*, April 1907.

32. *Wilshire's Magazine*, April 1906.

33. Haywood, *Bill Haywood's Book*, 193–94.

34. *Wilshire's Magazine*, April 1906.

35. *The Evening Journal*, 24 March 1906.

36. *New York Times*, 29 April 1907.

37. Upton Sinclair, *The Brass Check*, 9th ed. (Long Beach, Calif.: Author, 1928), 59.

38. *Justice*, 21 April 1906.

39. *The Socialist*, April 1906.

40. Lukas, *Big Trouble*, 289–91.

41. Ibid., 633–34.

42. Oliver Gramling, *AP—The Story of News* (New York: Farrar and Rinehart, 1940), 200.

43. Melville Stone, *Fifty Years as a Journalist* (Garden City, N.Y.: Doubleday, Page, 1921).

44. Lukas, *Big Trouble*, 636.

45. Ibid., 638–42.

46. Ibid., 435–37, 476.

47. Elliott Shore, *Talkin' Socialism: J. A. Wayland and the Role of the Press in American Radicalism, 1890–1912* (Lawrence: University Press of Kansas, 1988), 172–74.

48. George H. Shoaf, *Fighting for Freedom* (Los Angeles: Simplified Economics, 1953), 83.

49. *Industrial Union Bulletin*, 16 March 1907.

50. *Mother Earth,* July 1907.

51. Lukas, *Big Trouble,* 643.

52. *New York Times,* 17 May 1907.

53. *McClure's,* July 1907.

54. *Mother Earth,* July 1907.

55. *Appeal to Reason,* 20 April 1907.

56. *New York Times,* 7 May 1907.

57. Ibid., 10 May 1907.

58. Haywood, *Bill Haywood's Book,* 209.

59. *New York Times,* 4 June 1907.

60. *Appeal to Reason,* 8 June 1907.

61. *New York Times,* 5 June 1907.

62. Haywood, *Bill Haywood's Book,* 209.

63. Lukas, *Big Trouble,* 552–53.

64. Haywood, *Bill Haywood's Book,* 209.

65. *New York Times,* 6 June 1907.

66. *Appeal to Reason,* 15 June 1907.

67. *Wilshire's Magazine,* July 1907.

68. *Mother Earth,* August 1907.

69. *New York Times,* 29 July 1907.

70. *Wilshire's Magazine,* August 1907.

71. *Il Proletario,* 4 August 1907.

72. *Justice,* 3 August 1907.

73. *The Socialist,* September 1907.

74. George D. Brewer, *The Fighting Editor or Warren and the* Appeal (Girard, Kans.: Author, 1910), 70.

6

THE CASE OF SACCO AND VANZETTI (1921)

Arthur J. Kaul

"Long live anarchy."

"But what good is the evidence and what good is the argument? They are determined to kill us regardless of evidence, of law, of decency, of everything. If they give us a delay tonight, it will only mean that they will kill us next week. Let us finish tonight. I'm weary of waiting seven years to die, when they know all the time they intend to kill us."

[Nicola Sacco, 22 August 1927, 15 hours before his execution][1]

"If it had not been for these things, I might have lived out my life talking at street corners to scorning men. I might have died, unmarked, unknown, a failure. Now we are not a failure. This is our career and our triumph. Never in our full life could we hope to do such work for tolerance, for justice, for man's understanding of man as now we do by accident. Our words—our lives—our pains—nothing!

The taking of our lives—lives of a good shoemaker and a poor fish-peddler—all!"

[Bartolomeo Vanzetti, statement to a North American Newspaper
Alliance reporter, May 1927][2]

A sign in *The Daily Worker*'s office window at 12:25 A.M. on Tuesday August 23, 1927, simply read, "Sacco Murdered," replaced a few minutes later with another inscription: "Vanzetti Murdered." The electric-chair execution in the Charlestown, Massachusetts, prison of two alien Italian anarchists, Nicola Sacco and Bartolomeo Vanzetti, on that summer night was silently greeted by a dejected crowd of 5,000 in the streets of New York City while thousands of jeering picketers besieged the Boston Common to protest their deaths and to be conscientiously arrested by the score.[3]

Nearly 200,000 spectators watched a procession of 7,000 mourners plod eight miles through the streets of Boston behind the hearse carrying the immigrants' bodies to the Forest Hills crematory, where 10,000 persons gathered in a drizzling rain to hear Mary Donovan of the Sacco-Vanzetti Defense Committee bitterly declare, "Massachusetts and America murdered them."[4]

The grizzly finale to what the *New York Times* called "a legal and extra legal battle unprecedented in the history of American jurisprudence" sparked protests around the world.[5] Mobs looted and ransacked shops in Paris; demonstrators clashed with stick-wielding police in Hyde Park, London; crowds smashed $40,000 worth of plate glass in shops and the League of Nations building in Geneva, Switzerland; Communist authorities in the Soviet Union organized mass meetings in Moscow and Leningrad, vowing vengeance for two "innocent revolutionaries"; police charged angry rioters in Amsterdam when an attempt was made to pull down an American flag; a crowd marched on the American Legation in Copenhagen; labor leaders in Finland called for a boycott of American goods; the Republican guard was called out to quell a demonstration in Lisbon, Spain; American businesses in Buenos Aires were pelted with stones; Ford auto shops were bombed in Cordova, Argentina; protesters paraded in Mexico City; and 3,000 trade unionists marched through the streets of Sydney, Australia.[6]

The seven-year legal ordeal of Sacco and Vanzetti began in obscurity and radicalism and ended as an international cause célèbre that put American justice and its legal system on trial. Artists, agitators, clergymen, intellectuals, journalists, lawyers, radicals, and writers representing a dizzying array of ideologies and sentimentalities entered the debate over the judicial treatment of an inarticulate shoemaker and a philosophical fish peddler found guilty of killing a paymaster and his guard during an armed robbery in the streets of South Braintree, Massachusetts, on April 15, 1920.

Were they guilty of the crime or just two bomb-throwing Italian anarchists desperate for quick cash to finance their treacherous subversion? Or were they judicially murdered innocents, tried in a courtroom presided over by a prejudicial judge and a prosecutor who deployed perjured testimony, tampered evidence, and a dubious legal doctrine called "consciousness of guilt" to win a conviction congenial to the Beacon Hill establishment threatened by their radicalism during a paranoid season when America was coming apart at the seams?

The drama of Sacco and Vanzetti was staged in an America that had experienced massive class, economic and ethnic dislocation, and upheaval. Consumer prices doubled between 1914 and 1920, and per capita income fell below prewar levels; Henry Ford's $5-a-day wage in 1914 was worth $2.40 in 1919. The number of factory workers doubled in the first two decades of the twentieth century, rising from 4.7 million to more than 9 million, with much of the growth newly arrived, foreign born, ill educated, and desperately poor.

In 1919, a general labor strike in Seattle, followed by strikes of the Boston police, steelworkers, and mine workers, became emblematic of class and labor conflict in "the most strikebound year in American history," which witnessed an estimated four million workers participate in 3,000 labor actions. The *Boston Herald* called the police strike a "Bolshevist nightmare," while the *Boston Evening Transcript* found the steel strike strong evidence of the "extraordinary hold which 'Red' principles have upon the foreign born population in the steel districts."[7]

Six million immigrants arrived in the United States between 1900 and 1910, and the number of immigrants exceeded one million in six different years between 1905 and 1914, most from eastern and southern Europe who crowded into the squalid ghettos of eastern cities. More than 130,000 Italians arrived in 1908 alone, including Sacco and Vanzetti, gathering in urban ethnic enclaves derisively called "Little Italy" and "Dago Hill." By 1920, the populations of some eastern and midwestern cities were three-fourths foreign born. "Is it possible to contemplate a United States that is neither Protestant nor Anglo-Saxon," an observer asked in 1927, the question itself a token of nativist unease.[8]

The widespread distrust of newly arrived foreigners who disrupted the conventional Anglo-Saxon American social fabric was given a voice by people in very high places. President Woodrow Wilson's State of the Union Address in 1915, 18 months before entry into World War I, warned,

[T]he gravest threats against our national peace and safety have been uttered within our own borders [by those] born under other flags but welcomed under our generous naturalization laws . . . who have poured the poison of disloyalty into the very arteries of our national life. . . . Such creatures of passion, disloyalty, and anarchy must be crushed out. They are not many, but they are infinitely malignant, and the hand of our power should close over them at once.[9]

In June 1917, passage of the Espionage Act gave the president the legislation he sought. Congress obliged again in May 1918 with passage of the Sedition Act. Together, these acts empowered the federal government to punish false statements that could interfere with the war effort, promote disloyalty, obstruct recruitment, and prosecute those critical of the government. In the four years following passage of the Espionage Act, two-thirds of the states passed their own sedition laws, yielding more than 1,900 prosecutions and 800 convictions.[10]

The Bolshevik Revolution in Russia—journalist John Reed called it "Ten Days That Shook the World"—added to the national hysteria that a Communist-led domestic insurrection would erupt in the United States, destroy capitalist democracy, redistribute property, and install an anarchic authoritarian collectivism in its place. Evidence of subversion had appeared by way of a series of bombings, many attributed to Italian anarchists, in Boston, Milwaukee, New York City, and San Francisco between 1914 and 1918.[11]

In April 1919, 30 bombs were discovered, all intended for postal delivery to a wide array of private and public officials, including U.S. Attorney General A. Mitchell Palmer, Supreme Court Justice Oliver Wendell Holmes, and financiers John D. Rockefeller and J. P. Morgan. Mitchell secured an emergency appropriation of $500,000 to create an intelligence division within the Justice Department to investigate subversive activities, quickly producing 60,000 names in 100 days, 450,000 in 18 months.[12]

Hand-delivered bombs exploded on June 2, 1919, in seven cities, including at the Washington, D.C., residence of Attorney General Palmer, who escaped injury with a reinvigorated determination to wage his own war against radicalism. The bomber's body was blown to bits, part of his torso found on the cornice of a house a block away. Strewn in the debris were copies of an anarchist leaflet titled "Plain Words," printed on pink paper, that bore an incendiary message in response to the deportations and jailing of radicals and signed "The Anarchist Fighters":

There will have to be bloodshed; we will not dodge; there will have to be murder: we will kill, because it is necessary; there will have to be destruction; we will destroy to rid the world of your tyrannical institutions.[13]

Justice Department agents in November and December 1919 rounded up and arrested hundreds of aliens and seized radical literature in cities across the country. A group of 249 deportees seized in New York City were promptly separated from their families and put aboard the cargo ship *Buford,* one of the first ships to return from Europe with soldiers of the American Expeditionary Force and now dubbed "The Soviet Ark," and sent to Finland.[14]

The attorney general mounted a massive counteroffensive designed to roust subversion from American soil in one fell swoop on January 2, 1920, when federal, state, and local law enforcement officials in 33 cities in 23 states seized more than 4,000 alleged radicals and "Reds" within a few hours. Many were arrested, deported, or held incommunicado in jails.[15]

Into this swirling cauldron of national hysteria and paranoia entered two obscure alien Italian anarchists soon to become international celebrities in a politicized court battle that would become an icon of the times.

Ferdinando "Nicola" Sacco was born on April 22, 1891, in Torremaggiore (population: 10,000) in the spur of the boot of southern Italy. His father was a "republican," and a brother, Sabino, was a socialist. Nicola and Sabino Sacco arrived in Boston on April 12, 1908, 10 days before Nicola's seventeenth birthday, then moved to the Italian neighborhood of Milford, where Nicola earned a meager living doing construction work. Sabino Sacco returned to Italy a year later, entered his father's olive oil and wine business, married, and was elected mayor of his hometown in 1920; he never returned to the United States and died at the age of 92.

Nicola Sacco spent $50 for a three-month apprentice-like program to learn the skill of shoemaking (edge trimming), working with diligence and skill for seven years (May 1910 to May 1917) for Milford Shoe Company. In May 1912, he married Rosa Zambelli, and a year later they had a son, Dante Sacco. He joined an anarchist group in 1913 and subscribed to *Cronaca Sovversiva* (*Subversive Chronicle*) published in Lynn, Massachusetts, by Luigi Galleani, a militant Italian anarchist who eight years earlier published *La Salute e in Voi* (*Health Is in You*), a 46-page manual with practical instruction on making "dinamite." In August 1913, Sacco's name appeared in the newspaper's appeal for money. He participated in strike activities between 1913 and 1916, when he was arrested for disturbing the peace, convicted, and sentenced to three months in jail. A Massachusetts Superior Court judge overturned the conviction and dismissed the charges.[16]

Bartolomeo Vanzetti was born on June 11, 1888, in Villafalleto in the Piedmont region of northwestern Italy. His devoutly Catholic parents apprenticed him to a confectioner and pastry maker when he was 13 years old. "To tell the truth, I am tired of this miserable life," he wrote his parents. A bout of pleurisy ended his apprenticeship, and he returned to convalesce at home. The death of his mother of cancer at the age of 45 in 1907 was a crushing blow, and a year later he forsook Italy, arriving at Ellis Island on June 20, 1908, 10 days before his twentieth birthday. He worked at odd jobs in Connecticut and Massachusetts, returned to New York City to work as a pastry chef, then went to Springfield, Worcester, and, finally, Plymouth, Massachusetts, in search of work.

In his spare moments, Vanzetti was an avid reader of history, anarchist political philosophy, literature, and religion despite a well-developed anti-clerical attitude ("My religion needed no temples, altars, and formal prayers," he said.). He was particularly fond of St. Augustine—"The blood of martyrs is the seed of liberty" was a favorite quote—and Ernst Renau's *The Life of Christ*, which proclaimed that "Jesus was an anarchist."

In 1912, Vanzetti joined with fellow anarchists and sent a 25-cent contribution to support *Cronaca Sovverisiva*. He participated in the January 1916 strike at Plymouth Cordage Company (where he had briefly worked), made speeches, collected money, and sent strike reports to Cronaca. On May 5, 1917, three years to the day before his arrest, Vanzetti took out his first papers for American citizenship.[17]

The fates of Nicola Sacco and Bartolomeo Vanzetti were lashed together when they met for the first time at a gathering of Galleanist anarchists in Boston in May 1917, a month after the United States declared war on the Central Powers. Congress on May 18, 1917, passed a military conscription law requiring all 21- to 30-year-old males, whether citizen or not, to register. Aliens were required to register but were not liable for military service unless, like Vanzetti, they had begun the naturalization process. Failure to register could result in a one-year prison sentence.[18]

A week after their first meeting, Sacco quit his job of seven years, joining Vanzetti and 60 Galleanists who took refuge in Monterrey, Mexico, fearful of arrest, imprisonment, and deportation. With them in Mexico were Carlo Valdinoci, who later died delivering a bomb to the attorney general's home; Ameleto Fabbri, later a member of the Sacco-Vanzetti Defense Committee; and Mario Buda, who was with Sacco and Vanzetti on the night of their arrest. In September, the two returned to Massachusetts, Sacco to Stoughton, where he resumed his shoemaking trade with Three-K Shoe Company and managed to accumulate $1,500 in savings, and Vanzetti to Plymouth, where he became a fish peddler in the Italian neighborhood.[19]

Amid the headline notoriety of the November 1919 to January 1920 raids, arrests, and deportation of aliens and radicals, an attempted armed robbery went virtually unnoticed on Christmas Eve Day 1919 in Bridgewater, Massachusetts. Four men attempted to rob the L. Q. White Shoe Company payroll, one of the robbers firing a shotgun at the payroll truck. The robbery failed, and the bandits escaped. Three months later, the Justice Department detained without arrest or a warrant anarchist Andrea Salsedo, who had ties to *Cronaca Sovverivasa,* in New York City.

Then came another payroll robbery. Two men armed with handguns shot and killed Frederick Parmenter and Alessandro Beradelli, paymaster and guard for Slater & Morrill Shoe Company, in the streets of South Braintree, Massachusetts, on April 15, 1920, stealing $15,776.51 that was never recovered and escaping in a stolen Buick with several other men.

Meanwhile, Salsedo allegedly informed on his anarchist comrades, naming the Galleanni anarchists of Lynn, Massachusetts, as being responsible for the June 1919 bombings, before he leaped from a fourteenth-story window on May 3, 1920. His apparent suicide garnered extensive front-page headlines in the *New York Times:*

Red's Death Plunge, 14 Stories, Bares Long Bomb Trail / Andrea Salsedo, Informer in June Plots, Dashes Through Window / 'Pink Circular's' Author / Wearies of Aiding Government to Trace Men Who Tried to Kill Palmer and Others / Clues Oddly Pieced Out / Suicide Lifts Veil of Secrecy from a Search Extending to Europe.[20]

The stolen Buick used in the Slater & Morrill payroll robbery was found two days later near the home of Ferruccio Coacci, an anarchist scheduled for deportation the day of the robbery. His failure to appear at the appointed hour in East Boston for deportation, allegedly because his wife was sick and he needed to care for her, made immigration officials suspicious. An immigration inspector asked Bridgewater Police Chief Michael Stewart to investigate. The police chief arrived at Coacci's home on April 16, finding Coacci's wife in good health and Coacci packing his bags. Two days later, Coacci was deported to Italy. Stewart became suspicious that Italians, including Coacci, were involved in the Bridgewater and South Braintree holdups.[21]

Four days after the South Braintree robbery, Stewart returned to Coacci's residence, finding Mario "Big Nose" Boda, an anarchist who claimed to be a salesman and whose car was similar to the robbery vehicle. Boda told Stewart that the car was being repaired at the Elm Street Garage, prompting the police chief to visit the garage and to ask the owner to inform him when anyone came for the vehicle.

In a fearful panic that they might be implicated in a bomb plot, arrested, deported, or jailed after learning of Salsedo's suicide, Sacco, Vanzetti, Boda, and another anarchist comrade, Riccardo Orciani, on May 4 agreed to meet the next day at the Elm Street Garage, get Boda's car, and dispose of any evidence, especially incriminating anarchist literature. Earlier that day, Sacco went to nearby Boston to get a passport. When the four men arrived at the garage, the owner advised them against taking the car because the license tags had expired; his wife called police. Boda and Orciani left together on a motorcycle, and Sacco and Vanzetti took a streetcar to return home.[22]

A policeman boarded the streetcar as it pulled into Brockton about 10 P.M. on May 5 and arrested Sacco and Vanzetti because they appeared to be "suspicious characters." Both men were armed, Sacco carrying a loaded .32 Colt automatic and cartridges and Vanzetti a loaded .38 Harrington and Richardson revolver and some shotgun shells. Also found in Sacco's pocket was Vanzetti's handwritten note announcing a forthcoming meeting in Brockton to raise money for Salsedo's widow and children:

Workers, you have fought all the wars. You have worked for all the bosses. You have wandered over all the countries. Have you harvested the fruit of your labors, the price of your victories? Does the past comfort you? Does the present smile on you? Does the future promise you anything? Have you found a piece of land where you can live like a human being and die like a human being? On these questions, on this argument, and on this theme, the struggle for existence, Bartolomeo Vanzetti will speak.

Hour _____ Day_____Hall_____.
Admission free. Free discussion.
Bring the ladies with you.[23]

During police interrogation, Sacco and Vanzetti were evasive—and outright lied—about their political affiliations and beliefs, their guns, and their visit to the garage and denied knowledge of Boda and Coacci, repeating the lies the next day when questioned by Plymouth and Norfolk Counties District Attorney Frederick G. Katzmann. The prosecutor quickly developed a theory of the case that, like Police Chief Stewart, he would never abandon: The same men committed the Bridgewater and South Braintree robberies; Boda, who had eluded capture, served as gang leader with a car; Coacci supposedly took the money to Italy when he was deported; and Sacco and Vanzetti allegedly were gang members, Vanzetti the "shotgun bandit" at Bridgewater because he carried incriminating shotgun shells at the time of his arrest and Sacco because his Colt automatic was the same caliber gun used at South Braintree.

And besides, their suspicious behavior on the night of the arrest was evidence of "consciousness of guilt" regarding the South Braintree killings and robbery.[24]

In June 1920, Vanzetti went on trial in the Plymouth courtroom of Judge Webster Thayer, a member of the Worchester social elite who a month earlier had criticized a jury for acquitting an anarchist. Frederick Katzmann's prosecution was successful, and Vanzetti was found guilty on July 1, 1920, of assault with intent to murder and assault with intent to rob. The prosecution's evidence included identifications by several eyewitnesses, a shotgun shell found at the crime scene that supposedly matched one found at the time of his arrest, and "consciousness of guilt" at the time of his arrest. Vanzetti's defense attorney produced nearly a dozen Italian or Italian American witnesses who testified that they had seen Vanzetti the fish peddler deliver eels in Plymouth at the time of the Bridgewater holdup. Vanzetti never took the stand in his own defense, his attorney fearing that his alien Italian status and anarchist beliefs might be prejudicial. Judge Thayer gave Vanzetti a harsh sentence: 12 to 15 years in prison.[25] Sacco and Vanzetti were indicted on September 11, 1920, for the South Braintree robbery and murders.

Five days later, on September 16, Mario Boda retaliated for his comrades' arrest and indictment, detonating a huge bomb in a horse and buggy at the corner of Wall and Broad streets in the heart of New York City's financial district and causing an estimated 30 deaths, more than 200 injuries, and $200 million in damages. Boda escaped, eventually fleeing to Italy, never to return to the United States.[26]

Anarchist supporters quickly established a Sacco and Vanzetti Defense Committee and raised money to hire a defense attorney, Fred H. Moore, an abrasive Californian who had never tried a case in Massachusetts and who had a reputation for defending radicals. (Sixty years later, a son of one of the group that hired him disclosed that Moore was a cocaine addict supplied with the drug during the trial.[27]) Moore was assisted by two local attorneys, Jeremiah J. McAnarney and William Callahan. The Defense Committee would pay Moore $34,000 in legal fees and $88,000 in expenses.[28]

The trial of Sacco and Vanzetti for the South Braintree robbery and murder of the paymaster and his guard began on May 31, 1921, in Dedham. Judge Webster Thayer, who had tried and sentenced Vanzetti for the attempted Bridgewater holdup, once again presided, with District Attorney William Katzmann again the prosecutor, assisted by Assistant District Attorney Harold Williams. The six-week trial hinged on the prosecution's large claims and inconclusive evidence in three areas: witnesses identification, ballistic evidence, and consciousness of guilt.

WITNESSES IDENTIFICATION

The prosecution presented 11 eyewitnesses to the murder and robbery, seven identifying Sacco and four identifying Vanzetti. Of the seven witnesses identifying Sacco, three testified that they were unable to identify any of the bandits they had seen; one testified she saw Sacco lean out of the getaway car but denied on cross-examination saying at the preliminary hearing that she had doubts regarding her identification, even though her statement was in the record; one testified that Sacco was the "dead image" of the man in the getaway car, admitting on cross-examination that he had earlier told police that he had not witnessed the crime because he had run away scared; one witness testified that Sacco was the man working under a car in front of the shoe factory on the day of the crime, denying that during an earlier interview she said a picture of Sacco did not resemble the robber; and, finally, a witness testified that he had seen Sacco shooting from the car, but Judge Webster refused to allow the defense to introduce evidence suggesting that the witness's testimony was given in return for an agreement not to punish him for a larceny charge. Of the four witnesses identifying Vanzetti, one testified that he was the driver of the getaway car; one testified that Vanzetti was in the backseat of the car; and two others testified that they had seen Vanzetti in East Braintree on the day of crime, one saying he recognized the bandit was a foreigner by the way he ran.[29]

Both Sacco and Vanzetti had alibis. Sacco claimed, with corroborating testimony from a member of the Italian consulate, that he had applied at the consulate for a passport to return home to Italy on the day of the crime. Likewise, Vanzetti produced witnesses who testified that he was selling fish in his Italian neighborhood on the day of the crime. The prosecution countered with the argument that after a year's lapse, testimony with such precise recall could easily be mistaken.[30]

BALLISTIC EVIDENCE

The prosecution's expert ballistics witness, Captain William Proctor of the Massachusetts State Police, testified that the bullet that killed the paymaster's guard was "consistent with" being fired from Sacco's Colt automatic. Proctor later would admit that the prosecutor knew of his inability to match the weapons and bullets with certainty and that the prosecutor coached him to use the equivocal phrasing "consistent with" to give the impression of certitude in court. The defense presented its own expert witness to testify that Sacco's weapon did not fire the bullets that killed the paymaster's guard.[31] (Sixty years later, an analysis of the ballistics evidence introduced in the trial provided "substantial confirmation" for the theory that two of the bullets "were not genuine exhibits but were substituted by the prosecution" in an effort to frame the defendants.[32])

CONSCIOUSNESS OF GUILT

Like he had in the Plymouth trial of Vanzetti for the attempted armed robbery earlier, Katzmann argued that the behavior of Sacco and Vanzetti at the time of their arrest provided persuasive corroborating evidence. They fled when they could not get the car from the garage, they were armed when they were arrested, their weapons and ammunition were "consistent" with those used in the murders, and they lied about their political beliefs and about whom they were with on the night of their arrest. To counter this argument, the defense introduced their anarchist radicalism to explain that their fears of arrest, detention, and deportation—or, worse, the fate of their comrade Salsedo—led them to use the car to dispose of incriminating political litera- ture. They carried weapons for self-defense because Sacco occasionally worked as a night watchman and Vanzetti because he sometimes carried large sums of money as a fish peddler.

When Sacco and Vanzetti took the stand in their self-defense to explain their political beliefs, the prosecution used cross-examination to question their flight to Mexico and evasion of the draft as prima facie evidence of disloyalty and lack of patriotism.[33]

Consider this exchange between Katzmann and Sacco:

Katzmann: You love free countries, don't you?

Sacco: I should say yes.

Katzmann: Why didn't you stay down in Mexico?

Sacco: Well, first thing, I could not get my trade over there. I had to do any other job.

Katzmann: Don't they work with a pick and shovel in Mexico?

Sacco: Yes.

Katzmann: Haven't you worked with a pick and shovel in this country?

Sacco: I did.

Katzmann: Why didn't you stay there, down there in that free country, and work with a pick and shovel?

Sacco: I don't think I did sacrifice to learn a job to go to pick and shovel in Mexico.

Katzmann: Is it because—is your love for the United States of America commensurate with the amount of money you can get in this country per week?

Sacco: Better condition, yes.

Katzmann: Better country to make money, isn't it?

Sacco: Yes.

Katzmann: Mr. Sacco, that is the extent of your love for this country, isn't it, mea- sured in dollars and cents?[34]

Despite countless defense objections to this and similar lines of interro- gation, the prosecution's cross-examination of the defendants was able to exploit the patriotic fervor of the jury that would decide their fate. At 7:30 P.M. on July 14, 1921, the jury returned its verdict: guilty of murder in the first degree.

The verdict galvanized and outraged opposition on an international scale, prompting a flood of protest letters to American consulates and embassies in Europe and South America. Still more defense committees were formed in the United States and abroad to support appeals for a new trial. High-profile intellectuals publicly entered their protests. Within three months of Sacco and Vanzetti's conviction, Nobel laureate Anatole France wrote an "Appeal to the American People":

Listen to the appeal of an old man of the old world who is not a foreigner, for he is the fellow citizen of all mankind.

Sacco and Vanzetti have been convicted for a crime of opinion. It is horrible to think that human beings should pay with their lives for the exercise of that most sacred right which, no matter what party we belong to, we must all defend. Don't let this most iniquitous sentence be carried out. The death of Sacco and Vanzetti will make martyrs of them and cover you with shame.

You are a great people. You ought to be a just people. There are crowds of intelligent men among you, men who think. . . . I say to them beware of making martyrs. That is the unforgivable crime that nothing can wipe out and that weighs on generation after generation.

Save Sacco and Vanzetti.

Save them for your honor, for the honor of your children, and for the generations yet unborn.[35]

"Save Sacco and Vanzetti" became the most widely used protest slogan of the decade.

With Sacco and Vanzetti sitting in jail awaiting pronouncement of the mandatory death sentence, a protracted six-year appellate process got under way. Defense attorney Fred Moore withdrew from the case shortly after the guilty verdict to the great relief of Sacco and his wife, who both disliked and distrusted him. Many thought Moore botched the case, his abrasive courtroom style a constant irritant to the judge and jury and his inept preparation of defense witnesses allowing the prosecution free rein for highly prejudicial cross-examination. A conservative, prominent, and well-connected Boston lawyer, William G. Thompson, joined the defense to pursue the arduous appeals, assisted by an able young attorney, Herbert B. Ehrmann, whose postconviction investigation would provide compelling evidence of Sacco and Vanzetti's innocence of the South Braintree murders.[36]

The first of six motions seeking a new trial was filed nearly four months after the conviction. Five more would follow in the next two years:

- Ripley motion, November 8, 1921. The defense argued that the jury foreman brought .38-caliber cartridges into the jury room to show fellow jurors and filed an affidavit stating that the foreman's response to a comment that Sacco and Vanzetti might be innocent was, "They ought to hang anyway."

- Gould and Pelser motions, May 4, 1922. The defense argued that an eyewitness misidentified the defendants and another retracted his testimony. The witness who retracted his identification alleged that the assistant prosecutor persuaded him to make the identification.

- Goodridge motion, July 22, 1922. The defense sought a new trial based on the credibility of a prosecution witness, a felon who testified under a false name.

- Andrews motion, September 11, 1922. The defense argued for a new trial based on the retraction of an eyewitness.

- Hamilton motion, April 30, 1923. The defense argued for a new trial based on a weapon expert's affidavit stating that bullets in one of the murder victims and at the crime scene did not come from Sacco's gun.
- Proctor motion, November 5, 1923. The defense sought a new trial based on the prosecution's expert ballistics witness who admitted that the "consistent with" phrase was deliberately prearranged by the district attorney to give a false impression to the jury.[37]

A peculiarity of Massachusetts legal procedure allowed the motions for a new trial to be decided by the presiding judge of the original trial, Judge Webster Thayer, who many thought had baldly assisted the prosecution and had given prejudicial instructions to the jury. On October 31, 1924, Judge Thayer summarily denied all six motions for a new trial.

With Sacco in the Dedham jail was a young Portuguese immigrant, Celestino F. Maderios, convicted of murdering a bank cashier in Wrentham and awaiting the outcome of his petition for a new trial.

Maderios sent Sacco an extraordinary handwritten note, slipped to a trusty who delivered it between the pages of a magazine, on November 18, 1925: "I hear by confess to being in the South Braintree shoe company crime and Sacco and Vanzetti was not in said crime." Sacco gave the note to his lawyer, Thompson, who interviewed Maderios and took an affidavit. Maderios admitted having been in the South Braintree getaway car with a gang of Italians from Providence, Rhode Island, who made their living robbing railroad cars. Thompson dispatched his assistant, Herbert E. Ehrmann, to investigate.[38]

The assistant defense attorney's investigation produced information for a remarkably plausible alternative theory regarding the actual perpetrators of the South Braintree crime. Ehrmann traveled to Providence, talked to police who revealed their belief that the South Braintree crime was committed by professional criminals known as the Morelli gang, and discovered that gang leader Joe Morelli had been under federal indictment on five counts of robbing shipments of ladies' shoes from the Rice and Hutchins and Slater and Morrill, Inc., factories in South Braintree. The spotter who told the Morelli gang when shipments departed also could know about payroll deliveries. Maderios's accomplice in the Wrentham crime and another Maderios acquaintance confirmed Maderios's participation with the Morellis in the South Braintree payroll holdup. Finally, Joe Morelli bore a striking resemblance to Sacco; a Morelli gang member owned a weapon that the defense thought might have fired the bullets that killed the paymaster and his guard; and the defense could account for every member of the murder party, their motive, and even some of the stolen money.[39]

The Sacco-Vanzetti defense team filed a motion for a new trial based on the new evidence of Maderios's confession and information about the Morelli gang's activities on May 26, 1926, two weeks after the Supreme Judicial Court of Massachusetts upheld their conviction and an earlier rejection of motions for a new trial. On October 23, 1926, Judge Thayer denied the

Maderios motion, citing the unreliability of a convicted felon, Maderios, as a primary witness. Five years after the execution of Sacco and Vanzetti, assistant defense attorney and chief investigator Ehrmann called the failure to test in court the merits of the Maderios-Morelli theory of the South Braintree crime "the untried case."[40]

Harvard Law School Professor Felix Frankfurter, later a U.S. Supreme Court justice, published his assessment of the Sacco-Vanzetti case in the March 1927 issue of *Atlantic Monthly* that was given even wider distribution with subsequent publication in book form that month, then reprinted again in April. Frankfurter forcefully argued for a new trial and harshly criticized the judicial performance of Judge Thayer.

Frankfurter's review of the available Maderios-Morelli information led him to conclude, "Every reasonable probability points away from Sacco and Vanzetti; every reasonable probability points toward the Morelli gang."[41]

How did these facts appear to Judge Thayer? Frankfurter rhetorically asked. Based on what was included and excluded from Thayer's opinion on the Maderios motion, Frankfurter wrote, the uninformed reader would be "wholly misled as to the real facts of the case":

I assert with deep regret, but without the slightest fear of disproof, that certainly in modern times Judge Thayer's opinion stands unmatched, happily, for discrepancies between what the record discloses and what the opinion conveys. His 25,000-word document cannot accurately be described otherwise than as a farrago of misquotations, misrepresentations, suppressions, and mutilations. . . . The opinion is literally honeycombed with demonstrable errors, and infused by a spirit alien to judicial utterance.[42]

Frankfurter chastised Thayer for his unseemly characterization of Thompson's vigorous defense of the two Italians, quoting Thayer's remark: "Since the trial before the Jury of these cases, a new type of disease would seem to have developed. It might be called 'lego-psychic neurosis' or hysteria which means: 'a belief in the existence of something which in fact has no such existence.' "

Frankfurter continued,

And this from a judge who gives meretricious authority to his self-justification by speaking of the verdict which convicted these men as "approved by the Supreme Judicial Court of this Commonwealth"! The Supreme Court never approved the verdict; nor did it pretend to do so. The Supreme Court passed on technical claims of error, and "finding no error the verdicts are to stand." Judge Thayer knows this, but laymen may not. . . . No wonder that Judge Thayer's opinion has confirmed old doubts of the guilt of these two Italians and aroused new anxieties concerning the resources of our law to avoid a grave miscarriage of justice.[43]

Frankfurter's visible and vocal criticism, it would be revealed 50 years later, led to his phone being tapped by the Massachusetts State Police.[44]

The Sacco-Vanzetti Defense Committee weighed in when it published *Facing the Chair* (1927) by John Dos Passos, whose novel *Manhattan Transfer*

(1925) garnered critical acclaim. Dos Passos unleashed a portrayal of the besieged Italian anarchists as a metaphor for class oppression:

Sacco and Vanzetti are all the immigrants who have built this nation's industries with their sweat and their blood and have gotten for it nothing but the smallest wage it was possible to give and a helot's position under the bootheels of the Arrow Collar social order. They are all the wops, hunkies, bohunks, factory fodder that hunger drives into the American mills through the painful sieve of Ellis Island. They are the dreams of a saner social order of those who can't stand the law of dawg eat dawg. This tiny courtroom is a focus of the turmoil of an age of tradition, the center of eyes all over the world. Sacco and Vanzetti throw enormous shadows on the courthouse walls.[45]

The "garlic-smelling creed" of anarchism, Dos Passos wrote, had been for half a century "the bogy of American schoolmasters, policemen, old maids, and small town mayors." Many Italian immigrants had planted "the perfect city of their imagination in America," he wrote. "When they came to this country they either killed the perfect city in their hearts and submitted to the system of dawg eat dawg or else they found themselves anarchists."[46]

Dos Passos's personal encounter with Sacco in his jail cell revealed a man imprisoned in an incomprehensibly surreal world of deadly legal words and phrases:

The real world has gone. We have no more grasp of our world of rain and streets and trolleycars and cucumbervines and girls and gardenplots. This is a world of phrases, prosecution, defence, evidence, motion, irrelevant, incompetent and immaterial. For six years this man has lived in the law, tied tighter and tighter in the sticky filaments of law-words like a fly in a spiderweb. And the wrong set of words means the Chair. All the moves in the game are made for him, all he can do is sit helpless and wait, fastening his hopes on one set of phrases after another. . . . If they only make the right move, use the right words. . . . He is numb now, can laugh and look quizically at the ponderous machine that has caught and mangled him. Now it hardly matters to him if they do manage to pull him out from between the cogs, and the wrong set of words means the Chair.[47]

The novelist ended his defense with a plea to write to congressmen, political bosses, and newspapers; to call meetings to line up trade unions, organizations, and clubs; and to put up posters and "demand the truth about Sacco and Vanzetti." He concluded,

If the truth had been told they would be free men today. If the truth is not told they will burn in the Chair in Charlestown Jail. If they die what little faith many millions of men have in the chance of Justice in this country will die with them. Save Sacco and Vanzetti.[48]

Thousands obliged, including many renowned artists, intellectuals, and literati: Maxwell Anderson, John Dewey, Isadora Duncan, Albert Einstein, John Galsworthy, Thomas Mann, Katherine Ann Porter, Arthur Schlesinger, Sr., Ben Shahn, Upton Sinclair, Ida Tarbell, H. G. Wells, and Edmund Wilson, among others.

New York World columnist Heywood Broun's criticism of the case had grown so sarcastic and vitriolic that the *World*'s editorial board agreed to spike any more columns on Sacco and Vanzetti. *World* publisher Ralph Pulitzer inserted a signed statement in the space formerly occupied by Broun's "It Seems to Me" column on August 12, 1927, 10 days before the execution, saying that Broun's opinions on the case were expressed with such "utmost extravagance" that the newspaper was "exercising its right of final decision" and omitting any further columns.

Incensed, Broun quit. Five days later, the *World* relented, only to give Broun the opportunity to say farewell to his readers. "I am too violent, too ill-disciplined to fit into the *World*'s philosophy of daily journalism," he wrote. "In farewell to the paper I can only say that in its relations to me it was fair, generous and gallant. But that doesn't go for the Sacco-Vanzetti case."[49]

On April 7, 1927, two days after the Supreme Judicial Court of Massachusetts upheld the denial of the Maderios motion for a new trial, Sacco and Vanzetti entered the Dedham County Courthouse on April 9 to be sentenced to death. "Nicola Sacco, have you anything to say why sentence of death should not be passed upon you," the court clerk asked. Sacco responded in awkward and broken syntax:

I am no orator. It is not very familiar with me the English language . . . my comrade Vanzetti will speak more long. . . . I never knew, never heard, even read in history anything so cruel as this Court. . . . I know the sentence will be between two classes, the oppressed class and the rich class, and there will be always collision between one and the other. We fraternize the people with the books, with the literature. You persecute the people, tyrannize them and kill them. . . . Among that peoples and the comrades and the working class there is a big legion of intellectual people which have been with us for seven years, to not commit the iniquitous sentence, but still the court goes ahead. . . . As I said before, Judge Thayer know all my life, and he know that I am never guilty, never—not yesterday, nor today, nor forever.[50]

Likewise, Vanzetti again pleaded his innocence, concluding his lengthy courtroom oration:

This is what I say: I would not wish to a dog or a snake, to the most low and misfortunate creature of the earth—I would not wish to any of them what I have had to suffer for things that I am not guilty of. I am suffering because I am a radical and indeed I am a radical; I have suffered because I was an Italian, and indeed I am an Italian . . . but I am so convinced to be right that you can only kill me once but if you could execute me two times, and if I could be reborn two other times, I would live again to do what I have already done. I have finished. Thank you.[51]

On May 9, 1927, Vanzetti, on behalf of himself and Sacco, petitioned Massachusetts Governor Alvan T. Fuller, requesting that the governor "publicly investigate all the facts of our cases and set us free from that [death] sentence." Sacco was so dispirited that he refused to sign the petition. Vanzetti was explicit that neither he nor Sacco was asking for a pardon, which might imply forgiveness or convey a confession of guilt. "[H]ere we are asking not for mercy but for justice," the petition stated, concluding that they sought "most careful and unprejudiced consideration to the two grounds of our prayer—that we are innocent and that our trial was unfair."[52]

Responding to already intense and continually mounting public pressure, Governor Fuller, on June 1, 1927, appointed an advisory committee to review the case. The three-member committee was comprised of Harvard President A. Lawrence Lowell, a Boston Brahmin who descended from a wealthy family of mill owners; Massachusetts Institute of Technology President Samuel Stratton; and Massachusetts Judge Robert Grant. The "Lowell Committee" reexamined the evidence, some previously excluded from the trial; interviewed Judge Thayer in private and the remaining trial witnesses and 11 members of the jury; and heard testimony from others.

Life magazine drama critic Robert Benchley submitted an affidavit, previously published in the *Boston Evening Transcript* of May 5, 1927, to the Lowell Committee that cast serious doubt over the fairness of Judge Thayer's judicial conduct and corroborated charges of his prejudice. Benchley's affidavit and testimony delivered to the Lowell Committee related a conversation he had with an old acquaintance during a visit to his hometown of Worcester at the time of the 1921 trial. Benchley said that Judge Thayer had told his friend privately, "A bunch of parlor radicals are trying to get those Italian bastards off. I'll see them hanged and I'd like to hang a few dozen of the radicals, too."

Benchley's friend later denied that Thayer made the remark. "He thought I had violated the country club code of etiquette," Benchley commented. The episode tended to reinforce Dartmouth College Professor James Richardson's testimony that he had heard Judge Webster, a longtime friend, comment in 1924 during a football game, "Did you see what I did to those anarchistic bastards the other day? I guess that will hold them for a while."[53]

The Lowell Committee's July 27, 1927, report to Governor Fuller exonerated Judge Thayer and rejected out of hand any evidence that would undermine the guilty verdicts. The trial's stenographic report "gives the impression that the judge tried to be scrupulously fair," the committee wrote, acknowledging that:

the judge was indiscreet in conversation with outsiders during the trial. He ought not to have talked about the case off the bench, and doing so was a grave breach of official decorum.

But we do not believe that he used some of the expressions attributed to him, and we think that there is exaggeration in what the persons to whom he spoke remember. Furthermore, we believe that such indiscretions in conversation did not affect his conduct at the trial or the opinions of the jury, who, indeed, so stated to the Committee.[54]

The charge that police tampered with ballistics evidence to convict the defendants was rejected for lack of "credible evidence." Such an accusation may be dismissed without comment, the committee wrote, "save that the case of the defendants must be rather desperate on its merits when counsel feel it necessary to resort to a charge of this kind."

The committee found that affidavits corroborating Maderios's "worthless confession" did not "deserve serious attention." Sacco and Vanzetti's alibis were summarily dismissed as unbelievable, while the argument for "consciousness of guilt" was accepted. The Lowell Committee concluded that Sacco and Vanzetti were guilty beyond reasonable doubt.[55]

On August 3, 1927, Governor Fuller issued his own report, finding "no sufficient justification for executive intervention. I believe with the jury, that these men, Sacco and Vanzetti, were guilty, and they had a fair trial. I furthermore believe that there was no justifiable reason for giving them a new trial."[56]

The execution of Sacco and Vanzetti, twice postponed, was set for midnight, Monday, August 22, 1927, setting off desperate last-ditch appeals for a stay of execution and for clemency. Federal District Judge James M. Morton, Jr. denied a writ of habeas corpus, and U.S. Supreme Court Justice Oliver Wendell Holmes denied a stay of execution, stating in his refusal to intervene that he had "no authority to meddle" with a state case. Yet Holmes held out the faint hope that another Supreme Court justice might hold a different view. An appeal was made to Justice Louis B. Brandeis, who declined to intervene because of "personal relations with some of the people interested." Brandeis's wife had befriended Rosa Sacco. Chief Justice William Howard Taft, vacationing in Canada, and Justice Harlan Stone refused to act.[57]

The Citizens' National Committee for Sacco and Vanzetti sent a telegram with 150 signatures of prominent citizens to President Calvin Coolidge in Rapid City, South Dakota, asking for his intervention. The governor's office was being flooded with thousands of messages from all over the Western Hemisphere and Europe begging for clemency, including a petition signed by hundreds of "respected" professional men and women from 22 states and the District of Columbia. Meanwhile, Rosa Sacco and Luigia Vanzetti, Bartolomeo's sister from Italy, made a final, dramatic, and futile 90-minute appeal to Governor Fuller at the statehouse three hours before the execution. "I am sorry," the governor replied. "My duties are outlined by law."[58]

Three men were executed in Charlestown Prison that August night while thousands gathered in the streets around the statehouse and prison to protest the dying of light.

Celestino F. Maderios, who had won seven respites from the electric chair after he confessed to the innocence of Sacco and Vanzetti, had nothing to say. He was pronounced dead at 12:09 A.M.

Next, Nicola Sacco walked 17 steps from his cell into the death chamber, then cried out in Italian, "Long live anarchy." In English, he said, "Farewell, my wife and my child and all my friends." He was pronounced dead at 12:19 A.M.

Finally, Bartolomeo Vanzetti walked 18 steps from his cell to the death chamber and shook the hand of the warden, saying, "I want to thank you for everything you have done for me, Warden." To witnesses, he said, "I wish to tell you that I am innocent, and that I never committed any crime but sometimes some sin. I thank you for everything you have done for me. I am innocent of all crime, not only this, but all. I am an innocent man."

Vanzetti was pronounced dead at 12:26 A.M.

His last words: "I wish to forgive some people for what they are now doing to me."[59]

Fifty years after their executions, Massachusetts Governor Michael Dukakis declared August 23, 1977, "Nicola Sacco and Bartolomeo Vanzetti Memorial Day" and proclaimed that "any stigma and disgrace should be forever removed" from their names and from the Commonwealth of Massachusetts.

Without expressing a conviction regarding their guilt or innocence, the proclamation called on citizens "to reflect upon these tragic events, and draw from their historic lessons the resolve to prevent the forces of intolerance, fear and hatred from ever again uniting to overcome the rationality, wisdom, and fairness to which our legal system aspires."[60]

Were they guilty? Were Nicola Sacco and Bartolomeo Vanzetti guilty of the murder of two men in broad daylight on a street in South Braintree, Massachusetts, on April 15, 1921, during an armed robbery that yielded $15,772.51, never recovered? Or were they just "garlic-smelling" dagos and wops guilty of radical opinions about anarchism?

Were they guilty? Or was the verdict given for the wrong crime? Were they innocent of robbery and murder yet guilty of conspiracies whose anarchist bombs indiscriminately killed hundreds of innocents in a troubled time?

Were they guilty? Or were they trapped in a web of ideology and language that they, their accusers, and their champions could not ultimately comprehend, defend, or vindicate?

And what have we learned? Have we learned that the power of words cannot save us, that eloquence soothes but cannot assure justice, cannot protect the innocent, resurrect the dead?

What have we learned?

Edna St. Vincent Millay's protest poem "Justice Denied in Massachusetts," published in the *New York Times*[61] on the day of the execution, produced no requite of the soul, much less short-circuit an electric chair in the Charlestown prison.

Upton Sinclair's two-volume documentary novel on the Sacco-Vanzetti case, *Boston* (1928), concluded that the two Italians had become martyrs as Anatole France had earlier warned:

Mystic beings, with supernatural virtues, destined to become a legend. . . . And those two, the shining ones, the holy, who died to make freedom for the workers! Already one saw the history of martyrology repeating itself: the process of two thousand years crowded into one. Already they were canonized beings, concerning whom it was forbidden to speak any word but of praise. . . . And yet, obscurely, the symbol was working in the souls of men. A hundred million toilers knew that two comrades had died for them. Black men, brown men, yellow men—men of a hundred nations and a thousand tribes—the prisoners of starvation, the wretched of the earth—experienced a thrill of awe. It was the mystic process of blood-sacrifice, by which through the ages salvation has been brought to mankind![62]

Maxwell Anderson's final soliloquy of his verse play *Winterset* (1935), indirectly based on the Sacco-Vanzetti episode, admitted defeat:

This is the glory of earth-born men and women,
Not to cringe, never to yield, but standing
Take defeat implacable and defiant,
Die unsubmitting.[63]

John Dos Passos's "Camera Eye" episode in the final volume of his USA Network trilogy *The Big Money* (1936) quoted Vanzetti ("If it had not been for these things I might have lived out my life talking at street corners to scorning men.") and proclaimed:

America our nation has been beaten by strangers who have turned our language inside out who have taken the clean words our fathers spoke and made them slimy and foul their hired men sit on the judge's bench they sit back with their feet on the tables under the dome of the State House they are ignorant of our beliefs they have the dollars the guns they armed forces the power plants they have built the electric chair and hired the executioner to throw the switch. . . . We line the curbs in the drizzling rain we crowd the wet sidewalks elbow to elbow silent pale looking with scared eyes at the coffins we stand defeated America.[64]

His protest arrived like an epitaph from a distant place, too late to change the fated course of the stars.

Katherine Anne Porter, 50 years after the execution of Sacco and Vanzetti, wrote in her retrospective account, "The Never-Ending Wrong," with a wistful nostalgia for her loss of innocence:

I was still illusioned to the extent that I half accepted the entirely immoral doctrine that one should go along with the Devil if he worked on your side. . . . Two truisms: The end does not justify the means and one I discovered for myself then and there, The Devil is never on your side except for his own purposes. . . . In my whole life I have never felt such a weight of pure bitterness, helpless anger in utter defeat, outraged love and hope. . . . A darkness of shame, too, settled down with us, a most deplorable kind of shame. . . . Shame at our useless, now self-indulgent emotions, our disarmed state, our absurd lack of spirit.[65]

Were they guilty? What have we learned?
You decide, gentle reader, you decide.

NOTES

1. *Famous American Trials: The Trial of Sacco and Vanzetti* (http://www.law.umkc.edu/faculty/projects/ftrials, retrieved 29 June 2001).

2. Ibid.

3. *New York Times,* 23 August 1927.

4. Ibid., 29 August 1927.

5. Ibid., 23 August 1927.

6. Ibid., 24 August 1927.

7. Joseph P. McKerns, "Descent into Hell: The Red Crisis," in *The Press in Times of Crisis,* ed. Lloyd Chiasson, Jr. (Westport, Conn.: Greenwood Press, 1995), 129; Geoffrey Perrett, *America in the Twenties: History* (New York: Simon and Schuster, 1982), 31–49.

8. Perrett, *America in the Twenties,* 78; McKerns, "Descent into Hell," 122.

9. William Young and David E. Kaiser, *Postmortem: New Evidence in the Case of Sacco and Vanzetti* (Amherst: University of Massachusetts Press, 1985), 12.

10. McKerns, "Descent into Hell," 124.

11. Young and Kaiser, *Postmortem,* 137–38.

12. McKerns, "Descent into Hell," 125; Young and Kaiser, *Postmortem,* 140–47.

13. Paul Avrich, *Sacco and Vanzetti: The Anarchist Background* (Princeton, N.J.: Princeton University Press, 1991), 81.

14. McKerns, "Descent into Hell," 127; Perrett, *America in the Twenties,* 60–61.

15. McKerns, "Descent into Hell," 121.

16. Avrich, *Sacco and Vanzetti,* 9–30.

17. Ibid., 13–41.

18. Ibid., 58–59.

19. Ibid., 58–71.

20. Ibid., 188–95; *New York Times,* 4 May 1920; *Famous American Trials* (http://www.law.umkc.edu/faculty/projects/ftrials/SaccoV/SaccoV.htm).

21. *Famous American Trials* (http://www.law.umkc.edu/faculty/projects/ftrials/SaccoV/SaccoV.htm).

22. Ibid.

23. Avrich, *Sacco and Vanzetti,* 199.

24. Ibid., 202–3.

25. *Famous American Trials* (http://www.law.umkc.edu/faculty/projects/ftrials/SaccoV/SaccoV.htm); Young and Kaiser, *Postmortem,* 27.

26. Avrich, *Sacco and Vanzetti; Famous American Trials* (http://www.law.umkc.edu/faculty/projects/ftrials/SaccoV/SaccoV.htm); *New York Times,* 11 September 1920.

27. *Famous American Trials* (http://www.law.umkc.edu/faculty/projects/ftrials/SaccoV/SaccoV.htm).

28. Brian Jackson, *The Black Flag: A Look at the Strange Case of Nicola Sacco and Bartolemeo Vanzetti* (Boston: Routledge & Kegan Paul, 1981), 50–52.

29. *Famous American Trials* (http://www.law.umkc.edu/faculty/projects/ftrials/SaccoV/SaccoV.htm); Young and Kaiser, *Postmortem,* 46–63.

30. CrimeLibrary.com/Sacco/Saccomain.htm, retrieved 29 June 2001; Young and Kaiser, *Postmortem,* 78–84.

31. *Famous American Trials* (http://www.law.umkc.edu/faculty/projects/ftrials/SaccoV/SaccoV.htm); Young and Kaiser, *Postmortem,* 92–105.

32. Young and Kaiser, *Postmortem,* 106–23.

33. CrimeLibrary.com/Sacco/Saccomain.htm.

34. Jackson, *The Black Flag,* 33–34.

35. John Dos Passos, *Facing the Chair: Story of the Americanization of Two Foreignborn Workmen* (Boston: Sacco-Vanzetti Defense Committee, 1927; reprint, New York: Da Capo Press, 1970), 8.

36. CrimeLibrary.com/Sacco/Saccomain.htm.

37. *Famous American Trials* (http://www.law.umkc.edu/faculty/projects/ftrials/SaccoV/SaccoV.htm).

38. CrimeLibrary.com/Sacco/Saccomain.htm; Young and Kaiser, *Postmortem,* 134–57, esp. 141–50.

39. Herbert B. Ehrmann, *The Untried Case: The Sacco-Vanzetti Case and the Morelli Gang* (New York: Vanguard Press, 1933), 52, 67–84, 212–14. See also Herbert B. Ehrmann, *The Case That Will Not Die: Commonwealth vs. Sacco and Vanzetti* (Boston: Little, Brown, 1969).

40. Ehrmann, *The Untried Case.*

41. Felix Frankfurter, *The Case of Sacco and Vanzetti: A Critical Analysis for Lawyers and Laymen* (Boston: Little, Brown, 1927), 101.

42. Ibid., 104.

43. Ibid., 105–6.

44. The Sacco-Vanzetti Project (http://www.saccovanzettiproject.org/pages/summary.html, retrieved 2 July 2001).

45. Dos Passos, *Facing the Chair,* 45.

46. Ibid., 57.

47. Ibid., 69–70.

48. Ibid., 127.

49. Richard O'Connor, *Heywood Broun: A Biography* (New York: G. P. Putnam's Sons, 1975), 137–40.

50. *Famous American Trials* (http://www.law.umkc.edu/faculty/projects/ftrails/SaccoV/SaccoV.htm).

51. Ibid.

52. Ibid.

53. Babette Rosmond, *Robert Benchley: His Life and Good Times* (Garden City, N.Y.: Doubleday, 1970), 135–37.

54. *Famous American Trials* (http://www.law.umkc.edu/faculty/projects/ftrials/SaccoV/SaccoV.htm).

55. Ibid.

56. Ibid.

57. *New York Times,* 22 August 1927.

58. Ibid., 23 August 1927.

59. Ibid.

60. Young and Kaiser, *Postmortem,* 3–4.

61. *New York Times,* 22 August 1927.

62. Upton Sinclair, *Boston* (New York: Albert & Charles Boni, 1928), 754.

63. Maxwell Anderson, *Four Verse Plays* (New York: Harcourt Brace & World 1959), 133.

64. John Dos Passos, *The Big Money* (New York: New American Library, 1969), 468–69.

65. Katherine Ann Porter, "The Never-Ending Wrong," *The Atlantic,* June 1977.

7

THE CASE OF OSSIAN SWEET (1925–1926)

Elijah F. Akhahenda

"Niggers live there!"

Prohibition. The black bottom and the Charleston. Babe Ruth and Bobby Jones. Al Capone and the Untouchables. The Studz Bearcat, raccoon-skin coats, and rumble seats. The Roaring Twenties: a swinging, hell-raising, eclectic period marked by one of the most robust economic growth spurts in the history of the United States. Employment rose, industry expanded, and cities grew rapidly, most notably in the Northeast and Midwest.

As business grew and the stock market rose to giddying heights, salaries rose accordingly. Even the more menial jobs often paid well. Five bucks a day. Big wages for some during the Roaring Twenties. Big trouble for some too. Below the surface of the good times lay old problems.

Ironically, the robust economy did more than create employment. It fanned race hatred.

That proved the case in Detroit, Michigan, where the black population grew threefold, from 40,838 in 1920 to 120,066 in 1930. Many blacks that migrated into the city found employment in automotive assembly lines and related industries. They earned good wages, and consequently they looked for apartments to rent or homes to buy. Because the rapid increase in the black population put pressure on housing demand in predominantly black areas, black workers increasingly were forced to seek housing in predominantly white neighborhoods.

The opportunities that attracted blacks to the North also attracted white southerners, the majority with little or no education. They were especially attracted by the five-dollar daily wages Ford Motor Company began offering in 1915. They also received encouragement from the Ku Klux Klan, which advertised aggressively in southern newspapers to lure into their neighborhoods those southerners who shared their view about white supremacy.

As the legendary lawyer Clarence Darrow noted in his memoirs, whites who came north "brought with them their deep racial prejudice and they also brought with them the Ku Klux Klan, which was very powerful for a time in every northern city, except New York and Boston.[1] In Detroit, the Klan was so strong that it splintered into groups with innocuous names such as "The Improvement Club" and "The Neighborhood Association."[2] Their goal? To protect white communities from nonwhite encroachment. Fortifying the Klan's goals were private restrictive residential covenants that often make it illegal for white owners to sell their house to African Americans.[3]

Meanwhile, the rapid increase in black population put pressure on housing demand in black residential areas.[4] As housing tightened, blacks sometimes found it necessary to seek property outside congested black areas. But when they ventured into white districts, they discovered that the prejudice they thought dwelled solely in the South also resided in the North.

They found that house hunting in white areas could be risky business. While some property covenants prevented selling property to blacks, more worrisome was the enforcement of segregation by mob violence in several northern cities. Take the case of Oscar Depriest, a black congressman in Chicago. His house was bombed not once but several times.[5]

In Detroit, events led many blacks to believe that prejudice was ubiquitous and house hunting dangerous.

Consider the case of Dr. Alexander Turner, a black surgeon who purchased an expensive home on Spokane Avenue in a white section of northwest Detroit. A crowd quickly gathered, broke windows, tore tiles off the roof, and ripped lamps from the ceiling.[6] That done, they collected up his furniture and pitched it into a van. But that was not all. At the point of a gun, Turner signed away his interest in the property. When his wife refused, the crowd stoned Turner's automobile.[7] The physician and his wife barely escaped. They left the area.

Meanwhile, on Stopel Avenue, the Fletcher family had just moved into their new home. As they sat down at the dinner table, a white woman passing by the house noticed the occupants were black. "Niggers live there!" she yelled.[8] That was enough to marshal a crowd of 4,000. "Lynch them," someone in the crowd screamed as soda bottles pelted the house.[9] When a bottle smashed a window, someone in the home decided they had had enough. Fletcher got a gun and fired into the crowd. A bullet struck a teenager in the thigh. The police, who had not acted while the crowd was pelting the house with bottles and taunting the family with racial epithets, quickly arrested the Fletchers. The next day the Fletchers moved out of the neighborhood.

Dr. Ossian Sweet stood tall within the African American population in Detroit and anywhere else in the United States for that matter. He had degrees from Wilberforce Academy and Howard University and had studied radiology in France with Madame Curie as well as gynecology and pediatrics in Austria. In 1925, the Sweet family returned from Europe to settle in Detroit (Sweet, a native of Orlando, Florida, had married Detroit native Gladys Mitchell) and set about buying a house.

The Sweets did not begin looking for housing in a white neighborhood. Ossian Sweet explained he had only two conditions—an attractive home at an affordable price. "It made no difference to me whether it was in white neighborhood or a colored neighborhood," he later said, adding that he found nothing suitable "in the colored neighborhood."[10] When they purchased a brick two-story house on Garland Avenue for $18,500, trouble soon followed. Although they were only a few blocks from a heavily populated black section, their house sat in a working-class neighborhood inhabited by a mixture of residents from German, Polish, and Scandinavian heritage, the majority of whom apparently did not like the idea of an African American family further enhancing the diversity of the neighborhood.

The stress that usually accompanies house hunting should have ended when the Sweets made the deposit on the house. It did not. The woman who sold the house to the physician had not yet moved out when she received a telephone call from a representative of the Waterworks Improvement Association. The caller advised her not to let the black family move in. If they did, the caller said, she would be killed, the doctor would be killed, and the house would be blown up. The woman called Sweet and urged him not to move in, saying that the person who called represented the same group that ran off the Turners. She also reminded him of a meeting that had been organized by the same incendiary in a hall just opposite Dr. Sweet's new home. She described how more than 600 people had attended the meeting and pledged to "cooperate"[11] to enforce the restrictions against Negroes. Sweet knew about the meeting because an announcement of the time and venue appeared in the *Detroit Free Press* on July 12, 1925. It read,

To maintain the high standard of the residential district between Jefferson and Mack Avenues, a meeting has been called by the Waterworks Improvement Association for Thursday night in Howe School Auditorium. Men and women of the district, which includes Cadillac, Hurburt, Garland, St. Clair, and Harding Avenues are asked to attend in self defense.[12]

The association had crafted six "harmless" objectives: (1) to render constructive social and civic service, (2) to maintain a clean and healthy condition in streets and alleys, (3) to observe the spirit of the traffic ordinances for safety and protection of residents, (4) to cooperate with all city departments and all beneficial plans, (5) to cooperate with the police in the maintenance of law and order, and (6) to cooperate in the enforcement of the existing property restrictions and to originate such other restrictions as would preserve and protect the locality as a respectable community.[13]

In the spirit of fair play and truth in advertising, the association should have included a final objective summarizing the first six: "To guarantee, by hook or by crook, that no black ever set foot in a house in this clean, healthy, safe, and respectable community."

Even without the seventh objective, the association got its message across to Sweet and others. Sweet weighed his options. He could give up his right to own a home in a place of his choosing, or he could postpone moving in for some time in the hope that the hostility would subside. A third option, moving in, meant risking his life and the lives of his wife and two-year-old baby. He decided to postpone the move for three months.

After three months, the hostility showed no signs of subsiding. Sweet made his decision, saying, "I have to die like a man or live like a coward."[14] So Ossian Sweet moved into his new house, and he did so in the most unlikely of fashions. Along with plenty of groceries to fill the pantry, he brought nine guns and 400 rounds of ammunition. He knew he might need help, so he asked his two brothers as well as several friends to join him in the move.

On September 8, 1925, the day he moved in, 100 white people showed up at the house, stood in front, and stayed deep into the night. As the crowd dispersed at 3 A.M., a few threw rocks at the house. The following day, Gladys Sweet was in the kitchen preparing dinner. She had planned to serve roast pork, sweet potatoes, and mustard greens. Ossian Sweet was playing a game of cards with friends. "People—the people," someone in the house remarked.[15] They looked through the windows and saw a rising tide of humanity near the grocery store, in the alleys, and on nearby porches. As if someone had given a silent order, a barrage of stones suddenly pelted the house. The Sweets heard the crowd yell, "Niggers, Niggers, get them damn Niggers."[16]

Ossian Sweet had said he would die like a man defending his rights, but now he experienced overwhelming fear. Later, at the trial, he said that only a Negro who knew the history of black people could understand the fear that gripped him in that moment. He knew that history well; he had lived it growing up in Florida. He recalled the day he found the charred body of a Negro lynched in Polk County. He relived the day he saw a crowd of 5,000 whites attack Fred Rochelle, a black youth, near Bartow, Florida, on Peach River. Hiding in a nearby bush, Sweet watched the crowd pour kerosene on Rochelle and set him ablaze. Sweet remembered how the whites turned the occasion into what he termed a "Roman holiday." They drank alcohol, took pictures of the scene to commemorate their achievement, and grabbed bones from the victim as souvenirs.[17]

With their house under siege, the Sweets pulled down the blinds and turned off the kitchen lights. The barrage of stones continued, however. "Go raise hell in front. I'm going back," Ossian heard someone in the house say.[18] Ossian made his way upstairs as stones kept hitting the house. Utterly confused, he threw himself onto the bed.

At about this point, Henry Sweet and his friend John Letting stepped from the taxi. "Here's Niggers. Get them, get them,"[19] they heard the mob yell as people began to throw stones at the two blacks. When Henry saw the size of the crowd—now approaching 1,000 whites—close in on the house, he described the scene to the jury in simple but horrific terms. "It looked like death if we tried to hide, and it looked like death if we tried to get out."[20]

In his trial testimony, Ossian related how the two men rushed into the house and how the crowd surged forward "like a human sea." Ossian described how the stones keep coming faster, how he ran downstairs. "Another window was smashed. Then one shot. Then eight or ten from upstairs; then it was all over."[21]

One of the shots struck 33-year-old Leon Breiner, who was smoking a pipe on his friend's porch across the street from the Sweet residence. He dropped to the floor. "Boys, they've shot me," he said and breathed his last.[22] A second victim, Eric Haugsberg, suffered a bullet wound to the leg.[23] It took that level of pandemonium for the police, who had been posted to the scene, to act. They stormed into the home, turned on the lights, and arrested all 11 occupants. Each was later charged with capital murder and assault with intent to kill.

Arrested and charged were Ossian Sweet and Gladys Sweet; Ossian's brother, Dr. Otis Sweet; Henry Sweet; John Letting; Joe Mack, a chauffeur for Sweet; William Davis, a federal narcotics officer; Barnard Morse; Charles B. Washington; Morris Murray; and Leonard Morris. Three of the men, friends of Ossian, were there because trouble was expected. Henry and John Latting planned to stay until their return to Wilberforce Academy in Ohio. The rest were planning to room there.

Because of the racial climate in Detroit at the time, only the hardiest or most foolhardy judge would have been happy to see the Sweet case on his docket. As Judge Frank Murphy noted, "They see it as dynamite."[24] But Judge Murphy saw an opportunity, first for the liberal philosophy that had been gaining ground with the intellectual infusion of the Progressive movement and second for the integrity of the judicial system. He assigned himself to the case and set a hearing for October 30, 1925.

The state's case was based on a theory that lead prosecutor Robert Toms fleshed out in three hypotheses: (1) Ossian Sweet or someone in Ossian Sweet's house fired the shot that killed Leon Breiner, (2) Ossian Sweet aided and abetted the man who fired the shot that killed Leon Breiner, and (3) if Ossian Sweet aided and abetted one or more persons in the house who caused the death of Breiner, his act would be their act, and their act would be his act. The prosecution's contention was that the hypotheses were valid regardless of who fired the shot from Dr. Sweet's home.[25]

Lester S. Moll and Edward Kennedy, Jr. assisted Toms. The prosecution was confident that if it failed to prove the first hypothesis, it could prove the second and third. In his opening remarks, Toms painted a picture of a quiet evening in a tranquil neighborhood. In that idyllic neighborhood, residents were doing what they normally did, chatting in twos or threes or in small crowds. They visited on sidewalks, on their porches, and at the grocery store. Mr. Breiner was on his way from the store, Tom explained to the jury, when he paused to greet a friend. It was the kind of gesture one would expect from a tranquil, loving, quiet community member. As in every community, however, there exist a few mischievous boys, the prosecution conceded, harmless youths who throw stones for fun. It was such boys who indulged themselves at the expense of the Sweets, the prosecution concluded.

Youthful indulgence notwithstanding, explained the prosecution, the climate in the community was serene until the Sweets ruptured it without provocation by firing into the crowd. Toms gave some detail of the results of the shooting:

One [bullet] went through the eaves of Dove's house (where Breiner had paused to chat). Two others passed through the steps. One embedded itself in a small tree on the lawn and another cut through the glass door leading up to the second floor flat inside the house.[26]

Toms told the jury that no sizable crowd had gathered at the residence, adding, "The yard was untrampled, the hedge was unhurt, and even a rose bush was left blooming."[27] To leave no doubt this assertion was accurate, 70 witnesses corroborated the prosecution's version of what transpired the day Breiner was killed.

Like Judge Murphy, the National Association for the Advancement of Colored People (NAACP) recognized the civil rights significance of the case. The NAACP knew it needed a high-profile attorney because the case was high profile. It also knew it needed a white defense counsel. The organization therefore retained the services of two of the most distinguished attorneys in the country: Arthur Garfield Hays and Clarence Darrow. Hays was a noted civil rights lawyer. Darrow, hired as the lead counsel, had established himself as a formidable criminal defense attorney the year before in the highly publicized Leopold and Loeb murder-kidnapping trial. At that trial, Darrow put up a stout defense for teenagers Nathan Leopold, Jr. and Richard Lobe, even after they admitted to kidnapping and murdering 14-year-old Bobby Frank. Instead of the death penalty, both received life sentences.

Darrow's fame grew a year later with a case in Tennessee that was arguably the most highly publicized and dramatic trial in American history. In the small town of Dayton, Darrow defended John Thomas Scopes in what came to be known as the Great Monkey Trial. Scopes's trial commanded national interest because it pitted what America was becoming against what America had been. The early twentieth century saw the dawning of a brave new world filled with frightening implications and radical change. By the turn of the century, the country had completed its transformation from rural society to manufacturing colossus. But it had also become more secular. While the Great Monkey

Trial technically was about evolution, it fundamentally was about religion. For Darrow, the Scopes trial must have had much in common with the Sweet case. While the Sweet trial was technically about murder, it was fundamentally about race. It is no surprise then that the great Darrow was on hand to once again defend what appeared indefensible.

It was the same year as the Scopes trial that Darrow agreed to defend Sweet. Certain elements in the case intrigued him. He knew that the defense was up against a behemoth—the system. Forces behind the prosecution appeared so strong that it seemed unlikely anything could prevent the prosecution from sailing through the trial. But Darrow believed in man's ability to be both rational and just—a belief he incorporated in the Scopes defense—and believed it had the potential to produce an equal and opposite force sufficient to make the prosecution's task difficult. He also believed he could appeal to man's—and, he hoped, the jury's—more noble instincts. If he could, the Sweet case was destined to make history.

Hays delivered the opening statement for the defense. He began by asking the defendants to stand. He gave a biographic sketch of each before outlining the core of the case as the defense saw it:

The defense in this case faces and admits facts which are sometimes subject to equivocation and avoidance. We are not ashamed of our clients and we shall not apologize for them. We are American citizens; you men of the jury are American citizens; they are American citizens. Each juryman said he conceded equal rights to all Americans. On the basis of legal rights of the defendants we make our defense. We say this with the full realization of the sacredness of human life and having quite as much sympathy for the bereaved family of the defendant as has the prosecution.[28]

The defense sought to prove the right of self-defense, a right it said was rooted in Anglo-Saxon history. Quoting Lord Chatham, Hays reminded the jury about the sacredness of a person's home. Even the poorest man, he said, could in his cottage bid defiance to the crown. The house may be frail and its "roof may shake; the wind may blow through it; the storm may enter; the rain may enter; but the king of England can not enter; all his forces dare not cross the threshold of the ruined tenement."[29]

The defense's approach was disarmingly straightforward: If a man's home is sacred, then so is his right to defend it. The second part of the strategy drew attention to the state of mind that may have provoked the shooting. Again, the argument was simple: If the occupants of the house were in danger—real or perceived—if they were afraid or threatened, then whatever they did was an act of self-defense.

A third prong to the defense, less straightforward but crucial, developed as Hays and Darrow sought to establish that unless the state could identify from among the 11 defendants who fired the shot that killed Breiner, none could directly be tied to the crime. Moreover, even if it were determined that one of them fired the shot but fired not with the intention to kill a particular individual, whoever fired the shot could not be guilty of murder.

Since one strategy entailed showing the state of mind of those who perceived a threat, throughout the trial the defense attempted to show that a threat against the Sweets existed. This, of course, went directly to what Hays and Darrow stressed were the real, not the stated, goals of the Waterworks Improvement Association. It was this "association," the defense reminded the jury, that held several meetings, one of which attracted 700 people. The defense argued that the motive for the meetings—and, in fact, for the existence of the association—was to prevent blacks from moving into the neighborhood and, more specifically, the Sweets from occupying their new home.

To strengthen its argument, the defense produced as witnesses blacks beaten either while driving through the area or while near it. Darrow and Hays also produced witnesses who testified they heard people from the crowd shouting racial epithets and saying that "niggers" should be lynched or killed. Other witnesses said the crowd threw stones and various other objects at the Sweets' home. In addition, Henry Sweet and John Letting described the barrage of verbal and physical threats as they arrived at the house.

Finally, the defense drew attention to the role prejudice might have played. As Darrow said, he did not need to talk to the jury about race, prejudice, and the motives he knew were implicit in the case. He said he did not want to remind the court about "the terrible history" of bigotry in the United States. This is the way he presented his argument:

Here is [sic] eleven black people on trial before twelve whites, gentlemen. . . . Reverse this: Suppose one of you were charged with murder and you had shot and killed someone, while they were gathered around your home, and the mob had been a black mob and you lived in a black man's land and you killed a black man and you had to be tried by twelve blacks, what would you think? What would you think about it? You would probably think of pleading guilty and asking for the mercy of the court. Now, that is this case, gentlemen. I haven't any doubt but that this jury is as fair and has as good intentions as any jury I ever saw. It seems so to me but I don't care what your intentions are or how good you are or how intelligent you are, I know perfectly well that when you find a man who has no race prejudices you have got to find one out of a thousand.[30]

Darrow strenuously disagreed with the prosecution for calling Ossian a coward for loading his truck with food so that he could barricade himself in the house and for shooting at a crowd from the house. The prosecution had sarcastically asked the jury to excuse him for cowardice. In his summation, Darrow went straight to the point, calling Ossian a hero, not a coward.

Darrow then turned to the prosecution's argument that if Sweet's life was in danger, he should have called the police to protect him:

No man in any free country on earth is bound to call a policeman to defend his home or his life or his person or that of his friends. Under the laws of nature he has the right to stand and fight, and if he is a man he would rather die fighting than to cringe like a coward, and that is what he did.[31]

Darrow now had reached the most dramatic moment of the trial, when he asked the jury a question, one that echoed from the distant past and from a distant trial of 53 Africans and that still resonated with profound truth:

Imagine your face is black, would you have expected trouble? Why? Why? He is an intelligent man, he knew the history of his race, he knew that looking back to the terrible years that have marked their history he could see his answer; loaded like sardines in a box in the mid-decks of the steamers and brought forcibly from their African homes, half of them dying in the voyage; he knew they were sold like chattels as slaves and were compelled to work without pay. He knew that families were separated when it paid the master to sell them. He knew that even after he had got liberty under the Constitution and the law, he knew that bodies of dead Negroes were hanging from the limbs of trees of every state in the Union where they had been killed by the mob; he knew that in every state of the Union telegraph poles had been decorated by the bodies of Negroes dangling on ropes on account of race hatred and nothing else; he knew they had been tied to stakes in free America and the fire built around living human beings until they roasted to death; he knew they had been driven from their homes in the north and in great cities and here in Detroit and he was there not only to defend himself and his home and his friends, but to stand for the integrity and the independence of the abused race to which he belonged.[32]

Like a great thespian building to a climatic scene, Darrow told the jury that it held the power but that sometimes power was a two-edged sword: "[Y]ou may send him to prison if you like, but you will only crown him as a hero who fought a brave fight against fearful odds, a fight for the right, for justice for freedom, and his name will live and be honored when most of us are forgotten.

Darrow then charged the jury directly. "This is the only tribunal under our law that can take away the liberty or the life of a human being. . . . You have the power to judge."[33]

Passion flowing with every word, this was Darrow at his dramatic best. Speaking to each juror as though he were the only person in the room, Darrow's eloquence was intense and powerful. "No man has the capacity to judge—you must rid yourselves of prejudice, and you must be almost omnipotent and omniscient, to understand the other man, but you must judge, if the liberties go, it is the jury who is responsible for it, nobody else." The great lawyer concluded, "I urge you in the name of progress and of the human race to return a verdict of not guilty in this case."[34]

After Darrow's impassioned plea to the jury, Toms, perhaps reluctantly, stood before the jury to rebut Darrow and generate sympathy for Breiner. He summarily dismissed the defense strategy, saying, "Back of all your sophistry . . . back of all your prating about civil rights, back of your psychology and theory of race hatred lies the stark dead body of Leon Breiner with a bullet hole in his back."[35]

Toms then turned to Darrow and Hays, addressing them rather than the jury. "All your specious arguments . . . all your artful ingenuity born of many years of experience—all your social theory, all your cleverly conceived psychology, can never dethrone justice in this case." Then, "You can't make anything out of those facts of the defense gentlemen, but cold-blooded murder."[36]

It was now in the jury's hands. Because the jury was sequestered in a room adjoining the courtroom, those persons who lingered in the courtroom could hear animated exchanges in the jury room.

"What's the use of arguing with these guys?" someone asked rhetorically.[37]

"Two of you had these fellows convicted before you came here," another juror said.[38]

And another: "I will stay here 20 years, if necessary, and I am younger than any of you."[39]

Despite the judge's encouragement and despite deliberating 46 hours, the jury could not come to a consensus. Seven voted to acquit all defendants, while five insisted on manslaughter for the Sweet brothers—a hung jury and a mistrial.

The prosecution asked for a quick retrial. The defense successfully argued that the trials be separate. The prosecution decided to try Henry first since it contended that Henry either fired or was in the same building with the person who fired the killing shot, and since Henry was in a place that was not his residence, it followed that he must have gone to the house intent on committing violence.

The trial of Henry Sweet began April 19, 1926. It took five and a half days to impanel a jury. After the prosecution and defense had questioned 165 men from an initial list of 200 names, 12 men finally were selected. They represented a cross section of America except in two categories: gender and race. All were white. Charles Thorne, 82, was a steamship steward, retired after five years with the Detroit and Cleveland Navigation Company. William Brunswick was a locomotive engineer for Michigan Central Railroad. Edward W. Bernie, a young pharmacist, was serving jury duty for the first time. John A. Allen was a machinist; James Spencer, an electrician; William J. Simpson, an electrical engineer and contractor; Lewis Sutton, a watchman; Ralph Fuelling, a member of the water board and an Army veteran; Richard Adams, a retired lumberman; and Charles Dean, district manager of a grocery store. George Small, manager of Detroit Cunard Anchor Lines, was the jury foreman. Judge Frank Murphy, who presided over the first trial, wisely decided to sequester the jury, explaining that it was important to do everything humanly possible to get a fair trial.

The intense interest in the case was evident by the large crowds as well as their remarkable—for the times—diversity.

Josephine Gormon, a prominent civic leader in Detroit, noted the interest in the second trial by the number of people who attended the first day of the trial as well as the tension surrounding the event. Gormon noted that many civic leaders and organizations demanded the 11 blacks be punished to the fullest extent of the law so that "these Negroes be made an example."[40] Her summation of the trial's opening day: "A pin could have been heard dropping."[41]

When the case began, Toms and Moll sat at the state's table. Because Hays could not continue as defense counsel because of a previous commitment, the NAACP hired as a replacement a prominent black attorney, Thomas Chowke (Dr. Sweet had wanted Chowke before the NAACP took the first case).

Across the aisle little had changed. The prosecution's case differed only in that it focused on one person—Henry Sweet. The hypotheses were identical:

- Henry Sweet fired the shot that killed Leon Breiner.
- Henry Sweet aided and abetted the person who fired the shot that killed Leon Breiner.[42]

If Henry Sweet did aid and abet some one or more persons in the house who caused the death of Breiner, his act would be theirs, and their act would be his.

Apart from attempting to tie Henry Sweet to the shot that killed Breiner, the prosecution's greater challenge was to demonstrate to the jury that the now "infamous" Waterworks Improvement Association meeting was not a plotting session to evict the Sweets from their residence forcibly and that there was no unusual gathering at the Sweets' home the day of the shooting. This time the state outdid itself by producing 71 witnesses to corroborate these points.

The defense, on the other hand, did not want to rule out the possibility that Henry Sweet could have fired the shot that killed Breiner. It wanted to convince the jury that he did not. But in case someone on the jury panel thought he might have, the defense wanted to demonstrate that there was sufficient provocation. In his opening remarks, Darrow tied the theory to intent before the act:

If Henry Sweet went there or agreed after he got there to kill someone upon slight provocation, then he could be guilty of murder regardless of who fired the shot. But if he went there, as we claim, for the purpose of identifying his brother's home and family as it was not only his right, but his duty to do, or if he went there for that purpose and made a mistake and shot when in fact it wasn't necessary to kill, but he thought it was—he is innocent.[43]

Darrow also revisited the issue of cowardice brought up at the first trial:

They may have been gunmen. They may have tried to murder. But they were not cowards. Eleven people, knowing what it meant, with the history of the race behind them, with the knowledge of shooting and killing and insult and injury without end, eleven of them go into a house, gentlemen, with no police protection, in the face of a mob, and the hatred of a community, and take guns and ammunition and fight for their rights, and for your rights, and for mine, and for the rights of every being that lives. They went in and faced a mob seeking to tear them to bits. Call them something beside cowards.[44]

An essential component to Darrow's strategy, however, was to highlight inconsistencies in the state's testimony. He did so by using the state's own witnesses to support defense contentions. The cross-examination of a white resident that attended the meeting organized by the Waterworks Park Improvement Association illustrates how Darrow achieved this goal. During cross-examination, Alfred H. Andrews admitted that he attended the meeting before the riot and that a member of the Tireman Avenue Improvement Association was among the speakers. The following is how Darrow questioned Andrews:

Darrow: Did the speaker talk about legal means?

Andrews: I admitted to you that this man was radical.

Darrow: Answer my question. Did he talk about legal means?

Andrews: No.

Darrow: He talked about driving them out didn't he?

Andrews: Yes, he was radical—I admit that.

Darrow: You say you approved of what he said and applauded it, didn't you?

Andrews: Part of his speech.

Darrow: In what ways was he radical?

Andrews: Well, I don't myself believe in violence.

Darrow: I didn't ask you what you believe in. I said in what ways was he radical? Anything you want to say about what you mean by radical, that he advocated?

Andrews: No. I don't want to say any more.

Darrow: You did not rise in that meeting and say, "I guess I myself don't believe in violence," did you?

Andrews: No. I'd had a fine chance with 600 people there!

Darrow: What? You would have caught it, yourself, wouldn't you? You wouldn't have dared to do it at that meeting? (At this point, lead prosecutor Toms interrupted and asked the witness not to answer the question. He objected, and Judge Murphy sustained his objection. Undaunted, Darrow continued.)

Darrow: What did you mean by saying you had a fine chance? (Toms again interrupted. "Wait a minute. Did you hear the court's ruling?")

Darrow (apparently still undaunted): What did you mean by that?

Andrews: You imagine I would have made myself heard with 600 people there? I wasn't on the platform.

Darrow: What did you mean by saying you would have had a fine chance in that meeting where 600 people were present to make the statement that you said?

Andrews: I object to violence.

Darrow: Did anybody—did anybody in that audience of 600 people protest against advocating violence against colored people who had moved into the neighborhood?

Andrews: I don't know.

Darrow: You didn't hear any protest?

Andrews: No.

Darrow: You only heard applause?

Andrews: There was—as I stated—this meeting in the schoolyard.

Darrow: You heard nobody utter any protest, and all the manifestations you heard was applause at what he said?

Andrews: Yes, that is all.[45] (By now, Toms was quite disturbed by what Darrow's line of questioning had elicited. He tried to redirect the witness but with little success. Clearly, this was one of the high points in the trial for the defense.)

And Darrow's questioning of Eben Draper, another state witness:

Darrow: And you joined the club so as to do what you could—I am not saying that you did right or wrong—but to do what you could to keeping that a white district?

Draper: Yes.[46]

Cross-examination also raised questions about the credibility of the police. This time Chowke, who alternated with Darrow in cross-examination, smoothly led Lieutenant Paul Schellenberger to the brink of contradicting himself. As Chowke quizzed Schellenberger about the number of cars in the neighborhood that night, specifically asking why the police had diverted traffic on the street where Sweet lived, Schellenberger provided a litany of "no sirs," "I don't knows," and "I did nots."

Then, attempting to make clear that Schellenberger might be answering in a less-than-forthright manner, Chowke asked once again if traffic was getting heavy on Sweet's street:

Schellenberger: It appeared to me that people were getting curious. More so than anything else, and there was an unusual amount of traffic.

At this point, Chowke had led Schellenberger to the brink. Now he pushed him over:

Chowke: Then there was an unusual amount of automobile traffic there, wasn't there?[47]

Too late, the inspector realized that he had contradicted himself. Chowke had scored a point with the jury.

Darrow, however, was point man for the trial's most comical moment. That moment came when Darrow asked one of the patrolmen at the scene, a man named Schaldenbrand, to estimate the size of the crowd near the house.

When the patrolman said, "I didn't think," Darrow asked what he meant. "You didn't think? Don't policemen think?"

"No, a policeman is not supposed to think," Schaldenbrand said.[48]

The prosecution attempted to counter by emphasizing this was not a case about race or race relations, this was not a case about a neighborhood association, and this was not a case about prejudice. This was a case about murder, to which Darrow replied,

I haven't a doubt but what all of you are prejudiced against colored men—maybe one or two of you are not. We don't want to be prejudiced but we are. I fancy every one of you is, otherwise you'd have some companions in that race. I believe you've tried to rise above it, but to say there is no prejudice in this case is nonsense. You gentlemen bring these feelings into the jury box—they are part of your lifelong training. You needn't tell me you're not prejudiced. All I hope for is that you're strong enough, honest enough, decent enough to lay prejudice aside in this case. Would that mob have been standing in front of that house if the people there weren't black? Would anybody be asking you to send this boy to prison for life if he were not black? Is Mr. Moll right when he says prejudice has nothing to do with this case? Take hatred out of this case and you have nothing left.[49]

Darrow concluded simply, asking the jury to return a verdict of not guilty. This time he would receive a quick reply; after deliberating for three hours and 35 minutes, the jury reached a verdict. Judge Murphy summoned the jurors to court. Spectators who had scattered throughout the building magically filled Judge Murphy's court. Reporters raced back in. Clerks were secured. People gathered until the room choked beyond capacity. Judge Murphy asked the jury the customary question: "Have you gentlemen in the course of your deliberations reached a verdict in the case of Henry Sweet? And if so who will answer for you?"

Small, the foreman, stepped forward and announced, "We have and I will." He cleared his throat and announced, "Not guilty." His voice broke.

For a moment, counsels on both sides remained speechless. Then emotions burst forth. Tears rolled down the cheeks of Clarence Darrow and Henry Sweet. Families and friends hugged, sobbed, and laughed. Then, as the decision sank in, they congratulated one another.

Because the prosecution believed it had the strongest case against Henry Sweet, a verdict of not guilty for him essentially translated into a not-guilty verdict for all 11. The state soon dropped its charges against the rest of the defendants.

So ended the trials. But a verdict often has little to do with the public's attitude about the accused or the legal decision. Since the public usually is shackled to the media for the basic facts of any news event, media coverage was, to some degree, tied to public attitude. Since radio was still making the transition from experimental telecommunication technology to mass medium when the Sweet trials were held, the metropolitan newspapers of Detroit—the *Free Press,* the *News,* and the *Times*—became the major sources of news.

In general, coverage reflected greater support for the state than for the defendants, especially in the case of the *Free Press*. That newspaper ran stories that consistently leaned to or outright supported the prosecution, such as a report on how the lead prosecutor, Toms, was more aggressive than Darrow in the legal wrangling. At other times, state witnesses were described as so strong and convincing that Darrow failed to rattle them. In another story, the *Free Press* took great care to point out how witnesses corroborated the state's thesis about what happened the day Breiner was killed while providing little or no mention of the defense case for balance. In another story, Darrow was portrayed as exasperated and helpless at times.

On November 17, the *Free Press* ran a story that, although factually accurate, was more than a little provocative. According to the paper, testimony showed that a "Negro" married to a white woman had occupied the home that Dr. Sweet was alleging neighborhood residents did not want him to occupy. The story also suggested that the defense was unsuccessful in its argument about prejudice in the community since a black man previously resided there before. The paper was accurate about the black man residing there, but it failed to include the fact that neighborhood residents did not know that the woman was married to a black man.

In another story, the *Free Press* wrote that assistant prosecuting attorney Moll's presentation was brilliant, "a masterful summing up of the facts." Moll, wrote the newspaper, carried the jury systematically through the crime, provided them a glimpse into the childhood of Dr. Sweet, and "explored the remote psychological channels of the man's race mind and concluded that there was no justification, no excuse, for the shooting of Breiner."[50]

Newspaper coverage of the second trial was in many respects like coverage of the first trial. The *Free Press* seemed to cover events from the perspective of the state, while the *News* and the *Times* provided a more balanced view of what transpired inside the courtroom.

Few trials had the newsworthy ingredients of the Sweet trials. Both had conflict. Both had nationally famous attorneys. Both had novelty value regarding both defense and prosecution core arguments. Yet somehow interest outside Detroit was stunningly low. One would be hard pressed to find an editorial that challenged the system or questioned the obvious contradictions apparent in court proceedings. The appearance of a white mob, perhaps 1,000 strong, in front of a house occupied by a black physician who opens fire should have translated into truckloads of copy, especially coming on the heels of a major Supreme Court ruling against segregation by ordinance.[51]

Anything different would have been surprising, however. Media portrayals of blacks historically have exhibited a bias against blacks in both inadequate and unfavorable coverage.[52] Coverage of the Sweet trial proved nothing but consistent. As Hays observed:

The newspapers in Detroit had for a long period attributed lawless acts to negroes, and the comment in the press on the Sweet case seemed to indicate that on the night of the shooting the Sweet home was well protected by the police; that calm prevailed in the neighborhood and that the killing was wanton and malicious.[53]

If some in the Detroit press were guilty of the sin of commission by convicting the Sweets before the trial, the national press was guilty of sin by omission. That one of the great stories of the early twentieth century should be so neglected begs the question, Would the civil rights movement have mobilized decades earlier if the media had tended to its business more promptly, more objectively, and more humanely?

One might wonder then, in retrospect, how to apply the prosecution's wildly broad definition of cowardice. One might wonder just who, exactly, that scurrilous label best fits in the case of Ossian Sweet.

NOTES

1. Clarence Darrow, *The Story of My Life* (New York: Charles Scribner's Sons, 1932), 304.
2. Ibid.
3. Irving Stone, *Clarence Darrow for the Defense* (Garden City, N.Y.: Doubleday, 1941), 474.
4. Ibid.
5. Darrow, *The Story of My Life,* 304.
6. Douglas O. Linder, *Sweet Trials: An Account* (http://www.law.umkc.edu/faculty/projects/ftrials/sweet/background.html).
7. Ibid.
8. Linder, *Sweet Trials* (http://www.law.umkc.edu/faculty/projects/ftrials/sweet/sweetaccount.htm).
9. Ibid.
10. Stone, *Clarence Darrow for the Defense,* 474.
11. Ibid., 473
12. Linder, *Sweet Trials* (http://www.law.umkc.edu/faculty/projects/ftrials/sweet/sweetaccount.htm).
13. Arthur Garfield Hays, *Let Freedom Ring* (New York: Horace Liveright, 1928), 204.
14. Linder, *Sweet Trials* (http://www.law.umkc.edu/faculty/projects/ftrials/sweet/sweetaccount.htm).
15. Stone, *Clarence Darrow for the Defense,* 475.
16. Arthur Weinberg and Lila Weinberg, *Clarence: A Sentimental Rebel* (New York: Atheneum, 1987), 332.
17. Linder, *Sweet Trials* (http://www.law.umke.edu/faculty/projects/ftrials/sweet/h-jaccount.htm).
18. Stone, *Clarence Darrow for the Defense,* 475.
19. Ibid.
20. Linder, *Sweet Trials* (http://www.law.umkc.edu/faculty/projects/ftrials/sweet/background.html).
21. Hays, *Let Freedom Ring,* 226.

22. Linder, *Sweet Trials* (http://www.law.umkc.edu/faculty/projects/ftrials/sweet/sweetaccount.htm).

23. Eric Haugsberg's name is spelled differently by several sources. The *Detroit Free Press* spelled it "Haugsberg" twice in one story, and later in the same story a "k" was added to "Eric," and the last name was spelled "Hoberg." Other sources spelled it "Houghberg."

24. Stone, *Clarence Darrow for the Defense,* 476.

25. http://www.law.umkc.edu/faculty/projects/ftrials/sweet/h-jaccount.HTM#opening.

26. Douglas O. Linder, *The Trial of Henry Sweet: An Observer's Account* (http://www.law.umkc.edu/faculty/projects/ftrials/sweet/h-jaccount.htm#opening).

27. Ibid.

28. Hays, *Let Freedom Ring,* 214.

29. Ibid.

30. See Darrow's summation in the Ossian trial. Reconstructed by Douglas O. Linder (http://www.law.umkc.edu/faculty/projects/ftrials/sweet/Darrowsumm1.html).

31. See "I Need No Policeman," Darrow's summation in the Ossian Sweet trial (http://www.law.umkc.edu/faculty/projects/ftrials/sweet/Darrowsumm1.html).

32. Ibid.

33. See "You Owe It to These Eleven Defendants," Darrow's summation in the Henry Sweet trial (http://www.law.umke.edu/faculty/projects/ftrials/sweet/Darrowsum1.html).

34. See Stone, *Clarence Darrow for the Defense,* 485.

35. Weinberg and Weinberg, *Clarence,* 343.

36. Ibid.

37. Hays, *Let Freedom Ring,* 232.

38. Ibid.

39. Ibid.

40. Stone, *Clarence Darrow for the Defense,* 476.

41. Ibid., 484.

42. Weinberg and Weinberg, *Clarence,* 344

43. See speech excerpts organized by Douglas O. Linder (http://www.law.umkc.edu/faculty/projects/ftrials/sweet/h-jaccount.HTM#opening).

44. See "Who Are the Cowards in This Case?" taken from Closing Argument of Clarence Darrow in the Case of People v. Henry Sweet. In the Recorders Court, Detroit, Michigan Before The Honorable Frank Murphy, May 11, 1926. See also http://www.law.umke.edu/faculty/projects/ftrials/sweet/Darrowsumm1.html.

45. Linder (http://www.law.umkc.edu/faculty/projects/ftrials/sweet/h-jaccount.htm#opening).

46. Weinberg and Weinberg, *Clarence,* 336–37.

47. See Douglas O. Linder, *Case for the Defense, The Trial of Ossian Sweet: An Observer's Account* (http://www.law.umkc.edu/faculty/projects/ftrials/sweet/h-jaccount.htm).

48. Weinberg and Weinberg, *Clarence,* 345.

49. http://www.law.umkc.edu/faculty/projects/ftrials/sweet/h-jaccount.html#opening. For a more complete speech, see Richard J. Jensen, *Clarence Darrow: The Creation of an American Myth* (Westport, Conn.: Greenwood Press, 1992), 221–51.

50. *Detroit Times,* 25 November 1925, 1.

51. See *Buchanan v. Warley,* 254 U.S. 60 (1917).

52. See G. Stemple III, "Visibility of Blacks in News and News-Picture Magazines," *Journalism Quarterly* 48 (1971): 337–39; D. O. Sears, "Black Invisibility: The Press and the L.A Riot," *American Journal of Sociology* 76 (1971): 698–72; and Mary Alice Sentman, "Black White Disparity in Coverage by Life Magazine from 1937–1972," *Journalism Quarterly* 61 (1983): 501–508.

53. Hays, *Let Freedom Ring,* 200.

8

THE CASE OF CLAY SHAW (1967)

Robert Dardenne

"We gonna have Mardi Gras *and* the trial. Shee-it, what a time!"

Some people say New Orleans businessman Clay Lavergne Shaw was the unluckiest son of a bitch on the face of the earth. They say one day he was living his life as the respected founder and retired director of the International Trade Mart, as restorer and renovator of historic buildings, as part of a social circle of high-society folk eating in fine restaurants and drinking in good bars, and the next day? Well, the next day—that would be March 1, 1967—Jim Garrison accused him of conspiring to murder the president of the United States, arrested him, and, so they say, prosecuted him to death.

For the record, a jury two years to the day after Shaw's arrest, following a 40-day trial, took about 45 minutes to find him not guilty. Not that it did the poor sucker any good.

In early January 1969, the city that care forgot, the city of Jazz Fest, strip joints, take-out booze, po'boys, and just plain excess anticipated something other than Mardi Gras.

Oh, no, folks did not forget Mardi Gras, but neither could they ignore impending amusement, especially amusement on a grand scale. The central figure in this potential spectacle already proved his ability to produce drama and excitement. After all, hadn't he focused the whole world's attention on New Orleans? Hadn't he drawn hundreds of reporters to revel in the flesh and spirits of the city? Hadn't he been in every major newspaper and magazine and on every major television network? Hell man, he *was* the *Johnny Carson Show* one night. And why not? He had, after all, solved the mystery of the most incredible, most audacious, most dramatic crime of the century.

Hadn't he?

Let's see, now. How did that go?

At 12:30 P.M., November 22, 1963, at Dealey Plaza in Dallas, a team of at least seven members of the paramilitary right and anti-Castro fanatics, in precise fashion, fired a volley of shots, one of which killed President John F. Kennedy.

No. That's not exactly right, is it?

At 12:30 P.M., November 22, 1963, at Dealey Plaza in Dallas, besides men on the grassy knoll, at least two others fired from behind the president, one—not Lee Harvey Oswald—from the Dallas School Book Depository Building and one probably from the Dal-Tex Building. Counting people arrested near the grassy knoll and one man faking a fit, 11 people, four firing weapons, helped kill President John F. Kennedy.

As you well know, that's wrong, too.

At 12:30 P.M., November 22, 1963, at Dealey Plaza in Dallas, at least four gunmen fired six or more shots, and others abetted in killing President Kennedy by removing spent cartridges and creating diversions. Not one, however, was Oswald, the officially accused assassin. During the shooting, he likely stood outside the front door of the Book Depository watching the motorcade like hundreds of others who witnessed one of the century's most sensational crimes.

Okay, that's not it, either. But, not to take anything away from the hero of Oliver Stone's 1991 movie *JFK*, these scenarios, more or less, came from the impresario himself, New Orleans District Attorney Jim Garrison, in a single interview.[1] Other times he accused the CIA, the FBI, Vice President Lyndon Johnson, extremist groups, anti-Cuban revolutionaries, Texas oilmen, Dallas police, and, depending on your willingness to accept what some people say,[2] homosexuals. To cover all angles, Garrison also speculated that someone fired from in front of the president out of a manhole.

But, as you know, the government, supported by a supposedly exhaustive investigation, officially said a lone gunman, Oswald, on that November day, fired three shots from behind Kennedy, blowing away part of his head. The Dallas police, the Warren Commission, and others concluded that Oswald fired his mail-order Mannlicher-Carcano rifle that he perched on boxes arranged to steady his aim from a sixth-floor window in the Book Depository building. They agreed that Oswald abandoned his rifle, calmly left the building, and 45 minutes later killed Dallas patrolman J. D. Tippit. For two days, attention focused on this violent, wife-beating, self-proclaimed Marxist, recently returned from the Soviet Union, where he halfheartedly sought Soviet citizenship. Then attention dramatically shifted. Nightclub owner Jack Ruby,[3] watched by dozens of reporters and police and millions of viewers on live television, stepped in front of Oswald in the Dallas City Jail basement and shot him in the stomach with a Colt .38 revolver. Oswald died. Ruby went to jail, where he died of cancer in January 1967 awaiting the appeal of his murder conviction.

Meanwhile, Garrison, who accused so many people of having so many connections to the assassination and claimed in no uncertain terms to have solved it, eventually arrested only one person—in fact, the only one ever brought to trial in Kennedy's murder.

That would be the unfortunate Shaw.

Getting from Kennedy's assassination to Shaw's not-guilty verdict is a twisted and maybe demented journey through French Quarter backstreet bars; over the crowded and open Dealey Plaza in Dallas; across pages of the nation's newspapers, magazines, and books; and through the complex mind and personality of the eccentric and some say paranoid or even psychotic New Orleans district attorney. Wandering through all this are some of the most bizarre and unbelievable characters ever paraded through the pages of any book, at least any book that purports to be true.

And "truth" is definitely an issue here.

Already, too many people have put forward too many "truths" about this murder and this case. At the time, reporters and writers filled newspapers and magazines with articles, stories, commentaries, and analyses about the trial. And since then, hundreds, even thousands, of books and articles and an un-fathomable amount of "information" on the Internet offer readers support and even proof for dozens of scenarios in the death of John Kennedy, an imperfect man who seemed to embody a perfect hope. His death, perhaps because it so unexpectedly extinguished so much hope, was the first mass spectacle of the television age. Of all this violent era's murders and assassinations—Malcolm X, Martin Luther King, Jr., and Bobby Kennedy among them[4]—it remains the most laden with conspiracy speculation.

Garrison did not help serve truth when he declared early in the Shaw case, "The key to the whole thing is through the looking glass. Black is white; white is black. I don't want to be cryptic, but that's the way it is."[5] Garrison critics say it is the only thing he had right.

Neither did it help that all this was set in New Orleans, a city formed in fantasy, nurtured in the surreal, and addicted to festivity and amusement. It is, to be fair, a city of many dimensions. People live, work, and play as every-where else. But because New Orleans nourishes its vices and tolerates almost anything, few people stand out, creating an environment that appeals to those who wish to be invisible. One might conclude after reading about the Shaw trial that the city teemed with anti-Castro activity, harbored secret training grounds for potential invaders of Cuba and other hot spots, and attracted a staggering array of undercover political intrigue. In steamy, smoky bars, smelling of Herbsaint, Angostura bitters, and decades of urine and spilled long-neck Dixies, sticky with grenadine and sugar water splashed out of countless hurricanes, CIA, FBI, anti-Castro revolutionaries, and multitudes of other covert operatives smoked unfiltered cigarettes, drank Worcestershire- and Tabasco-laced Bloody Marys, and planned secret operations, imaginary or otherwise. And sitting among them, in bars pouring out cheap draughts in big plastic cups; serving fried catfish, shrimp, and oysters and bowls of gumbo; or featuring naked women swinging over the streets through open windows and couples simulating sex acts on stage, were militant-extremist whackos; potheads and acidheads and probably cokeheads and horseheads, too; panhandlers, transvestites, homosexuals, prostitutes, vagrants, runaway kids, and bums; lawyers, businesspeople, winos and drunks, restaurant and bar workers, locals and visitors; and passels of googly-eyed tourists from Nebraska in button-down collars and light cotton dresses not really sure whether to shit or go blind.

In short, New Orleans was, is, no place to seek truth or establish reality, no place to be too serious, and no place to muck with people's amusements. So, obviously, it was the perfect place to try Clay Shaw for conspiring to kill the president of the United States.

Why shouldn't this weird case be tried against the backdrop of chicken hearts and bat blood and New Orleans voodoo? After all, it's filled with magic. Didn't the extra rifles disappear from the Book Depository building? Didn't the examination notes from Parkland Hospital disappear? Didn't autopsy reports and X rays disappear? Didn't records and documents and boxes of other evidence disappear into the national archives? Didn't the president's brain disappear? And didn't that magic bullet stop and change direction in midair? Certainly a magician fired that many precise shots in that little time?

The president's brain? His body lies in Arlington National Cemetery, but his brain apparently doesn't. It disappeared at some unknown point after they wheeled him into Dallas Parkland Hospital. It's true. Well, it is as true as things can be when you talk about John F. Kennedy. His brain is not a major issue, but those who devote their lives to solving Kennedy's murder— they'd be the ones insisting it isn't solved now—find significance in everything, particularly things missing, of which there's no shortage.[6] The missing brain, for example, likely provides incontrovertible evidence that assassins shot Kennedy from the front, not the back, as must be the case if Oswald is the true and lone assailant. That Kennedy was killed from the front is what Garrison sought to prove when he brought Shaw to trial. Why? Because it would prove a conspiracy, and Shaw was on trial for conspiracy, and because it would prove the Warren Commission wrong, and Garrison really, really wanted to prove the Warren Commission wrong.

Now that you're into this, it's easy to see what you are thinking. But, sorry, it's unlikely Garrison stole the brain because neither he nor anyone else has proved that Oswald did not kill Kennedy. And certainly, jurors in the Shaw trial, after being sequestered in a reasonably cheap and cramped New Orleans motel for 40 days and 40 nights, when given the chance, pronounced him not guilty in 45 minutes and got the hell out of Dodge.

How did it come to that?

Let's start with Jim (formerly Earling Carothers) Garrison, a six-foot-six, slightly hunched over New Orleans fixture and celebrity who, in 1969, was the district attorney of Orleans Parish (county), a husband and father, a politician to watch and watch out for, and a charismatic and loquacious charmer with a smooth voice, local connections, and big ideas. And, despite his efforts at cleaning up what many considered to be a very dirty city, he had time on his hands. So, after he connected Oswald to New Orleans and when then-U.S. Senator Russell Long told Garrison that he thought the Warren Commission Report was flawed, Garrison stoked up his own investigation, starting with Oswald's New Orleans activities.

Some newspapers and magazines looked askance at Garrison and his investigation, and some attacked him, claiming he made up the case and mistreated and even abused Shaw. A few diehards today claim the person mistreated was Garrison, the man standing up against the press, the military-industrial complex, the U.S. government, the Communists, the CIA, the FBI, and the secret all-powerful forces really running the country and the world. Certainly Garrison thought that or made it appear that he did. His genius, or his paranoia, gave him the impetus and support he needed, as a parish attorney, to undertake this unprecedented investigation. That the Secret Service, the FBI, the CIA, the Dallas police force, the Warren Commission, and others had already investigated the assassination did not faze him.

They were wrong. They misled, mishandled, distorted, lied, and even murdered to keep the truth from the American public, a wrong Garrison would right. He would find the truth despite personal threats from government representatives, which he describes in his books (*Heritage of Stone* and *On the Trail of Assassins*); despite government operatives in his office who turned over confidential prosecution strategy to the defense and office documents to the FBI and manipulated key defections and embarrassing leaks; despite suspects and witnesses disappearing or dying; despite concerted efforts by U.S. authorities to deny him assassination evidence; and despite a massive government/media campaign to smear his good name and his just cause. Many believed him. They thought the Warren Commission wrong or, worse, a sham. Garrison, knowingly or not, tapped in to that obviously massive store of discontent and bought wide latitude in building his case, in part against Shaw but mostly against his own government.

Although he said the investigation began in November 1966, the *New Orleans States-Item* broke the news on February 17, 1967. That article led to the following:

- New Orleans becoming headquarters to hundreds of representatives of the national and international press. Garrison seemed to revel in their attention as they latched on to him as a media personality, especially in Europe, where people eagerly followed the investigation.

- Garrison realizing that public records left him exposed. He created Truth or Consequences, a group of prominent New Orleans businesspeople who put up substantial funds to privately finance his very public investigation, thereby effectively removing some public scrutiny and creating an ethical and possible legal dilemma.

- Garrison attracting attention of dozens, if not hundreds, of people with "information" about the assassination. He would say the Warren Commission and other investigators ignored, misrepresented, or missed these sources. Garrison foes would say they were a parade of crackpots and crazies bizarre enough to excite even the most jaded New Orleans Mardi Gras aficionados.

Here's the case.

The state said three men—Shaw, Oswald, and David Ferrie—met at Ferrie's apartment at 3300 Louisiana Avenue for a party and, after most guests left, discussed killing Kennedy. That discussion, plus one move toward carrying out the plan, under Louisiana law, constituted a conspiracy for which Shaw was arrested. The key witness for the prosecution was Perry Raymond Russo, who claims to have been a friend of Ferrie's and the remaining party-goer when the discussion occurred. The defense said Clay Shaw never knew Oswald or Ferrie or Russo, never went to a party in Ferrie's apartment, and never discussed killing the president anywhere with anyone.

State witnesses swore they saw Shaw with either Oswald or Ferrie or both, trying to prove Shaw lied. Because the state believed that Shaw used the alias "Clay Bertrand" and that Bertrand was connected to the assassination conspiracy, it brought witnesses to tie Shaw to "Bertrand." Because the state attempted to prove that Kennedy died as the result of a conspiracy, it brought witnesses to prove assassins fired shots in Dallas from several directions. The defense countered testimony from state witnesses, often discrediting and in one case devastating them, and was forced to support Warren Commission findings that Oswald fired the only shots at Kennedy.

Why did the state fail? Critics say Garrison, who hardly ever attended the trial between opening and closing arguments, chose Shaw to prosecute essentially by pulling a name from a hat and then offered testimony from liars, crazies, drug addicts, and otherwise highly unbelievable witnesses. They may be mostly right. Garrison and his aides offered an unconvincing case with witnesses of questionable character and credibility. Further, it was a schizophrenic case, declared against Clay Shaw but aimed at the Warren Commission and the U.S. government. The state could never reconcile the two, nor could the jury.

The case started badly. Really badly. The district attorney's suspect dropped dead.

When Garrison announced that arrests were imminent because he had solved the Kennedy assassination beyond all doubt, he had in mind not Shaw but David Ferrie—a hairless pilot, self-proclaimed psychologist and chemist, private investigator, and pianist rumored to have CIA and anti-Cuban ties. Probably a brilliant man, Ferrie was peculiar. He lived in, by most accounts, a filthy and cluttered apartment where he kept rats for experiments he hoped would lead to a cure for cancer. He practiced hypnosis and concocted potions and experimented on willing and other subjects in his effort to find an aphrodisiac for homosexuals. He also apparently worked with Russo selling pornographic films from Cuba.[7] Accounts in books and throughout the Internet connect Ferrie with paramilitary fringe groups for which he flew or trained pilots and soldiers. Eastern Airlines fired him as a result of an arrest on homosexual charges, although he was never convicted. No one knew how he lost all hair, perhaps through illness or something connected to flying. He glued odd patches of reddish hairlike material to his head and brows or used greasepaint for eyebrows and was "physically filthy,"[8] thereby creating an appearance that could draw attention even in a city that celebrates such weirdness.

Ferrie occasionally worked for Louisiana Mafia leader Carlos Marcello, which makes him of interest for those who connect Kennedy's assassination to the Mafia.[9] Ferrie was, in fact, in court with Marcello the day Kennedy died. What he did after that court session convinced Garrison that he was in on the plot.

Garrison originally ran across Ferrie's name when he looked into Oswald's New Orleans connections shortly after the assassination and, in fact, had arrested Ferrie and turned him over to the FBI, which questioned and cleared him. Three years later, when Garrison began his serious investigation, he went back to Ferrie, uncovering, unsurprisingly, another cast of fascinating characters. At the core was investigator and alleged drunk[10] Jack Martin (a.k.a. Edward S. Suggs). On the day Kennedy died, Martin, a talker, got drunk and got pistol-whipped by former FBI agent and private investigator Guy Banister. In the months before, he may have made unauthorized long-distance calls on Banister's account and thought that Ferrie ratted him out on the calls.

Let's get this straight. Martin makes unauthorized calls, Ferrie tells on him, Kennedy gets killed, Martin and Banister drink all day, Banister beats up Martin; then Martin calls the FBI, the district attorney, and by some accounts a bunch of other people and tells them Ferrie is connected to the president's assassin. He told Garrison that Ferrie and Oswald served in the Civil Air Patrol together and that Ferrie taught Oswald how to shoot a rifle.

Banister, who died in 1964, is of interest because Garrison claimed that he was a CIA operative deeply involved in anti-Castro activities, because some sources link Oswald and Ferrie to Banister, and because Banister resembled Clay Shaw enough for some to think people might have confused the two. Wise readers will keep in mind that it is possible Banister was not CIA, Oswald never knew him, and no one ever mistook him for Shaw. But when Martin, the pistol-whipped drunk, told everyone Oswald and Ferrie were connected, he drew rapid and intense attention on himself and those around him, including Banister. Martin had told New Orleans police that Banister beat him because of the long-distance calls. He told Garrison that he lied to police because he feared Banister's reaction if he told the truth, which was that he knew Banister and Ferrie were connected to the assassination. The district attorney's investigators found Martin's information compelling in part because they heard it from several sources, all of whom may have heard it from the loose-tongued and highly unreliable Martin, who either lied to police or lied to Garrison and may have lied to everyone.[11]

In any case, Garrison focused on Ferrie and knew that on the day Kennedy was shot, he drove several hours with two acquaintances to Houston's Winterland Ice Skating Rink. Curiously, he didn't skate but stayed near the telephone. That Ferrie may have known Oswald and Banister, that Banister beat up Martin, that Martin said Ferrie and Banister were connected to the assassination, and that Ferrie took the mysterious trip to Texas were enough for Garrison to hone in on Ferrie as a suspect. Ferrie, he thought, may have been the getaway pilot and the rink a kind of communications center.

Unfortunately for Clay Shaw, as it happened, Ferrie turned up dead on February 22, 1967. *Washington Post* reporter George Lardner said he interviewed Ferrie four hours late into the night on February 21 in the sloppy Louisiana Parkway apartment. Apparently, soon after he left, a vein burst in Ferrie's brain, killing him pretty much instantly. The pilot's demise left Garrison with an investigation apparatus in full swing, inflated expectations among the many who believed he would expose government involvement and cover-up and solve the killing, and an increasing number of media people salivating over what might come next.

Ferrie's death, while initially a blow, legitimized Garrison's investigation for those who wanted to believe in a conspiracy. The coroner ruled Ferrie died naturally; however, Garrison called two unsigned notes found in Ferrie's apartment "suicide notes" and referred to the death as a suicide and sometimes hinted at murder.[12] Anti-Garrison people say authorities may have planted the notes. The death seemed a remarkable coincidence, and the press, sensing something sensational, renewed its interest in Garrison's quest, which, of course, put more pressure on him to produce something to meet suddenly and dramatically increased expectations. At the same time, people in New Orleans, sensing a major pre–Mardi Gras diversion, followed the case through big headlines in the local papers and speculated about it at bars and parties. They were in for a big shock.

While good conspiracy fodder, Ferrie's passing left Garrison without any suspect. How he acquired one is not entirely clear, and you may or may not be pleased to know the story is no less bizarre than any other connected to this case.

A round, jive-talking lawyer and associate district attorney from a neighboring parish was laid up in a hospital with pneumonia and on medication the day Kennedy died. Dean Adams Andrews, Jr. captivated the press with his ubiquitous sunglasses and jive attitude and lingo. He once said of Garrison, "I don't know what he's up to. He's pickin' me like chicken, shuckin' me like corn, stewin' me like an oyster . . . I'm trying to see if this cat's kosher, you know?"[13] Andrews said, among other things, that Oswald had visited his office several times in the past, probably sent by "Clay Bertrand," whom he knew from previous contacts and who helped local gay kids. He also said that on November 22, 1963, he got a call from Bertrand asking him to go to Dallas and represent Oswald.[14]

That's likely the introduction of "Clay Bertrand" into the case, although Garrison, unsurprisingly, claims something different. By now, however, astute readers might be unwilling to take all Garrison's claims (or anyone else's in this case) at face value. Still, Garrison, in his search for a suspect, decided Clay Bertrand and Clay Shaw were one and the same. David Chandler, a reporter for *Life* magazine who worked early on with Garrison, told author Edward Jay Epstein that he heard Garrison tell his staff, when puzzling over the name, that Clay Shaw stuck out of a list of possibilities because the first names were the same, because Shaw was homosexual and had homosexual associations, and because Bertrand befriended homosexuals.[15] Another author said Garrison knew Shaw was gay and that provided the link to Ferrie, also gay.[16] It is also possible Garrison heard Shaw's name officially, as various people claim that the FBI interviewed him during the 1963 investigation. U.S. Attorney General Ramsey Clark, in fact, told the press in 1969 that Shaw had been investigated and cleared, but the attorney general's office apologized later and said that Clark spoke incorrectly and that Shaw had not been investigated.

To pro-Garrison people, Clark's gaff, of course, screamed cover-up. They and Garrison[17] insist the FBI did interview Shaw, that many in the French Quarter knew him as "Clay Bertrand," and that Shaw was heavily involved with the CIA. To prove the CIA connection, Garrison and his supporters look to *Paese Sera,* a left-wing Italian newspaper that, on March 4, 1967, reported that Centro Mondiale Commerciale, a Rome trade-promotion organization from 1958 to 1962, was a CIA front. Guess who was on the board of directors? The paper also reported Perimindex, another organization, was CIA controlled. Guess who was on that board, too? Yep, Clay Shaw. CIA records (as revealed throughout the Internet and in many publications) show that Shaw, as did other businesspeople and travelers, routinely provided information to the CIA from 1948 to 1956. An article published on-line out of *Studies in Intelligence,* from the Center for the Study of Intelligence at the CIA, claims that the *Paese Sera* article was a successful Communist disinformation effort to discredit the United States.[18] The article confirmed that Shaw provided information to the CIA but denied he was an agent and denied that Centro Mondiale Commerciale was a CIA front.

Anti-Garrison people point to the article and others like it as proof positive that the district attorney and his supporters grossly exaggerated and even lied about Shaw's CIA connections.

Looking-glass truth, indeed. Garrison, who has proved to be at least unreliable and at worst criminal, claimed evidence shows one thing, and the

CIA, the agency Garrison tried to tie to Kennedy's assassination, said Garrison's evidence was Communist disinformation. Garrison supporters produce bits and scraps of files showing or hinting at Shaw's CIA involvement, an affiliation of which there appeared to be no shortage in 1960s New Orleans. Anti-Garrison people cite official CIA statements denying any relationship with Shaw beyond what was common for many others in his position and build their cases on lack of substantial proof that Shaw was CIA. The whole thing muddies the investigative waters as writers bolster their claims by repeatedly quoting obviously biased sources. Add to all this universal Internet access, the technology to easily fake documents and the large number of them that circulate in conspiracy cases, the ability to put massive amounts of material on-line without substantiation or much accountability, and the apparently heavy emotional and perhaps intellectual investments by many people firmly convinced of one side or the other, and you have more than muddied waters. You have mud.

Mud or not, the Bertrand issue came to be the core of the case. Star witness Russo brought up the name "Clem Bertrand" in the March 26, 1967, preliminary hearing, at which three judges, based almost entirely on what he said, determined that enough evidence existed for Shaw to stand trial. Or, as pro-Shaw people claim, Garrison and his staff implanted it in his mind through hypnosis and truth-serum treatments. Further, an officer getting information at Shaw's arrest said he signed a card acknowledging he used the alias Bertrand. But at the trial, Judge Edward Haggerty found the testimony unbelievable and refused to allow it or the signed card in evidence. A mailman testified that mail he delivered to a forwarding address for Shaw included letters to Clay Bertrand. Defense lawyers fed the mailman fictitious names, which he also admitted delivering to that address, thereby losing some credibility. Finally, a woman at an airline courtesy room identified Shaw as the man who signed the name "Clay Bertrand" on the check-in register, but in court, a defense handwriting expert said it was not Shaw's writing. Records from Garrison's office quoted and displayed on many on-line sites and books show that his investigators could not find evidence of the existence of a Clay Bertrand in New Orleans, and purported FBI records show that its investigators also came up empty. Garrison claimed after the trial to have found many people who knew Shaw used the name "Clay Bertrand"[19] routinely, and pro-Garrison writers[20] make the same claims. Garrison produced none of these sources at the preliminary hearing or the trial.

No one can authoritatively state that he knows the truth in this matter, in part because none of the Bertrand stories holds up without doubt, including that of Andrews. A compulsive talker and publicity seeker, he said over time that Bertrand called to get him to represent Oswald, that he made up the name Bertrand out of "solid air,"[21] that Bertrand might or might not have been Clay Shaw, that Bertrand certainly was not Clay Shaw, and that Bertrand was French Quarter bartender Eugene Davis. He also said that Clay Bertrand was a man who helped homosexuals in court cases and was a "lawyer without a suitcase,"[22] that Bertrand accompanied Oswald to his office, that Bertrand owed him money, and that Bertrand had fled the last time he saw him. Bartender Davis, called to the stand, denied he was Bertrand or ever used the name. That Garrison convicted Andrews of perjury over the matter is of little consequence, as Garrison seemed to use perjury as threat of retaliation. And that Andrews's final version of his story was that no Bertrand existed seems hardly more believable than any other version.

Garrison, however, had enough to question Shaw, whom he brought in and asked to take a lie detector test. Shaw agreed, but only the next day after resting. Garrison, perhaps angered, arrested Shaw immediately and searched his house, finding, among other things, masks and whips, which the district attorney attributed to a perverse lifestyle and found significant because several figures he connected to the conspiracy were homosexual. Shaw said the masks and whips were parts of old Mardi Gras costumes. But it did not matter. Garrison had an arrest, one that shocked, even staggered, the good citizens of New Orleans. Naturally, this was good. Accusing a prominent civic leader for conspiring to kill the president has incredible potential for diversion spectacular enough to fill idle hours with gleeful speculation as the good citizens of New Orleans awaited the main course Mardi Gras bacchanalia.

Nobody is this crazy. Nobody arrests a leading citizen of the city without having a solid case. Therefore, one statement of excitement and anticipation reverberated throughout the city, the nation, and even the world:

"He must have something."

Well, he had Clay Shaw, although by most accounts not much else.

Unless you count numerous letters and calls from people with every manner of zany notion, some of which Garrison apparently announced to the press as "evidence" he had collected. But the big district attorney (the press called him "Big Jim" and "The Jolly Green Giant") did not have to wait long for one of these contacts to score big. He stumbled on Perry Russo, a Baton Rouge insurance salesman with Equitable Life Assurance Company, who had known Ferrie in the summer and early fall of 1963 and, as so many others in this case, liked to talk. But, as you will soon see, Russo, the all-too-willing witness, was essentially a work-in-progress. How Garrison completed that work resulted in one of the biggest controversies in the case and turned mild Garrison critics, even in the press, into hard-core Garrison haters. And it turned one reporter into a witness for the defense.

Russo, after reading about Ferrie's death, sent a letter to Garrison offering information, and by the time he got together with Garrison investigator Andrew "Moo" Sciambra, he had already talked to a Baton Rouge newspaper, a New Orleans television station, and other news media. Among other things, he said Ferrie, whom he met through Civil Air Patrol and befriended even after Ferrie threatened to kill him, had said Kennedy would be easy to kill and, "We will get him, and it won't be long."[23] Russo also said he hadn't heard of Lee Harvey Oswald until the assassination. Sciambra interviewed him and gave Garrison the results in a memo.

That's the simple version, and wouldn't it be nice if, just for once, things stayed simple? Well, they don't.

Remember that Russo was the star witness in the case. Remember he's the one who said he overheard Ferrie, "Leon" Oswald, and Shaw in the front room of Ferrie's apartment discuss assassination plans. Remember he testified to this at the preliminary hearing. Remember he said the same thing at the trial. Many authors noted problems with his testimony; Russo himself told various people he was not confident of several things, including even his identification of Shaw; and, at the trial, he characterized the overheard discussion as a bull session rather than a conspiracy.

But there's more. And it's worse. James Phelan, a former *Saturday Evening Post* reporter covering the trial for *True* magazine who had written favorably about Garrison before, asked the district attorney for an interview sometime after the preliminary hearing. Garrison, often eager to speak to journalists and looking for rest, invited Phelan to meet him in Las Vegas. Phelan, in his *Post* article,[24] said Garrison, who allowed various journalists access to files and even evidence, gave him the memo Sciambra wrote after the Baton Rouge interview with Russo. What Phelan didn't find in that memo startled him and, in the long run, did as much as anything to destroy Garrison's case.

But before we learn what Phelan didn't find, here's some things he did. Russo identified three pictures. One was Arcacha Smith, the leader of a New Orleans anti-Castro group, who Russo said closely resembled an actor in one of the Cuban pornographic movies he sold with Ferrie. The second was Oswald, whom he said Ferrie introduced as "Leon," his roommate. The third was Shaw, whom he said he had seen twice before in New Orleans, once with Ferrie at a service station Ferrie owned and once in a crowd listening to John Kennedy speak at Nashville Wharf.

Here's what he didn't find in that more-than-3,000-word memo:[25] Nothing about a party in Ferrie's apartment at which people talked about assassinating the president, nothing about ever meeting Shaw, nothing of Clay Bertrand. In other words, he found nothing in the memo relating to Russo's most damaging testimony against Shaw. If Russo didn't tell Sciambra about Shaw in Baton Rouge, when did he tell him? And why, given this is the case's most important piece of evidence, didn't Russo tell him, or, if he did, why didn't Sciambra put it in his memo?

Phelan, the reporter, turned decidedly and publicly anti-Garrison. He joined *Newsweek*'s Hugh Aynesworth and *Playboy*'s James Kirkwood as mainstream Shaw supporters who themselves became media sources of pro-Shaw sentiment. Kirkwood appeared on a New Orleans television program just as the trial began and said, among other things, "I became involved because I strongly believe—I have no way of knowing, of course, it's just my personal belief—that he's completely innocent of the charges against him."[26] Phelan appeared on a June 19, 1967, NBC program highly critical of Garrison and could not cover the trial for *True* because he became a defense witness. If we wanted to muddy up these waters more, and we do, we'd find on the Internet FBI documents showing that Phelan, the freelance reporter, contacted the bureau and turned over the Sciambra memo,[27] which he had copied without Garrison's knowledge, and other materials from Garrison's files.

Whether or not Phelan actively worked for intelligence agencies, the crucial information missing from the memo hurt Garrison's credibility, even though Russo testified with certainty that Shaw was the man in the apartment. Sciambra said he forgot; or included the information in other, now destroyed notes; or gave the information to Garrison outside the memo. Critics, including Phelan, claim that the district attorney's assistants, especially Sciambra, essentially created Russo's testimony about Bertrand and the party during extensive hypnosis and truth-serum treatments, which Garrison claimed were routine and used only to enhance his memory and ensure he was telling the truth.

However Russo knew the story, he told it well in the preliminary hearing and trial and except for various lapses clung more or less to its fundamentals until his death on August 16, 1995. He supposedly recanted in January 1971, when he was said to have told Shaw's attorneys that he thought Shaw wasn't the man at the party and that he probably thought it wasn't Shaw when he testified.[28] In later interviews, and certainly for the Oliver Stone movie, he reiterated his preliminary hearing and trial testimony. In a brief but rambling interview conducted in 1993, Russo, then a cab driver, shed little light on the case but didn't deny or refute anything he said in court 25 years earlier.[29]

Russo wasn't the only person to testify that he overheard Shaw talk about killing Kennedy, just the sanest.

Charles Spiesel, a New York accountant, testified directly and firmly about meeting whom he took to be an old acquaintance, the hairless Ferrie, in Lafitte's Blacksmith Shop, a backstreet French Quarter bar. They went to a nearby apartment, joining Shaw and other people. In a remarkable development—a kind of early Mardi Gras parade that seemed to delight local citizenry—Spiesel led judge, jury, prosecution, defense (including a seemingly bemused Shaw), and spectators on a tour through part of the French Quarter to identify the building and apartment he claimed to have visited years before. Here, truly, was a spectacle almost worthy of Mardi Gras as people hung out windows and tooted car horns. Spiesel, coincidentally, identified, albeit tentatively, an apartment in a building perhaps sharing the same grounds but certainly adjacent to Clay Shaw's residence. Spiesel told the court that on that May 1963 evening, the conversation around an oval kitchen table turned to Kennedy and how he could be assassinated. Spiesel said Shaw suggested that Ferrie, the pilot, might aid the escape by flying the assassins out.

This well-dressed, well-spoken professional man could devastate Shaw's defense. But, you are surely not shocked to learn, things worked out differently in a quite sensational way.

Unflinching and precise, Spiesel answered questions in cross-examination. What happened to his income tax return business?

Well, it had to do with the $16 million lawsuit he had filed against a psychiatrist and New York City. Hmmmm.

Why had he filed it?

Because police officers and other people hypnotized him 50 or 60 times against his will, planting certain thoughts in his mind, giving him the illusion they were true. They used sophisticated techniques to follow him, tap his phones, torture and harass him, pass him by quickly in the streets to make him think they didn't want to talk to him, make him and his family members out to be Communists, link him to various crimes, and make him break the law. They "surrounded him with competitors in the tax return business, and hired 'plants' to work in this office, who then acted intoxicated and annoyed and frightened his customers."[30] In fact, so good did his antagonists become at substituting their own people for his family members that the poor man repeatedly fingerprinted his own daughter to assure himself of her identity.[31] All this, of course, adversely affected Spiesel. He lost his ability to perform normal sexual functions, and he lost his tax return business.

And, as you might imagine, he lost all credibility. The prosecution played it thoroughly; they made sure jurors understood he had also lost his mind. This startling defense cross-examination didn't come purely as a stroke of genius or good luck. Tom Bethell, a young investigator in Garrison's office, became disenchanted with the prosecution and handed over to the defense the district attorney's witness list,[32] and *Newsweek*'s Aynesworth, further entangling himself in the case, not only showed defense lawyers a witness list he had obtained but also sent a special-delivery letter urging the defense to investigate Spiesel and suggested two private investigators.[33]

Not all prosecution witnesses were whackos, of course. Garrison also used a heroin addict. Vernon Bundy, cooking up two caps of heroin on the Lake Pontchartrain shore, saw two men whom he identified as Shaw and Oswald conversing. He said Shaw gave Oswald what appeared to be money. Bundy, also a convicted thief, said he recognized Shaw in part by a stiffness in his walk, which was demonstrated to judge, jury, and spectators when, in a minor dramatic moment, Shaw was made to walk across the courtroom. Bundy stuck to his story, but two people, including another thief, said he made it up to curry favor with Garrison. And various researchers and writers say that documents released in the 1990s show that original interviews with Bundy, as with so many other witnesses, reveal different and less incriminating information than that to which he testified in the trial.

Garrison once said he used less-than-desirable witnesses because bank presidents generally are not party to such crimes. And, while he didn't bring up bank presidents, he did offer a law enforcement officer and three other seemingly normal upright citizens from Clinton, Louisiana, a small East Feliciana Parish town near Clay Shaw's hometown of Kentwood and about 125 miles north of New Orleans. These four diverse and believable people made various consistent connections among Shaw, Oswald, and Ferrie. All speaking about the same day in Clinton, the three said they saw Shaw in a black Cadillac with Oswald as a passenger; one identified Ferrie as being with them, and one said Ferrie might have been with them. The jury thought they told the truth, most reporters seemed to think they told the truth, and some years later the House Select Committee on Assassinations, in its report, stated that testimony of the Clinton witnesses probably indicated that Shaw, despite his denials, knew Oswald, Ferrie, or both.

By now, however, you readers are more careful, wiser even. You know that Garrison was, indeed, correct when he said nothing is the way it appears. The Clinton witnesses seemed sincere and may well have been, but various writers cast doubt on their testimony using found documents, heretofore unseen notes, and probable and improbable connections and affiliations involving the Ku Klux Klan and the Congress for Racial Equality (C.O.R.E.). Patricia Lambert (in her book *False Witness*) claims to have uncovered original notes from the first district attorney investigators in Clinton that show, among other things, that their interviews do not include identifications of Shaw or Ferrie or people who looked like them, and the Oswald person was originally identified as a widely known local man. Shaw, Ferrie, and Oswald emerged as characters in the Clinton scenario later, after the district attorney's investigator Sciambra got involved.[34]

Further, Lambert and others think the likely motive for claiming that the three were in Clinton, which had racial and integration problems, was to discredit C.O.R.E., then involved in civil rights activities, by soiling its reputation through association with the Communist Oswald. Even in the 1960s, those opposed to equal rights for people of color commonly tried to taint civil rights organizations by claiming they had Communist affiliations. Presumably, the black witness was motivated by fear. Lambert and others[35] attempt to tie Garrison to extreme right-wing and even racist politicians and operatives, suggesting that these ties explain why the Clinton witnesses testified the way they did.

The 40-day trial included dozens of other witnesses, including many testifying as to the events of November 23, 1963, on Dealey Plaza as Garrison attempted to prove a conspiracy to complete the case against Shaw and discredit the Warren Commission. Many Shaw witnesses to the Dallas shooting had been overlooked or not believed during the Warren Commission investigation. Garrison's team also showed for the first time in public, against vehement defense objections, the Zapruder film, the clearest and most complete images depicting Kennedy's assassination. In fact, the prosecution showed the film 10 times. The defense feared that the horror it depicted might prejudice jurors against Shaw. The film seems to show the president's head snapping backward, as if hit from the front. Although this has been explained four or five different ways, Garrison used it to bolster his conspiracy case. All the Dallas testimony is the subject of millions of words on-line and in books and articles about bullet angles and trajectories, possible locations of shooters, powder burns, head wounds, autopsy reports, and a hundred other pieces of assassination information and lore.

In the end, jurors may have believed that more than one person shot at Kennedy, and they may have been unsure if Clay Shaw knew Oswald or Ferrie, but they were quite sure Shaw did not conspire to kill the president. Press reactions, as you'll see, came quickly and decisively. The verdict vindicated the national press, which came down hard on Garrison, as did the local press, finally, after the trial.

Garrison, however, blamed the press for many of his problems, saying he was "vilified in the press as a publicity-seeking politician, a charlatan, and a communist."[36] He said the verdict showed the American people weren't ready to hear the truth. However, truth was so important to him that the day after the trial, before Shaw could do much more than sigh, Garrison arrested him again—this time for perjury. He said Shaw lied when he denied knowing Oswald and Ferrie. Most accounts describe Shaw by this point almost broke, if not broken, but here he was again, sending lawyers to court to fight off charges brought by a district attorney who seemed intent on destroying him.

Shaw did, in the end, prevail, sort of. A district court judge in a rare decision enjoined Garrison from ever prosecuting Shaw in connection with the Kennedy assassination. Shaw subsequently filed a civil suit against Garrison but died on August 15, 1974, before the suit was resolved. Who's to say the lengthy and grueling case didn't prematurely end Shaw's life? Some on-line writers try to find Shaw's death mysterious, but most claim that as the target of an unsupported and perhaps criminal attack for years, his death was no mystery at all.

Garrison, on the other hand, won reelection as district attorney, lost the next election, and eventually became a state judge. He wrote three books and consulted on Stone's *JFK*, which revived interest in the case and probably led to legislation that opened many assassination records to the public in the 1990s. Critics argue that neither the book nor the film is good history, and various Web sites and books easily show more or less provable fallacies in both. Garrison died on October 21, 1992.

Did he, in the end, have something?

Answers to this question proved a dilemma for the press because some reporters desperately wanted him to have something and others were sure he had nothing. Both groups wanted to do more about it than journalism tradition and ethical practice generally permitted.

Some did. Therefore, you may think the Shaw case was not the finest hour for the U.S. press. After all, *Life* and other reporters joined Garrison's investigation by assisting his staff in following up tips and agreed to share information. That most fled Garrison in favor of Shaw does little to restore journalistic integrity; they simply went from one indefensible position to another. Garrison gave some reporters original documents (some got them other ways) that they later turned over to Shaw's lawyers or to federal investigative agencies. It is even possible some journalists on the Shaw case worked with the CIA. Watergate journalist Carl Bernstein has claimed that some 400 journalists supplied information to the CIA since the 1950s.[37] And, as you might expect, Garrison claimed that the CIA "had on its payroll journalists ostensibly working for the major media but in fact disseminating propaganda for consumption by the American people."[38]

Kirkwood, the up-front, self-admitted Shaw supporter, describes in the highly readable *American Grotesque* how reporters flagrantly supported Shaw; their meaningful glances at crucial points; their disappointed, dismayed, and sometimes irate reactions when things seemed to go against Shaw; and their gleeful celebration when things seemed to go the defendant's way. He described his own and others' visits to Shaw before, during, and after the trial; their words of encouragement; their disgust with the district attorney's case; and their fears that Garrison might prevail. He and Phelan even confronted executives of the New Orleans papers and complained that their papers were too soft on Garrison.[39] With Shaw supporter Aynesworth abetting the defense, no wonder *Newsweek*'s trial coverage ridiculed Garrison and his case, often referring to them in circus terms. For example, the case was "Big Jim's headline-hunting side show"[40] and Garrison an "extraordinarily imaginative barker in promoting his assassination side show in New Orleans."[41] Witnesses were an "exotic array of stars . . . trotted out for public showing,"[42] and while the outcome of the trial acquitted Shaw, it "convicted" Garrison of "incompetence and irresponsibility as a public official."[43] That Aynesworth, Kirkwood, and perhaps even Phelan, the freelance reporter who testified for the defense, deeply believed that Garrison fraudulently prosecuted Shaw and that they, in the end, correctly reported various circumstances of the case leads anti-Garrison writers and others to overlook their journalistic indiscretions or applaud them for fighting the just fight. Perhaps they had a responsibility to expose what they considered to be massive abuse of power, but press behavior in the Shaw case, even in the social and cultural environment of the 1960s, challenged notions of journalistic objectivity and ethics. *Columbia Journalism Review*, in its spring 1969 issue, singled out three journalists for possibly stepping outside normal journalistic bounds. Besides Phelan and Aynesworth, it named Art Kevin, a California radio reporter who sat with the prosecutors during the trial.[44]

Time magazine also called the trial a sideshow, saying Garrison, "known for his erratic behavior," used "circus tactics" and has "tried to foster the belief that he has something up his sleeve besides Russo's testimony."[45] After the verdict, *Time* said, "In his closing argument, Garrison tried to wrap up with sheer demagoguery what he had been unable to deliver in fact."[46] NBC and CBS strongly criticized Garrison and the case against Shaw in lengthy reports. Garrison got airtime to reply to the NBC report. The *Saturday Eve-*

ning Post and other magazines generally criticized Garrison, and the larger newspapers, including the *New York Times,* took occasional shots as they covered the case more or less factually, usually without fanfare. The *Times* did strongly condemn the prosecution in a posttrial editorial.

Ramparts and other alternative publications, usually focusing on the conspiracy aspect, tended to sympathize with Garrison, as they shared his distrust of the Warren Commission report. The two New Orleans Newhouse newspapers, the *States-Item,* which originally broke the story of the Garrison investigation, and the *Times-Picayune,* frustrated Shaw supporters by taking aggressively neutral stances, which, in the end, seemed to favor Garrison, whose charges and claims got big headlines, straight reporting, and no editorial comment. They reported Spiesel's testimony about overhearing Shaw, Ferrie, and the others discuss the assassination for almost 30 paragraphs before mentioning hypnotism, family substitutions, a destroyed sex life, and other paranoia that had overshadowed everything else he said. Because the two papers published little negative news about the case, at least one Garrison foe, the New Orleans Metropolitan Crime Commission, bought ads to air its views.

The papers, in front-page editorials after the trial, denounced Garrison and said they were bound by the judge's order to limit opinion and undue publicity to ensure a fair trial. The *States-Item* wrote,

District Attorney Jim Garrison should resign. He has shown himself unfit to hold the office of district attorney or any other office.

Mr. Garrison abused the vast powers of his office. He has perverted the law rather than prosecuted it. His persecution of Clay L. Shaw was a perversion of the legal process such as not often seen.

Mr. Garrison's conspiracy case was built upon the quicksands of unreliability and in the end it did not stand up. . . .

Mr. Shaw has been vindicated, but the damage to his reputation caused by Mr. Garrison's witch-hunt may never be repaired. It is all too shameful.

This travesty of justice is a reproach to the conscious of all good men and must not go unanswered. Mr. Garrison himself should now be brought to the bar to answer for his conduct. . . .

This newspaper has been constrained from comment on the case by the guidelines set out by judge Haggerty to insure a fair trial, guidelines which Mr. Garrison himself has consistently ignored. We have had to bite our tongue in the face of the injustice that unfolded before us.

But that is the case no more. The jury has spoken. Clay L. Shaw is innocent. And Mr. Garrison stands revealed for what he is: A man without principles who would pervert the legal process for his own ends.[47]

You already know what good that did. Garrison, unmoved and undaunted, immediately arrested Shaw for perjury. And the two papers? Well, they further incensed Shaw supporters by reporting the arrest as though those editorials had never been written.

The question history may fail to answer is, What serves the public better under these circumstances: a traditional, objective approach to the news that allows the trial proceedings and, at least in this case, public officials to control the tone and content of the coverage, or a subjective approach in which the reporter takes control of the tone and coverage? We already know that reporters aided both sides and openly revealed their biases in print and on the air. That they may have been correct in some or even most of their assumptions doesn't necessarily validate their actions because journalists don't always know what's true and what's real.

And surely the Shaw trial and the volumes of materials resulting from it tell us that we can't take truth and reality for granted.

It seems to be a legacy of the Kennedy assassination and the Shaw trial that few things can be proved untrue, or, perhaps, nothing can be proved untrue to everyone's satisfaction. And if that doesn't make everything true, it at least makes nothing necessarily untrue. And that makes a mess of both history and journalism.

The assassination, including the Shaw case, created an industry now populated by every kind of data in every kind of media imaginable. So many people write so much about the assassination and Garrison's investigation, and they write with such authority, that we have solved the crime a dozen times over. Contributors symbiotically depend on each other not only for quotes and citations but also as foils to keep their various opinions, perspectives, and obsessions afloat. They depend on a handful of pivotal sources who have told so many different stories that too many researchers simply use the versions that best suit their premises and discard or denigrate the rest.

Lambert, for example, who claims to finally tell the true story, cites sources, finds missing evidence, and, from an anti-Garrison perspective, is plausible and convincing. However, as we've come to see, the case is littered with crackpots, braggarts, compulsive talkers, liars, opportunists, the mentally ill, the vane, and the confused, and their facts, stories, and even testimonies shift and change, sometimes dramatically and without discernible pattern. This forces Lambert and other authors trying to make the case against Garrison to choose, for example, Dean Andrew's vow that he made up the name "Clay Bertrand" to show that Shaw could not have been Bertrand. Then they denigrate Garrison's case that Shaw was Bertrand by saying that no Bertrand existed because Andrews, who also claimed he knew Bertrand, was a liar and braggart.

This circumstance is not unique to the Kennedy assassination, the Shaw trial, or authors who end up opposing Garrison, but few occurrences have generated so much interest and so much material. One would have reason to hope that the volume of material would lead to if not definitive answers then at least more definite ones. *Newsweek,* of all publications, confronted this issue of definite answers some three weeks after the Shaw trial, saying the law is "an imperfect instrument for laying ghosts to rest,"[48] whether they be Kennedy's or Martin Luther King's. The author, arguing that James Earl Ray's guilty plea robbed the public of a trial, said that while trials are overrated as a means to the truth, they might help provide story endings that people demand and "satisfy the impulse to make some sense of the absurd, to impose order on the anarchy of events."[49]

Garrison may or may not have been a deranged demagogue who deliberately destroyed an innocent man's life, but he surely exposed and perhaps exploited a massive national skepticism and even distrust that seems to have continued virtually unabated. So many people wanted to believe Garrison because they didn't believe the government. The trial, indeed, proved to be an imperfect instrument to get at the truth, and since then, writers and researchers, in analyzing all available materials and perhaps making up some of their own, offer an ever-increasing array of scenarios, assassins, charges, and countercharges. No doubt they impose sense and order, maybe even eliminating more possibilities than they kindle, but much absurdity and anarchy prevails.

In the end, the press reflected the muddle and confusion. Maybe that's not bad. It reminds us that we probably ought to learn to be comfortable with uncertainty, even as we keep searching for the truth.

And in the end, New Orleans got what it wanted, too. Judge Haggerty even arranged for a private balcony so the sequestered jurors could watch the parades on Fat Tuesday. As sometimes happens, a cab driver had summed it all up before the trial even started:

"We gonna have Mardi Gras *and* the trial. Shee-it, what a time!"

NOTES

1. Garrison interview, *Playboy,* October 1967. Transcripts and excerpts of the interview are readily available at numerous Internet sites. The reader is certainly aware that specific Internet site addresses don't last forever. Those given in these notes were operative as of 2002. But the Kennedy assassination and Shaw trial have inspired hundreds of sites and searches using various relevant key words eventually provide results that would likely satisfy even the most demanding researcher (at least the most demanding researcher who understands the strengths and limitations of online materials).

2. James Phelan, *Scandals, Scamps, Scoundrels: The Casebook of an Investigative Reporter* (New York: Random House, 1982), 150. Pro-Garrison people imply that Phelan was too biased against Garrison to believe. He writes damaging comments about Garrison, much of it out of an interview in Las Vegas.

3. Josh Alan Friedman, "Jack Ruby: Dallas' Original J.R.," on-line at http://www.wfmu.org/LCD/20/ruby.html. Jack Ruby doesn't turn up again in our story, but he has a remarkable afterlife in books, articles, and on-line, usually in alleged connections to the Mob. This Friedman piece, a variation of which once appeared in *Hustler* magazine, is one of the more interesting and refreshing. Also archived at WFMU's Web site at http://www.wfmu.org.

4. John Siegenthaler, *A Search for Justice* (Nashville: Aurora Publishers, 1971), 8–9.

5. Rosemary James and Jack Wardlaw, *Plot or Politics?* (New Orleans: Pelican Press, 1967), 47. Also found in New Orleans *Times-Picayune,* 26 February 1967.

6. Edward Jay Epstein, "Epitaph for Jim Garrison: Romancing the Assassination," *The New Yorker,* 30 November 1992. Also on Edward Jay Epstein's Web site at http://edwardjayepstein.com/archived/garrison2htm.

7. Edward Jay Epstein, *Counterplot* (New York: Viking Press, 1969), 49. Epstein, whose wonderful *Between Fact and Fiction: The Problem of Journalism* (New York: Vintage Books, 1975), not about Shaw or Kennedy, is considered by many to be one of the more dependable writers in the Kennedy/Shaw area.

8. James and Wardlaw, *Plot or Politics?,* 42.

9. See John H. Davis, *Mafia Kingfish: Carlos Marcello and the Assassination of John F. Kennedy* (Ontario: Signet/Penguin Books, 1989), for one of the most interesting and comprehensive books making a case for Mafia assassins.

10. See Gerald Posner, *Case Closed: Lee Harvey Oswald and the Assassination of JFK* (New York: Random House,1993), 139, 438, and Patricia Lambert, *False Witness* (New York: M. Evans and Company, 1998), 23–24, 29–30, 277–79, and elsewhere. Both have some detail about Martin. Lambert's book appears to be well researched and has gained much favor with Garrison critics.

11. Lambert, *False Witness,* 30.

12. Jim Garrison, *On the Trail of Assassins* (New York: Warner Books, 1988), 167. Garrison critics, of which there are many, consider this book fanciful or delusional. It is, however, well written and compelling, which no doubt attracted Oliver Stone and resulted in the movie *JFK,* which further incensed Garrison critics.

13. Posner, *Case Closed,* 431.

14. Epstein, *Counterplot,* 26.

15. Ibid., 42.

16. Posner, *Case Closed,* 432.

17. Garrison, *On the Trail of Assassins,* 173, 174.

18. Max Holland, "The Power of Disinformation: The Lie That Linked CIA to the Kennedy Assassination," *Studies in Intelligence,* no. 11 (fall–winter 2001) (on-line at http://www.jfkassassination.net/sii.htm).

19. Garrison, *On the Trail of Assassins,* 98–100.

20. William Davey, *Let Justice Be Done* (Reston, Va.: Jordan Publishing, 1999), 119–20. Davey is one of several writers who continue to support Garrison's case. He has at least one book and other publications and, along with most of the others, has an on-line presence.

21. Dave Reitzes, "Who Speaks for Clay Shaw" in a four-part on-line series. He quotes Edward Jay Epstein as saying that Andrews made the name up out of "solid air" (http://mcadams.posc.mu.edu/shaw1.htm). Reitzes is a prolific online contributor to the Kennedy/Shaw debates.

22. Lambert, *False Witness,* 36.

23. Bill Bankston, "Russo Says on TV Didn't Know Oswald before Assassination," *Baton Rouge State-Times,* 24 February 1967 (also on-line at http://mcadams.posc.mu.edu/russo.txt).

24. James Phelan, "A Plot to Kill Kennedy? Rush to Judgment in New Orleans," *Saturday Evening Post,* May 6, 1967 (also on-line at various sites, including http://www.jfkassassination net/phelan.htm).

25. Various sites claim to display the memo, including http://www.jfkassassination.net/russo2.txt.

26. James Kirkwood, *American Grotesque* (New York: Simon and Schuster, 1970), 91. The Kirkwood book is solely about Clay Shaw and the trial and, despite its obvious biases, is probably the most entertaining and valuable book written on the subject. It is comprehensive, informative, and fun to read.

27. See Lisa Pease's ardently pro-Garrison Web site at http://www.webcom.com/~lpease/index2.htm.

28. Lambert, *False Witness,* 173, relates this, as do several Web sites, including http://www.jfk-online.com/russorecants.html. Note that it is always possible that many claims originate with the same primary source.

29. See interview by William Matson Law at http://www.jfklancer.com/Perry.html.

30. Kirkwood, *American Grotesque,* 238. See pp. 231–45 for a full description of the testimony.

31. Epstein, "Epitaph for Jim Garrison," http://edwardjayepstein.com/archived/garrison2.htm.

32. Kirkwood, *American Grotesque,* 246–47.

33. Ibid., 248.

34. Lambert, *False Witness,* 196, 197.

35. See the prolific Dave Rietzes, a Garrison critic, at http://www.jfk-online.com and many other places on-line.

36. Garrison, *On the Trail of Assassins,* xv.

37. From a 20 October 1977 *Rolling Stone* article available on-line at http://www.webcom.com/~lpease/ index2.htm.

38. Garrison, *On the Trail of Assassins,* 332.

39. Kirkwood, *American Grotesque,* 481–83.

40. *Newsweek,* 27 January 1969, 27.

41. Ibid., 17 February 1969, 34.

42. Ibid.

43. Ibid., 10 March 1969, 36.

44. Roger M. Williams and Michael Parks, "The Clay Shaw Trial: Reporter-Participants," *Columbia Journalism Review,* spring 1969, 38–41. The authors also said that the Shaw trial had more journalistic participation "and more journalistic passions than the Scopes trial, the missile crisis or the Viet Nam negotiations—more, in fact, than any other story we know about."

45. *Time,* 31 January 1969, 40.

46. Ibid., 7 March 1969, 23.

47. *New Orleans States-Item,* 1 March 1969.

48. *Newsweek,* 24 March 1969, 28.

49. Ibid., 29

9

THE CASE OF MANUEL NORIEGA (1991–1992)

Nancy McKenzie Dupont

"I Fought the Law and the Law Won."

Christmas Eve, 1989: One of the most bizarre scenes in the history of American warfare unfolds. Hundreds of heavily armed U.S. soldiers surround the Vatican embassy in Panama City, Panama, and take control of the area with an iron grip. They shut down traffic, lay barbed wire in the streets around the embassy, and set up a team of sharpshooters in a nearby parking garage.[1] They cut shrubbery around the embassy to improve their view and clear a nearby soccer field so helicopters can land to deliver fresh troops and supplies. And when the soldiers fail to get what they came for, they set up loudspeakers in a vacant lot across the street from the embassy and begin playing rock music, including popular tunes with not-so-subtle messages: "You're No Good," "I Fought the Law and the Law Won," and "Working on a Chain Gang."[2] For variety, the loudspeakers occasionally break away from a ditty by The Pretenders to blare radio news reports and excerpts from speeches by President George H. Bush.[3]

The goal of these eccentric exercises is the capture of General Manuel Antonio Noriega, the former Panamanian dictator, who sits in a room inside the embassy, a U.S. federal indictment against him and a million-dollar bounty on his head. Only a few days earlier, on December 20, a U.S. force of 24,000 invaded Panama by air and sea. It took only a few hours for the troops to secure the small country and the Panama Canal. President Bush told Americans that "Operation Just Cause" had been launched to protect American lives, to defend democracy, to ensure that the Panama Canal treaty was followed, and to stop drug trafficking. And to get that pesky Noriega fellow.

U.S. officials believed that Panama's chief drug trafficker was Noriega; they'd accused him of racketeering and drug trafficking by taking money to protect cocaine shipments through Panama for much of the 1980s. Despite the overwhelming use of force, however, U.S. troops did not capture Noriega in the invasion. He escaped and hid in various locations, including a graveyard. He believed Americans wouldn't search a graveyard in the dark: "Americans are afraid of death even during the day, let alone in the shadows," he stated in 1997.[4]

The next day, Noriega jumped into a Vatican flag-bearing car at a Panama City parking lot and was driven to the embassy, where he hoped to be granted protection from the U.S. forces. He was armed with an Uzi and a hand grenade.[5]

Who was this man hiding in the Vatican embassy? Was he, as he claimed, the military leader of a small country who was not involved in drug trafficking but who became a U.S. prisoner of war in an American move designed to keep control of the Panama Canal?[6] Was he, in the view of the intelligence head for the Joint Chiefs of Staff, "a corrupt, debauched thug"?[7] Was he an insane voodoo-practicing pervert whose seized stash of animal parts, sex toys, and cash was displayed by U.S. Army troops to American television audiences?[8] Or was he just an unfortunate Latin American official who had refused to play ball with the United States?[9]

This much was known about Noriega: He had been indicted in February 1988 on 11 counts of drug trafficking, conspiracy, and money laundering. The government said he had accepted $4.6 million in bribes to protect cocaine shipments from the Medellin cartel in Colombia through Panama and then into the United States. He had gone to Cuba to meet with Fidel Castro in 1984. And there was some not-so-secret speculation that he had once been so close to high-ranking U.S. officials that he had been on the government payroll.

There are many ways to judge Manuel Noriega, as many today as there were in 1989. In 2002, Noriega is 10 years into the 30-year sentence he received at his U.S. trial in 1992. Should he live to be released, he faces 90 years in a Panamanian prison for convictions on homicide, drug trafficking, and other charges.[10] He waits for what he calls fair play, hoping "that people will come to understand the colossal injustice of what happened."[11] Of all the questions Noriega asks about his indictment, arrest, and trial, perhaps none is more enduring and puzzling as this one: Does one nation have the right to invade another country, capture a fugitive, and take him to justice outside his own country?

When Noriega went into the Vatican embassy, he proved to the world he was no fool. He was seeking sanctuary in a sovereign state that considers itself a moral leader in a secular world. As long ago as Old Testament times, accused criminals used churches and church-established institutions to gain protection from law officers and others trying to find them. Later, during medieval times, all a fugitive had to do was grab a ring attached to a church to gain religious protection.[12] Noriega's flight into the Vatican bought him time and forced the United States to negotiate for his surrender. Those negotiations took place at the highest levels in Washington, D.C., and Rome and even caused the U.S. ambassador to the Vatican to miss part of Christmas Eve Mass at St. Peter's Basilica.[13]

But as the talks continued, so did the loudspeaker blasts. "They're a form of torture, meant to drive him crazy," said a man who lived near the embassy. "And they could drive him crazy."[14] Noriega claimed to be unaffected by the noise, but it bothered Vatican Ambassador Jose Sebastian Laboa so much that he told the Americans he could not negotiate amid the noise.[15] In the United States, television viewers saw the spectacle and laughed at the concept of rock music being used as psychological warfare. The *Toronto Star,* in a tongue-in-cheek editorial, called the military's strategy proof that rock music was the equivalent of bamboo slivers being driven under the fingernails. No human being that age, the newspaper wrote, "should be subjected to Hit Parade music with speakers turned full up even if he is a dope-dealer, a dictator, an abuser of human rights and an all-round rotten person."[16] On the third day of the music marathon, the Vatican issued a statement saying that an occupying force could not interfere with the work of diplomacy.[17] The Pretenders, Carly Simon, and others stopped singing.

Noriega finally had silence but few options. He could not stay at the Vatican embassy indefinitely. The Vatican had made that clear when it proclaimed Noriega had neither political nor diplomatic asylum; he was "a person in refuge against whom there were political charges."[18] He could give himself up to Panamanian authorities and try to avoid being taken to the United States. The new Panamanian president, Guillermo Endara, who had been installed in office by U.S. troops during the invasion, said he would not extradite any Panamanian citizen, that he would put Noriega on trial in his homeland. The last option for Noriega was to surrender to U.S. troops, and, inside the Vatican embassy, that is what he was being encouraged to do.

Ambassador Laboa met with Noriega on January 2, 1990. The priest told the general about Americans threatening to remove immunity from the Vatican embassy, thereby opening doors and allowing angry Panamanian mobs to lynch Noriega, à la Benito Mussolini. Noriega remembered Laboa's words: "There's nothing I can do."[19] Before Noriega surrendered the next day, Laboa gave him a Bible and a rosary and told him God would not abandon him.[20] Noriega gave Laboa a letter addressed to the pope, thanking him for the sanctuary and "for the bright light that you gave me."[21]

Noriega negotiated a few terms for his surrender. He was assured that he would not face the death penalty in the United States. He asked for and received a telephone to make two calls: one to his wife and family, the other to his mistress. He was allowed to change from the undershirt, green shorts, and sneakers he had worn during most of his time in the embassy[22] into a full Panamanian military uniform. His weapons, including the Uzi he had kept under his pillow, were confiscated by workers in the embassy. Finally, Noriega was allowed surrender to a U.S. officer of equal rank. When he reached the embassy gate, he was seized, searched for weapons, and put on an army helicopter for the flight out of Panama.

Noriega had not yet had his day in court, but the cost of his capture was mounting. The invasion left 26 American service personnel dead and 300 wounded. The United States claimed 516 Panamanians were killed. Critics said the number was much higher.[23] In monetary terms, the price was staggering. The Defense Department estimated the invasion cost $163.6 million.[24]

The American people had heard thousands of news reports about the Panamanian strongman and his criminal government, his murderous Panamanian Defense Forces, and his millions in drug-running profits. In addition, U.S. law enforcement agents had worked countless hours and more than two years to put Noriega in a U.S. courtroom. In the end, all efforts to get him out of power without force had failed. In *Divorcing the Dictator,* author Frederick Kempe wrote that Noriega was "a new breed of despot: a combination of ghetto street-fighter, Oriental mystic, intelligence agent, and Mafia godfather."[25] He had, perhaps, been made larger than life in the eyes of some Americans, including one of the federal agents working on the case against him. Kenny Kennedy, a Drug Enforcement Administration (DEA) investigator in Miami, said that when Noriega landed in Miami in chains, he was surprisingly small and ugly with skin like a "horned toad."[26]

News reporters descended on Miami as soon as word of Noriega's surrender was out. Television satellite trucks filled the Miami courthouse parking lot; 200 journalists and courtroom sketch artists signed up for the 40 seats reserved for the press at the arraignment.[27] The hearing was scheduled before Judge William Hoeveler, a Carter appointee who had been assigned the Noriega case two years earlier. He had not thought this day would come, having told his wife, "It'll never go to trial. They'll never get him."[28] But at age 67, Hoeveler was about to handle perhaps the toughest, longest, and most contentious case of his career.

U.S. Attorney Dexter Lehtinen and his chief assistant, Myles Malman, headed the prosecution. Noriega's team was led by Frank Rubino, who had represented Noriega in negotiations with the United States before the invasion. Miami lawyer Steve Kollin provided assistance. Rubino and Kollin had a plan for the first hearing: keep Noriega out of the courtroom. Judge Hoeveler, however, was having none of that.

"Where is the defendant?" Hoeveler asked.

"At this time, General Noriega would waive his right to appear," Rubino replied.

"This is not a case I want to go by waivers," the judge said, and he ordered Noriega into the courtroom.[29]

Noriega's comments in court that morning were in Spanish and were translated for the judge by an interpreter. Rubino told Hoeveler that Noriega would not enter a plea, that he was in court under protest. Noriega was a political prisoner, Rubino argued, adding a caveat that became the core defense argument. Noriega, explained Rubino, should have immunity under his status as Panama's head of state. Judge Hoeveler entered a plea of not guilty on behalf of the court, and the first hearing in the case of the *United States v. Manuel Antonio Noriega* was completed in 20 minutes.[30]

On February 8, 1990, Judge Hoeveler ordered Noriega to stand trial on drug-trafficking charges.[31] For the first time, Noriega appeared in court with five codefendants named in his drug-trafficking indictment in February 1988. But Noriega was clearly the focus of the bond hearing, and the proceedings that day would be anything but routine.

Noriega dressed as he had the day of his arraignment: green army slacks with a short-sleeved shirt bearing the four stars that signify a general's rank.[32] His choice of clothing was calculated apparently to provide a backdrop for the fireworks display Rubino would soon launch. Moments into the hearing, Rubino walked to the lectern before the judge.

"His name is Manuel Antonio Noriega," Rubino deadpanned. "His rank is four-star general. His serial number is 0001. . . . The government of the United States must immediately repatriate General Manuel Noriega to a third country or to his own homeland. General Noriega, commander-in-chief of the Panamanian Defense Forces of the Republic of Panama, hereby claims the status of prisoner of war."[33] Rubino's goal? Blanket Noriega in the special rights afforded by the Geneva Convention.

Observers in the courtroom may have been shocked to hear such a pronouncement at a bond hearing, but Judge Hoeveler remained unperturbed. "I don't find that under the Geneva Convention I must divest myself of jurisdiction," the judge responded. Noriega maintained a tranquil persona too, calmly thumbing through a Spanish-language copy of the Geneva parleys.[34]

Later in the day, Rubino made formal his charge that the court had no jurisdiction in the case, filing a motion claiming Noriega to be a prisoner of war. "The plain and simple truth is that no prisoner of war has even been brought before a nonmilitary tribunal of the detaining power to be tried for a crime that was allegedly committed prior to the armed conflict,"[35] the motion stated.

Rubino's comments for the press proved less articulate but more colorful: "I ain't going to take it sitting down."[36] In a matter of days, the prisoner-of-war question became two separate issues: whether Noriega was a prisoner of war and whether a U.S. federal court could hear his case.

Prosecutors wasted little time in clarifying the first issue when they announced the United States would not object to treating Noriega as a prisoner of war and giving him privileges described by the Geneva Convention. On February 16, the newly declared prisoner of war got his first visit from the International Committee of the Red Cross. Noriega had been moved from his holding cell in the Miami courthouse to the Federal Metropolitan Correctional Center just outside the city limits. In keeping with Red Cross traditions, a delegate and a medical doctor toured the prison, inspecting the cells and the kitchen. Then they met with Noriega. "We have private talks, and it is very important that they be without witnesses," said Jean-Marc Bornet, a Red Cross delegate in Latin America. But he assured the press the conversation concerned prison conditions: "It may be about food, about being allowed to go out, or to have contact with families or about medical treatment."[37]

The answer to the question of a federal court hearing a prisoner-of-war case would have to wait. Noriega's lawyers decided to launch an attack on a new front by questioning the invasion that led to Noriega's capture. Their argument that the invasion was overkill received a public relations boost from an unexpected source on March 29. Former President Jimmy Carter told the Atlanta Press Club that he condemned the invasion, saying the United States should have used diplomatic measures to get Noriega out of power.[38] Four days later, Rubino again stood before Judge Hoeveler with what he believed was strong evidence that the United States had acted inappropriately.

Rubino used the news media to make his point. He played videotapes of the invasion used by ABC, CBS, and NBC, stating, "All of the death and destruction the court has seen is for the arrest of one man."[39] Rubino then cited a 1974 federal appeals case in which the court ruled that shocking behavior during an arrest could be grounds for dismissal of the charges.[40] "If this conduct is not shocking, I don't know what is, except nuclear weapons and leveling the earth. Do I have to bring my client here with no arms and legs? The intent was there,"[41] Rubino concluded.

Former U.S. Attorney General Ramsey Clark, speaking as head of the Independent Commission of Inquiry on the U.S. invasion of Panama, then testified. "We have reports of people being cut in half . . . by either something running over them or sometimes by just a slice of metal."[42]

Hoeveler called it a moving argument but paid close attention to the response of U.S. Attorney William Bryson. "You don't punish society by letting a presumptive criminal go to make another point,"[43] he told the judge.

The green Miami spring turned into the green Miami summer as Judge Hoeveler considered the pretrial motions. The media debate over Noriega's guilt or innocence faded into a discussion of the morality of the Panama invasion. Even those who supported the invasion had to wonder how effective U.S. forces had become. On July 2, the *New York Times* reported that a U.S. Air Force general had failed to inform superiors that a bomb dropped during the invasion missed its target by as much as 160 yards. The newspaper also reported that General Robert Russ knew of other problems with F117A fighter-bombers but kept quiet. This disclosure followed the Pentagon's admission of mishandling invasion press coverage by keeping reporters out of the combat zone.[44] That the target of the invasion had yet to go to trial had to be a major embarrassment in the top levels of American government.

Noriega spent the long spring days in a secluded cell, afraid of what might happen if other prisoners at the Federal Metropolitan Correctional Center came in close contact. They jeered and threatened him when he arrived at the center, and his lawyers confirmed he was unnerved by the animosity.[45] Personal insults abounded, such as the nickname "Pineapple Face" (because of his bumpy complexion). He believed the American media unfairly portrayed him as a dangerous, drug-dealing, banana-republic dictator. He wrote to a group of Los Angeles schoolchildren, "The press of your country . . . has misinformed and distorted the image of a nationalistic and patriotic leader who struggled, struggles and will struggle for the sovereignty of his country."[46]

But fear of what could happen to him outside court and inside prison haunted Noriega, perhaps for good reason. He received a letter from Carlos Lehder, a former leader of the Medellin drug cartel, who blamed Noriega for his own drug-smuggling charges. From a prison in Illinois, Lehder suggested to Noriega that he plead guilty and bargain for a cell that would protect him from enemies. "The sorrow of the men of your race whom you turned over to the agents of the DEA awaits you,"[47] Lehder warned Noriega.

During pretrial maneuverings, two new issues emerged. First, since Noriega had worked for both the CIA and the DEA and had contacts with Cuban leader Fidel Castro, the drug cartels of Colombia, and the contras and the Sandinistas in El Salvador, the evidence against him might include information classified by the U.S. government. Since the prosecution wanted to keep as many top-secret documents sealed as possible, a catch-22 came into play.[48]

The *Miami Herald* twice protested Judge Hoeveler's orders to seal documents. "[W]e've got to let the judge know that the press has an interest in these proceedings and all the documents in them, and before the documents are sealed or hearings closed, we are entitled to a hearing," argued *Herald* attorney Jerry Budney.[49] For the defense, the problem proved even more daunting since the Classified Information Procedures Act prohibits the disclosing of classified information to anyone, including defense attorneys. Now for the real kicker: Tens of thousands of classified documents existed that might be used by both the prosecution and the defense.[50]

Paying the defense team became the second issue. Noriega's assets had been frozen by the U.S. government, leaving him with no access to cash. On April 30, the defense team asked to be removed from the case because Noriega could not pay his bills, and it accused the United States of sabotaging Noriega's defense. To try Noriega without legal fees was like "shooting a fish in a barrel,"[51] Rubino told the press.

But on May 21, prosecution and defense reached a back-scratching deal: The government would pay Noriega's legal fees, which could run as high as $3 million, and the defense would not subpoena documents that might show the CIA and other federal intelligence agencies had paid him for information. Addendum to the deal: If Noriega is acquitted, his assets will be returned, and he pays the legal bill.

U.S. Attorney Lehtinen called the agreement "reasonable"; David Keating of the National Taxpayers Union in Washington called it "incredible" and questioned how the government could agree to pay the legal bills of "one of the most notorious accused criminals of our time."[52]

Murky waters further muddied when on May 24 Judge Hoeveler said the agreement was illegal and Noriega would have to pay his lawyers. Hoeveler's decision hit both sides hard. Prosecutors faced the highly embarrassing probability that they would have to reveal Noriega had been paid millions of dollars for his cooperation—by the United States. A prosecutorial nightmare awaited: explain in open court how the government had a dictator on its payroll yet spent millions of dollars and lost American lives just to try him in a federal court.

The defense lawyers surely viewed their situation as far worse. They might not get paid. They faced the possibility that Hoeveler would provide Noriega with court-appointed attorneys and that they would never be paid the fees for the work they had done since January. "This is manifestly unfair," the acerbic Rubino said in court. "This man is only indigent and unable to pay his lawyers because of action by the U.S. Justice Department in seizing his property."[53]

To the American taxpayers, the Noriega case appeared to be one of the strangest criminal cases on record. And rightly so. But news is a fleeting, incorporeal thing, particularly when it becomes the minutiae of a pretrial legal fight. The flashy holiday season invasion of Panama and the Christmas Eve race to the Vatican embassy were fading from the public mind, and the images plastered across front pages and on television nightly news was that of three-piece suits carrying briefcases into a federal court. The remaining images of Noriega? Two stale pictures: a drawing by a courtroom sketch artist of a short, pock-faced man in a general's getup or television file footage of the belligerent dictator raising what looked like a sword above his head. And those images would soon dissolve with the emergence of a bigger, badder story as the United States slid toward another international crisis with a man named Saddam Hussein.

Judge Hoeveler ruled in early June: The U.S. district court had jurisdiction over the Noriega case. "Given the serious nature of the drug epidemic in this country, certainly the efforts of the United States to combat the problem by prosecuting conduct directed against itself cannot be subject to the protest of a foreign national profiting at U.S. expense,"[54] the judge wrote in his dismissal of the defense argument.

As for the defense contention that Noriega's arrest had been shocking, Hoeveler wrote, "Noriega's complaint is a challenge to the very morality of war itself. This is a political question."[55] The same day, one of Noriega's codefendants pled guilty and agreed to testify that Noriega assisted him in operating a drug-trafficking ring—a double whammy for the defense.

On the other hand, all was not bad for the defense. Noriega's lawyers would be paid. Hoeveler ruled that Noriega needed his frozen funds to pay for his defense, and on June 20, the government agreed to free up $6 million of his assets.

In this goofy case, however, good news always seemed to preface bad news. And it did once again when the new Panamanian government informed Judge Hoeveler it would sue Noriega for extortion, fraud, and murder, charging him specifically with killing the leader of a failed coup attempt just two months before the American invasion.[56] It would be a civil lawsuit asking for more than $5 billion of Noriega's assets. (The actual lawsuit filed in November asked for $6.5 billion.) Even his loudest detractors did not say he had that much. At least not yet.

Media attention quickly shifted away from Noriega in early August as Iraq invaded Kuwait. Comparisons between Iraqi warlord Saddam Hussein and Noriega proved inevitable, however, as editorial writers speculated how President Bush would handle this latest international crisis. "Unfortunately, because of the American hatred of Iran during the 1980s, the U.S. government backed the Iraqi leader to the hilt, making him today the Mideast equivalent of Manuel Noriega," wrote Robert Hunter, a vice president at the Center for Strategic and International Studies, in *Newsday*.[57] "The issue underlying President Bush's moves in the Persian Gulf is not Kuwait or Saudi Arabia or even oil. It is Saddam Hussein, the Noriega of the Middle East,"[58] opined Harvard's Bernard Trainor in the *New York Times*.

Washington Post columnist William Raspberry wrote that Hussein had replaced Noriega as "the number one barbarian of the Universe . . . [but] the point is to avoid the American habit of substituting villains for solutions."[59] Sam Keen, the author of *Faces of the Enemy: Reflections of the Hostile Imagination*, saw strong similarities between the dehumanization of Hussein and Noriega. "All the talk about voodoo and weird pants made it easier for us to forget how long Noriega was on our payroll."[60] Meanwhile, Noriega's date with justice crept ever further into the future. Judge Hoeveler had set a January 27, 1991, date for the trial, but behind the scenes the legal system had ground to a halt. Rubino complained that Noriega was facing a bureaucratic and diplomatic tangle in trying to get access to his money. Rubino also complained that all requests for top-secret government documents were tied up in sealed motions before the court.[61]

Inside the Federal Metropolitan Correctional Center, Noriega had telephone privileges that allowed him to make long-distance calls through his lawyer's office. That privilege would soon ignite a firestorm, delay the legal process further, and return Noriega to the front page.

On Tuesday, November 6, two reporters from CNN went to Rubino's office for an interview. Marlene Fernandez and John Camp played an audio recording for Rubino in which Noriega discussed his legal strategy with defense investigator Jim Hawkins. But how could this be? Surely the government knew that recording such a conversation violated attorney–client privilege. Didn't the government understand it jeopardized its own case by leaking illegal material to the press?

A month earlier, unidentified sources had told the news media that Noriega was passing coded messages to his supporters in Panama. But the idea of government eavesdropping on Noriega's discussion with his legal team infuriated Rubino. "It's the most grave violation of constitutional rights I have ever seen," he told CNN.[62] Before the end of the day, Rubino approached Judge Hoeveler to ask that the court stop CNN from airing the tapes. By 7 A.M. the next day, the world knew what CNN had. The network aired a report saying that Noriega had been planning a coup in Panama and that the Bush administration had found out about it by recording his telephone calls.[63]

Hours later, CNN aired excerpts from the tapes despite the fact that Judge Hoeveler had issued a ban on playing the recordings. In the tape, Noriega could be heard talking with a member of his defense team. CNN was violating two of Judge Hoeveler's orders: to stop airing excerpts and to turn the tapes over to the court. Rubino smelled a possible dismissal of the charges against Noriega. "The government is an eighty-headed snake,"[64] he said in raging Rubinese.

But the public would learn more about CNN's First Amendment rights than Noriega's Sixth Amendment rights. Newspapers and broadcast networks came to CNN's defense, pointing out the newsworthiness of the tapes and how the court had no right to prevent them from being aired (apparently forgetting that they were aired in defiance of court orders, thereby breaking the law). "Let's remember, there's an important news story here and the news story is that the government may have acted improperly by listening to conversations between the defendant and his counsel,"[65] said Timothy Dyk, who represented the National Association of Broadcasters and the American Society of Newspaper Editors.

Despite the support, CNN lost its appeals in the 11th Circuit and the U.S. Supreme Court. For the first time, the Supreme Court formally upheld an order barring the publication or broadcast of information.[66] CNN said it was stunned by the decision, and free-speech advocates condemned the court's action. "The court that decided the Pentagon Papers case would not have done this,"[67] said Gene Nichol, dean of the law school at the University of Colorado.

The CNN tapes diverted attention only temporarily from the defense attorneys' pay crisis. After 11 months without compensation, Noriega's lawyers pled with Judge Hoeveler for relief and tried a new tactic: have Noriega speak to the judge. Neither Hoeveler nor the prosecution objected when, on November 16, Rubino asked Noriega to step up to the lectern. In his full military uniform, with its four stars, Noriega stood erect and spoke in Spanish.

"When I was brought to the United States in a U.S Army airplane, I mistakenly believed that I would be able to receive a fair trial,"[68] Noriega said. "The U.S. government has done as much as possible to deprive me of a fair trial . . . the government of the United States does not wish that I defend myself."[69] Complaining of "psychological warfare" and how the government still blocked the release of his funds, he explained how he was prevented from hiring lawyers of his own choice. He then dismissed government explanations of diplomatic problems with foreign banks. "I know that when the government of the United States wishes something to be done, they obtain it,"[70] he said. Noriega portrayed himself as the victim. "The battle I am facing is very similar to the invasion my country suffered. And this battle is unfair, also. I find myself at the mercy of a totally unfair system."[71]

Judge Hoeveler listened silently as Noriega spoke, and a few moments passed before he responded. When he did reply, he assured Noriega he would have "top flight" defense attorneys. "I want the defendant to understand he is not being cast adrift by the court, the judicial system. So I say this for his benefit, the case will not lag. He is entitled to a trial. He is entitled to a fair trial."[72]

Before the end of the month, two separate newspaper reports would put the pretrial posturing and courtroom dramas into some sort of perspective. *La Prensa* (Panama City) wrote that in the year since the U.S. invasion of Panama, impressions of the invasion had changed in Panama. According to the journal, in January 1990, 89 percent of the nation favored the invasion; in December, only 37 percent believed the invasion brought more benefits than problems to Panama.[73]

On December 12, 1990, *USA Today* published an investigative report showing Noriega's worth to be at least $31.5 million at the time of the invasion. The money rested safely in 16 separate accounts in Luxembourg's Bank of Credit and Commerce International (BCCI).[74] In addition, BCCI officials had pled guilty to laundering cocaine money in January.

Richard Koster, author of *In the Time of the Tyrants,* said Noriega probably had more money in other bank accounts.[75] Combined with his two homes in Panama; his property in Israel, the Dominican Republic, Venezuela, and Japan; and his business interests, Koster said, Noriega was no millionaire but a billionaire.

Rampant speculation followed. What, exactly, was this guy? A crooked politician or just a crook? Or both? Worth $163 million of American taxpayers' hard-earned dollars to bring to justice? Perhaps. Panamanians answered no, but Americans would have to wait and see.

In the days leading up to Operation Desert Storm, American newspapers speculated as to when the U.S.-led coalition forces would attack Iraq. Readers may have missed a small article in mid-January, something about the U.S.

government admitting to having this Noriega guy on its payroll for 31 years. It seems that from 1979 to 1985, the CIA paid Noriega just under $2,000 a month. But the good news was that his income was supplemented by the U.S. Army. Although the government never revealed what the payments were for, it provided a total earning statement not unlike a W-2 form: $320,000 received in cash and gifts.[76]

For months, there had been speculation that the United States had paid Noriega millions of dollars for his help in the war on drugs. The ever-brash Rubino termed the total far too low, candidly adding that the "prosecutors knew less than I thought."[77]

In early January, the start of Noriega's long-awaited trial was delayed. Again. The pretrial proceedings had gone on for more than a year, and the *New York Times* described the judge as "weary and angry."[78] Hoeveler set a new trial date for June 24. Meanwhile, defense attorneys continued to claim that the airing of the CNN tapes had damaged Noriega's right to a fair trial. At a January 11 hearing, Rubino questioned Michael P. Sullivan, now leading the prosecution team, about how the government had handled the taping of Noriega's conversation. "Mr. Sullivan is the most adverse witness I've faced in 17 years of practicing law,"[79] Rubino snapped. It was, as the *Times* put it, "a growing hostility."[80]

But good news arrived from Austria. That European country, hidden safely away from the never-ending story that came to define the Noriega case, released $1.6 million from one of the Panamanian general's bank accounts. Finally, the defense's angst could be somewhat assuaged.

The fight(s) over government documents continued. In April, Rubino dropped another bombshell, saying that government documents seized in the Panama invasion proved Noriega helped in the war against drug trafficking. It was a prelude to a request that the government release other documents that Rubino said outlined assassination plots against Noriega and his predecessor, General Omar Torrijos. Noriega rose to power in Panama after Torrijos died in a 1981 plane crash. The defense also asked for files detailing Noriega's meeting with then Vice President George H. Bush. Prosecutors objected, saying they had already given defense attorneys 7,000 pages of government material.[81]

Judge Hoeveler considered the defense demand until May. He summed up the problem for Rubino and his team: "What you are seeking is a couple of truckloads of materials, about 98 percent of which would not be admissible in any way." The flamboyant Rubino, demonstrating his ability to manufacture a quote in almost any circumstance, felt compromising. "Let us scale it down. I am not going to try to stand here and feed you some garbage. . . . We are more than willing to go back to the drawing board . . . and try to scale it down."

The scale-down strategy worked, and by the middle of May the judge had given the defense team much of what it wanted.[82] But haggling over specific documents continued throughout July, putting off the trial. Again.[83]

As any lawyer will say, a delay need not be a hurdle but rather a stepping-stone. And the prosecution had used the delays to build an impressive case. Through a series of plea bargains, a long list of witnesses who might be able to connect Noriega directly with the Medellin drug cartel had been compiled.

An attorney for a Noriega codefendant, Amet Paredes, said, "They [the prosecution] have left no stone unturned. The slimmest of eels and the most honest types, they've knocked on all their doors and given away the courthouse—within the rules, of course."[84]

The biggest gun in the prosecution's arsenal was secured just before the trial began. On August 28, Ricardo Bilonick, the Panamanian ambassador during the Torrejos and Noriega administrations, pleaded guilty to drug charges and agreed to testify that Noriega took $10 million to protect almost 15 tons of cocaine bound for the United States. The defense publicly dismissed Bilonick as another criminal with a "get-out-of-jail-free" card.[85]

September 4, 1991. More than 20 months after Noriega had surrendered to U.S. forces in Panama City, more than 20 months after rock music had rocked the Vatican embassy, the once-powerful Panamanian dictator waited, meekly, for his trial to begin. Finally.

Noriega sat quietly, listening via headphones to a Spanish-language translation of the proceedings. He took notes on a legal pad. The courtroom filled with journalists, but few curiosity-seeking spectators attended, a staple at high-profile trials. "Es nada,"[86] one man told a reporter outside the courthouse.

Inside, Rubino hammered away at what he considered a crucial point—Noriega's right to a fair trial. He could not receive one, Rubino claimed. Why? Because one of Noriega's attorneys was a government informant when he encouraged the general to surrender on January 3, 1990, Rubino explained. Raymond Takiff had resigned from the defense team shortly after Noriega's arrival in the United States, but it was months later when the public learned that in 1989 Takiff began working for the Justice Department as part of a plea agreement to avoid tax evasion charges.[87]

As for the possibility of Noriega copping a plea, that matter had ended with finality two weeks before. Rubino offered up a guilty plea on one count in exchange for time served. "You have to be kidding,"[88] was the prosecution's response. Sullivan was willing to offer 10 to 15 years for a guilty plea on two charges. "Sorry," Rubino replied, "my client is innocent."[89]

As the trial began, public attention turned elsewhere. U.S.-led forces liberated Kuwait from the clutches of Saddam Hussein, while on the home front politics became the topic of conversation as the Democratic Party searched for someone to defeat President Bush.

But many in the media still saw the Noriega trial as pure drama with a sleazy sideshow, a performance rife with the possibilities of backroom deals embarrassing to the U.S. government. The defendant's physical bearing—short and physically unattractive—provided novelty value. Then there was the occult/religious thing. As Otis Pike of the *Seattle Times* wrote, "The prosecution contended that Noriega had placed voodoo curses on the trial judge and the prosecuting attorney. That sure gets an impartial jury in Miami. . . . Noriega's lawyers say he has become a born-again Christian. A spell in the pokey before trial often brings out the best in folks."[90]

Jury selection took six days. Gender breakdown: nine women and three men. Racial makeup: eight blacks, two Hispanics, and two whites not of Latin origin.[91] When they walked into the courtroom on the first day of the trial, several appeared visibly shaken by the number of reporters and courtroom artists present.[92] More than 50 news organizations had representation, but only a few covered the case from gavel to gavel.

Then at 10:07 A.M., September 16, 1991, the trial of the *United States v. Manuel Antonio Noriega* began.

The prosecution wasted no time in telling the jury Noriega was a "crocked cop." While Noriega may have never seen or used cocaine, "he recruited others to engage in illegal conduct, and he was paid for it."[93] Sullivan said that while Noriega may have tried to stop narcotics traffic at one time, the Medellín cartel changed that in 1982. "They sat down and decided to either eliminate him or buy him. They decided to buy him,"[94] Sullivan said. The prosecution, Sullivan claimed, would prove Noriega had gone bad. Lehder would testify, he said, that Noriega received $400,000 per load for allowing aircraft to carry drugs through Panama.[95]

Rubino waived his opening statement. He believed that if the trial lasted months as predicted, the opening statement would be lost and forgotten in a fog of testimony, objections, and bench deliberations when it came time for the jury to deliberate.[96]

Judge Hoeveler then ruled testimony would begin the following morning, September 17. The first day's testimony set the pattern for the prosecution's case as well as for how the defense would counter. The government presented witnesses who had pleaded guilty for drug crimes; the defense attacked their credibility. First up: Luis del Cid, a long-time Noriega associate who said he delivered cartel payments to the general. Then came Max Mermelstein, a former member of the Medellín cartel, who confessed to playing a role in three drug-related murders.[97] Mermelstein told the court he had seen Noriega's name on a cartel drug-distribution payment book.

Rubino hammered back, hard: "When all is said and done, you have never in your life met General Noriega and you've never seen him commit a crime." Mermelstein's curt answer: "That's correct."[98] His testimony seemed further weakened when it was learned the Bush administration had paid him $250,000 to analyze drug-smuggling ledgers.[99]

The first week went badly for the prosecution. "Although experts still believe General Noriega will be convicted, it is emerging that the government's case may not be as strong as earlier imagined,"[100] the *Independent* of London wrote. By the second week, however, the prosecution linked Noriega to payoffs from the Medellin cartel when Floyd Carlton, a Panamanian pilot, took the stand. Carlton said cartel leaders Pablo Escobar and Gustavo Gaviria had asked him in 1981 about flying drugs from Colombia to Panama.

According to Carlton, Noriega asked what his cut would be. When he told Noriega between $30,000 and $50,000, Carlton testified that Noriega asked whether "I was crazy or they were crazy." No less than $100,000 would suffice for Noriega, Carlton said.[101] Carlton testified that he gave Noriega $100,000 for one flight and $150,000 for a second. In cross-examination, Rubino pointed out that Carlton's testimony hinged on conversations with no corroborating witnesses. Noriega, Rubino explained, received funds but offered no service in return. In short, he provided no protection for the drug flights even though the cartel paid for them.[102]

Adding to the prosecution's woes was another of its own witnesses. Ricardo Tribaldos admitted on the stand that he thought Noriega had not known about the Medellin drug deals being routed through Panama.[103]

In November, the prosecution played to its strength. Enrique Pretelt, a former Noriega associate, said the general had volunteered to be the "Godfather" of the Medellin cartel's leader in Panama.[104] But the prosecution still had not played its trump cards. The "trial without focus" soon would turn dramatic with testimony from former Colombia drug kingpin Carlos Lehder.

Serving a life-plus-135-year prison sentence for dealing cocaine, Lehder was taken from his Illinois prison cell to Miami. Referring to the defendant as "the criminal, corrupt policeman, officer Noriega,"[105] the flamboyant Lehder unveiled the details of the cartel's dependence on Panama after the DEA closed the cocaine route from the Bahamas into the United States. He testified that Noriega received five cents on every dollar's worth of cocaine the cartel flew through Panama. In return, Noriega would "protect" the operation with his police force.[106] Once again, a catch-22 set in for the prosecution. Once again, a seemingly strong government witness helped the defense with his testimony that the Medellin cartel had given U.S.-backed contras in Nicaragua $10 million during the 1980s. This gave credence to the defense claim that some Central American drug trafficking was allowed by the United States to help the contras.[107] One step forward, two steps back for the prosecution.

The prosecution rested—perhaps thankfully—on December 17. After calling 60 witnesses, it had established a direct link between Noriega and his alleged drug money. At a casual meeting with the judge before the defense began presenting its case, Sullivan joked—one can only assume it was a joke— with Judge Hoeveler: "We want to recall all of our previous witnesses."[108]

Rubino had asked for a delay in presenting his case, saying he needed more time to prepare. That he got. During a break for the holidays, Judge Hoeveler failed a medical stress test and underwent triple-bypass open-heart surgery, pushing the date for resuming the trial from January 6 to at least January 27.[109]

It was during the long break that both defense and prosecution became aware of a tidbit that could blow the case wide open. A DEA plan called

"Operation Negocio" (Operation Business) to curtail drug smuggling in Central America revealed that Noriega had provided the agency with information about drug cartel money being routed through Panama.[110]

Meanwhile, the media used the extra time for further editorializing. "Happy Second Anniversary of Operation Just Cause. Forget that one already?"[111] asked *Newsday*. "Noriega may be the last of a breed. He is fabulously, enchantingly ugly. He is a scared animal, with eyes you can't see into, a face like a stamp canceled by testosterone," wrote the *Washington Post*. [112] And the *Boston Globe* theorized, "If Noriega had raped an individual, instead of just a country, we'd have heard more about his crimes. From this distance, and from what we hear on the grapevine, the Justice Department turned the case against Noriega into a case of refried beans."[113] And a juror, as if to make a silent statement that the case had dragged into infinity, was found wandering in a daze outside the federal courthouse. She was dismissed from the case, as had been two others, for medical reasons.[114]

When it finally had the chance, the defense took only slightly more than one month to present its case. Rubino framed a simple message for the jury: If my client is a criminal, he is a criminal only because he tried to help your country stop Central American drug trafficking.[115] The witness list included 16 U.S. government agents, ensuring that some defense witnesses would be hostile. It was a calculated gamble by the defense—pit the government against its own people.[116]

At this point, the defense dropped a bombshell, announcing Rubino would no longer serve as lead counsel. Replacing him was Jon May, an attorney with less courtroom experience but a more scholarly demeanor than Rubino's.[117] Three days later, Rubino was back in the lead position for good. "I hope you haven't forgotten me over the last seven weeks," he quipped to the jury.

"I think the government hopes they have," joked Hoeveler.[118]

One by one, Rubino questioned the witnesses. Some admitted they did not want to be there. Some testified that Noriega had helped the U.S. government in its antidrug efforts. One, a former CIA chief in Panama, detailed a meeting between Noriega and then CIA Chief William Casey in 1984 at which Noriega gave Casey details of Castro's statements about the United States in Central America.[119]

Interestingly, details of the defense's case are difficult to find in newspaper archives. In an *ABA Journal* article, "No Longer News: The Trial of the Century That Wasn't," Jack Doppelt of the Medill School of Journalism at Northwestern University claims the trial had become a journalistic afterthought.[120] "Coverage of the trial fell off so dramatically that news organizations had their official press credentials revoked. Only the wire services, the Panamanian news organizations, the *New York Times, Miami Herald, Fort Lauderdale Sun-Sentinel* and National Public Radio kept reporters there gavel to gavel."[121] Even CNN was gone. The *Wall Street Journal* left after three weeks. But they'd all be back, hoping for testimony from the celebrity of the case, Noriega.

It was not to be. At a meeting with his defense lawyers, Judge Hoeveler, and several journalists who had been allowed to observe, Noriega announced his decision to stay off the stand. "I am prepared to testify mentally and physically, but based on the laws of the country of the United States, and based also on the Geneva talks for prisoners of war, I would like to take my right not to testify,"[122] Noriega stated. But, he continued, "I would not want the prosecution or the lawyers present here to interpret my waiver of not testifying as thinking I am hiding from anything."[123]

In closing arguments, Rubino, true to form, claimed the case to be politically motivated and morally wrong. He put his arms around a crying Noriega and asked the jury, "Are you going to find him guilty of being a military dictator, or are you going to find him guilty of that indictment?"[124]

In less dramatic fashion, prosecutor Miles Malman reminded the jury of the ties between Medellin and Panama. "The cartel was comfortable in Panama. It was their back yard,"[125] he explained.

After four days of closing arguments, the fate of Manuel Antonio Noriega finally, thankfully, was placed in the hands of the jury.

For five long days, the jury deliberated in a Miami hotel, alternately crying, praying, and arguing. They pored over the testimony. One juror drew diagrams trying to show how Noriega and the Medellin cartel could be connected.

"We were sick to our stomachs. We had headaches,"[126] a juror said later.

On the fourth day, the jury had a message for Judge Hoeveler: It was deadlocked. One woman juror, it seemed, had made her decision before the deliberations even began.[127] Hoeveler was having none of it. He ordered jurors back into deliberation with a promise: "[N]one of you are going home tonight."[128]

Thirty hours later, the verdict was read. Guilty in 8 of 10 counts. Wearing his four stars as he had throughout the trial, Noriega displayed no emotion. Sullivan said it was all worth it. Rubino countered that the United States should not be playing "the world's policeman."[129] President Bush proclaimed the conviction a victory against the drug lords.

On July 10, 1992, Noriega was sentenced to 40 years in prison for his conviction in the Miami indictments. He read a statement at his sentencing hearing, in Spanish, claiming President Bush had wanted him dead.[130] His defense attorneys promised to appeal, but government attorneys felt relief that the man who, in their words, "put tons and tons of powdery white death"[131] on the streets of America would be residing in a prison cell for a long, long time.

The Tampa indictment against Noriega was eventually dropped. On December 19, 1994, CNN read a statement repeatedly throughout the day, saying it had been in error when it aired the tapes of Noriega's telephone conversations from prison. In 1999, Noriega's attorneys finally won a small victory in the appeals process when his sentence was reduced from 40 to 30 years.[132]

Noriega now lives in a four-room enclosure at the Miami Federal Correctional Institution. He speaks to his wife and mistress by telephone regularly. He is still the only prisoner of war being held in the United States.[133] He is still the only federal prisoner allowed to wear a military uniform. He is still the only federal prisoner to receive regular visits from the International Red Cross.

In 1997, Noriega published his memoirs with ghostwriting help from Peter Eisner, the reporter who covered the trial for *Newsday*. In that book, Noriega still maintains his innocence, insisting that the United States has imprisoned neither his soul, nor his ideals, nor his faith, which "exists in a flight of eternal liberty."[134]

NOTES

1. Lee Hockstader, "Troops Blare Music at Papal Nunciature," *Washington Post*, December 28, 1989, A28.

2. David Harris, *Shooting the Moon: The True Story of an American Manhunt Unlike Any Other, Ever* (New York: Little, Brown, 2001), 366, and Kevin Buckley, *Panama: The Whole Story* (New York: Simon and Schuster, 1991), 247.

3. Steve Albert, *The Case against the General: Manuel Noriega and the Politics of American Justice* (New York: Macmillan, 1993), 85.

4. Manuel Noriega and Peter Eisner, *The Memoirs of Manuel Noriega: America's Prisoner* (New York: Random House, 1997), 175.

5. Harris, *Shooting the Moon*, 365.

6. Noriega and Eisner, *The Memoirs of Manuel Noriega*, 16.

7. Albert, *The Case against the General*, 77.

8. Ibid., 76.

9. Noriega and Eisner, *The Memoirs of Manuel Noriega*.

10. *Seattle Times*, September 1, 2001, A15.

11. Noriega and Eisner, *The Memoirs of Manuel Noriega*, 208.

12. Don Lattin, "Vatican Sanctuary Has Medieval Roots," *San Francisco Chronicle*, December 27, 1989, A18.

13. Kevin Buckley, *Panama: The Whole Story* (New York: Simon and Schuster, 1991), 246.

14. Hockstader, "Troops Blare Music at Papal Nunciature," A28.

15. Noriega and Eisner, *The Memoirs of Manuel Noriega*, 181.

16. Gary Lautens, "Not Even Noriega Deserves the Torture of Modern Music," *Toronto Star*, January 3, 1990, A2.

17. Buckley, *Panama*, 249.

18. Ibid., 250.

19. Noriega and Eisner, *The Memoirs of Manuel Noriega*, 183.

20. Ibid.

21. Albert, *The Case against the General*, 85.

22. Buckley, *Panama*, 251.

23. Independent Commission of Inquiry on the U.S. Invasion of Panama, *The U.S. Invasion of Panama: The Truth behind Operation "Just Cause"* (Boston: South End Press, 1991), 40.

24. "Capture Cost $163 Million," *St. Louis Post-Dispatch,* September 17, 1990, A6.

25. Frederick Kempe, *Divorcing the Dictator: America's Bungled Affair with Noriega* (New York: G. P. Putnam and Sons, 1990), 422.

26. Harris, *Shooting the Moon,* 370.

27. Albert, *The Case against the General,* 87.

28. Ibid., 89.

29. Ibid.

30. Ibid.

31. Richard L. Berke, "Judge Rules Noriega Trial Must Proceed," *New York Times,* February 9, 1990, A12.

32. Albert, *The Case against the General,* 115.

33. Ibid.

34. Berke, "Judge Rules Noriega Trial Must Proceed," A12.

35. Ibid.

36. Ibid.

37. "Red Cross Delegates Pay Their First Visit to Noriega in Prison," *New York Times,* February 17, 1990, A13.

38. "Carter Condemns Invasion of Panama," *St. Louis Post-Dispatch,* April 1, 1990, D12.

39. Albert, *The Case against the General,* 131.

40. Jeanne DeQuine, "Dismissal Sought for Noriega," *USA Today,* April 3, 1990, A4.

41. Albert, *The Case against the General,* 131.

42. DeQuine, "Dismissal Sought for Noriega," A4.

43. Albert, *The Case against the General,* 132.

44. "US Report Highlights Failures in Panama," *Times* (London), July 3, 1990, A13.

45. Christine Toomey, "Noriega Spins a Tangled Web for Court Defense," *Sunday Times* (London), May 20, 1990, A18.

46. Ibid.

47. Ibid.

48. Andrew Blake, "Noriega Case to Spawn Clash over Disclosure of U.S. Secrets," *Boston Globe,* April 23, 1990, A3.

49. Ibid.

50. Albert, *The Case against the General,* 105.

51. Jeanne DeQuine, "Noriega Lawyers Beg Off over Pay," *USA Today,* May 1, 1990, A4.

52. Ibid.

53. Robert L. Jackson, "Judge Rejects Agreement to Pay Noriega's Legal Fees," *Los Angeles Times,* May 25, 1990, A4.

54. "U.S. Has Jurisdiction over Noriega, Judge Rules," *New York Times,* June 9, 1990, A8.

55. Ibid.

56. Jeanne DeQuine, "U.S. Frees $6 Million for Noriega," *USA Today,* June 21, 1990, A1.

57. Robert E. Hunter, "Step One: Cut Off Iraq's Cash," *Newsday,* August 5, 1990, 1.

58. Bernard E. Trainor, "Saddam Hussein, Mideast's Noriega, Has to Go," *New York Times,* August 12, 1990, A21.

59. William Raspberry, "The Villain," *Washington Post,* August 22, 1990, A21.

60. Sam Keen, quoted in Don Lattin, "The Enemies We Love to Hate," *San Francisco Chronicle,* August 30, 1990, B3.

61. Peter Eisner, "Noriega Case Dragging Along," *Newsday,* October 21, 1990, 8.

62. Albert, *The Case against the General,* 169.

63. Ibid.

64. Ibid., 172.

65. Timothy Dyk, quoted in Ruth Marcus, "Media, Press Groups Rally behind CNN in Its Noriega Tapes Case in High Court," *Washington Post,* November 15, 1990, A6.

66. David G. Savage and John M. Broder, "Justices Refuse to Allow Airing of Noriega Tapes," *Los Angeles Times,* November 19, 1990, A1.

67. Gene Nichol, quoted in ibid.

68. Albert, *The Case against the General,* 177.

69. Manuel Noriega, quoted in Robert L. Jackson, "Noriega, in Court, Blames U.S. for Freeze on Funds, Pleads for Fairness," *Los Angeles Times,* November 17, 1990, A2.

70. Ibid.

71. Ibid.

72. Albert, *The Case against the General,* 178.

73. *La Prensa,* quoted in *Los Angeles Times,* December 2, 1990, A18.

74. Sam Meddis, "The Noriegas' Global Shopping Spree; Paper Trail Shows Fortune of $31 Million," *USA Today,* December 12, 1990, A1.

75. Ibid.

76. Albert, *The Case against the General,* 185.

77. Ibid.

78. David Johnston, "Five Month Delay in Noriega Trial," *New York Times,* January 11, 1991, A11.

79. Ibid.

80. Ibid.

81. "Noriega's Lawyers Say He Aided Anti-Drug Effort," *New York Times,* May 1, 1991, A19.

82. Albert, *The Case against the General,* 218.

83. Ibid., 228.

84. Douglas Frantz and Robert L. Jackson, "The Spooks, the Kooks, and the Dictator," *Los Angeles Times,* July 21, 1991, A8.

85. Sam Meddis, "'Noriega's Noose Tightens,'" *USA Today,* August 29, 1991, A3.

86. Rick Bragg, "Few Show Interest as Noriega Appears in Court," *St. Petersburg Times,* September 5, 1991, A1.

87. Sam Meddis, "Noriega Trial Opens with Legal Punches," *USA Today,* September 5, 1991, A3.

88. Albert, *The Case against the General,* 232.

89. Ibid.

90. Ibid.

91. Albert, *The Case against the General,* 238.

92. Ibid., 248.

93. "Drug Lords 'Bought' Noriega, Trial Told," *Toronto Star,* September 17, 1991, A22.

94. Ibid.

95. Ibid.

96. Albert, *The Case against the General,* 252.

97. Deborah Sharp, "Witness Links Noriega, Cartel," *USA Today,* September 18, 1991, A3.

98. Ibid.

99. David Adams, "Gaffes Weaken Noriega Trial," *Independent* (London), September 21, 1991, 10.

100. Ibid.

101. Anne Moncreiff Arrarte, "Witness: Drug Cartel Paid Noriega," *Newsday,* September 27, 1991, 15.

102. Ibid.

103. Peter Eisner, "Looking Good Noriega," *Newsday,* October 29, 1991, 15.

104. "Noriega Had Offered to Be 'Godfather,' " *Independent* (London), November 6, 1991, 11.

105. Peter Eisner, "For Drug Boss, the Court's His Stage," *Newsday,* November 24, 1991, 15.

106. Albert, *The Case against the General,* 325.

107. Laura Myers, "Witness: Cartel Had Money Ties to Contras," *USA Today,* November 26, 1991, A3.

108. Albert, *The Case against the General,* 353.

109. "Noriega Trial Delayed," *Newsday,* December 28, 1991, 8.

110. Albert, *The Case against the General,* 348.

111. Jim Dwyer, "All in the Name of a Just Cause," *Newsday,* December 16, 1991, 2.

112. Henry Allen, "We Find the Defendant . . . Everywhere," *Washington Post,* February 12, 1992, C1.

113. David Nyhan, "A Keystone Kops Kase," *Boston Globe,* March 12, 1992, 15.

114. Ben Smith, "Noriega Jury Hears of Drug Crackdown," *Atlanta Journal and Constitution,* February 25, 1992, 3.

115. K. Michael Fraser, "Noriega Drug Trial: Defense Takes Stand," *Christian Science Monitor,* February 3, 1992, 8.

116. Albert, *The Case against the General,* 359.

117. Ibid., 355.

118. Ibid., 363.

119. Peter Eisner, "When Noriega Met Casey," *Newsday,* March 3, 1992, 4.

120. Jack Doppelt, "No Longer News: The Trial of the Century That Wasn't," *ABA Journal,* January 1993, 4.

121. Ibid.

122. "Noriega Won't Testify at Trial," *St. Petersburg Times,* March 11, 1992, A5.

123. Ibid.

124. Sam Meddis, "Noriega Jury Confronts 'Big Question Mark,' " *USA Today,* April 3, 1992, A7.

125. Ibid.

126. Larry Rohter, "Trial within the Noriega Trial: Jurors Tell of Their Ordeal," *New York Times,* April 11, 1992, A7.

127. Peter Eisner, "Noriega Jury Deadlocked," *Newsday,* April 9, 1992, 7.

128. Ibid.

129. Sam Meddis, "Bush Calls Noriega Conviction 'Victory against Drug Lords,' " *USA Today,* April 10, 1992, A1.

130. Ben Macintyre, "White House Sighs with Relief as Court Imprisons Noriega," *Times* (London), July 11, 1992, A1.

131. Ibid.

132. Harris, *Shooting the Moon,* 4.

133. At the time of this writing, Noriega was the only prisoner of war held in the United States. This may have changed given events since September 11, 2001.

134. Noriega and Eisner, *The Memoirs of Manuel Noriega,* 206.

10

THE CASE OF MATTHEW SHEPARD (1999)

Alfred N. Delahaye

"Guess what? We're not gay and you're going to get 'jacked."

The passing mountain biker who discovered a limp form tied to a fence at a lonely spot just outside Laramie, Wyoming, thought he had happened upon a scarecrow. But the five-foot-six, 105-pound form was that of Matthew Shepard, unconscious and barely breathing. The date was Wednesday, October 7, 1998. Only the day before, Shepard had been an active University of Wyoming freshman, attending classes, visiting off-campus hangouts, and helping a campus organization plan Gay Awareness Week.

The first police officer on the scene mistook Shepard for a 13-year-old. He was really 21, but he had been so brutally beaten that blood covered his face except where tears had washed it away.

Early news reports echoed the scarecrow image. They told of his having been tied to a fence like a dead coyote, of his having been left for dead for 18 hours before anyone found him. He was suffering from hypothermia and various injuries, including a two-inch depression in his skull. Gay leaders called the assault an antigay hate crime.

The prompt arrests of two young roofers and their girlfriends and then the victim's death five days later further stoked media and public interest. To many, Matthew Shepard quickly became an icon, a metaphor, a martyr, a lightning rod, a gay-rights messiah, or the patron saint of hate-crime legislation. Conversely, to others he was a wuss, a sinner, or just another faggot whose misfortune had been blown out of proportion by the news media.

Meanwhile, the Shepard story began to appear in newspapers and on television throughout the country and abroad. Among those on trial in the court of public opinion for more than two years were homosexuals and heterosexuals, liberals and conservatives, the city of Laramie, the state of Wyoming, state and national lawmakers, and the news media.

Laramie and Wyoming were uncomfortable in the national and international spotlights. Laramie residents resented suggestions that their city was the capital of hate crimes, and Wyoming citizens rejected the occasional designation of "hate state." Laramie is a city of about 29,000 population (including almost 10,000 university students) in the southeastern corner of Wyoming, about 50 miles west of the capital city, Cheyenne.

The University of Wyoming, the state's only university, dominates Laramie. The university's symbol is the rodeo rider, its student newspaper *The Branding Iron*. Wyoming is also known as the Cowboy State; in fact, the silhouette of a bronco buster has appeared on state license plates since 1936. With about 480,000 residents, Wyoming has the lowest population density in the country. The Equality State, as Wyoming is known, enfranchised women long before any other place. It has no income tax and no law against openly carrying a gun. It has no openly gay bars and, since 1977, no sodomy laws.

Young Shepard chose Laramie and the University of Wyoming in part because he thought he would feel safe there. He grew up in Caspar, Wyoming, but when he was a high school sophomore his family moved to Dhahran, Saudi Arabia, where his father was an oil safety engineer. Because there were no American schools there, young Matthew attended the American School in Switzerland.

During his senior year, he visited a coffeehouse in Morocco one night and, on the way home, encountered a gang of locals who raped him six times. Thereafter he would suffer from periods of paranoia. Generally, he did not hide his homosexuality from friends or make it known to strangers.

After high school, young Shepard briefly attended college in North Carolina and then Caspar College. There an instructor introduced him to an outgoing lesbian, and, when she moved to Denver, he followed, working briefly as a telemarketer selling vitamins. Because he suffered from periodic clinical depression, he considered entering an assisted-living home in Denver operated by mental health professionals. Instead, he entered the University of Wyoming, his parents' alma mater, to major in political science and to minor in languages. To visit a gay bar in Fort Collins, Colorado, Shepard sometimes hired a limousine, feeling a bit uncomfortable about such extravagance.[1]

Shepard's last evening as an active university student begins at 6:30 on a Tuesday when he telephones a friend to cancel plans to see a movie with him. He says he has to study for a French class. Then he attends the weekly meeting of the Lesbian, Gay, Bisexual, and Transgendered Association. During the Tuesday gathering in the university union, the group, usually numbering from 10 to 20, goes over the last-minute details of Gay Awareness Week, scheduled to begin the following week.[2]

Once the meeting ends, the group, as is its custom, goes out for coffee at the Village Inn. Shepard sits at one end of a crowded table and eats cherry pie. He tries to persuade his friends to accompany him to the Fireside Bar and Lounge, but no one says yes. A friend drives him to his apartment, watches him enter, and believes he is in for the night.

But sometime after 10 P.M., Shepard, dressed in jeans and a sport coat, enters the Fireside alone, sits at the bar, drinks a Heineken, and chats with the bartender, Matt Galloway, a university junior. Galloway knows Shepard to be amazingly polite and soft and well spoken. Shepard's last beer costs $2.50, but Galloway says, "Just give me two bucks." Shepard gives him three.

Also sometime after 10, two roofers, both 21 years old and grungily dressed, enter the bar, having earlier downed two pitchers of beer at another bar. They order a pitcher of beer and count out $5.50 in quarters and dimes. The dirty hands of one of them bothers Galloway. They command the bartender to "gimme this, gimme that."

At one point, the roofers disappear in the direction of the pool tables. At another point, they and Shepard strike up a conversation. The roofers, supposedly with robbery in mind, tell Shepard they are gay. The three leave the bar at midnight or shortly thereafter.

As roofers, Aaron McKinney and Russell Henderson earn roughly $7.50 an hour. McKinney and his girlfriend live in an apartment with their four-month-old son. McKinney is awaiting sentencing, having pleaded no contest about two weeks earlier to a felony burglary charge. McKinney, about five-foot-six and 145 pounds, is known to friends as "Dopey" because of his big ears and his close association with drugs. When he was 16, McKinney's mother died because of a botched operation; later he received just under $100,000 in a settlement.

Henderson, having recently turned 21, delights in going to bars. Although he completed Eagle Scout requirements as a youngster, he has a police record that includes two drunken-driving convictions. He and his girlfriend live in an aging trailer, paying $340 monthly rent.[3]

Outside, the three young men get in a pickup truck owned by McKinney's father. Inside the truck is a pistol the roofers had tried to sell earlier in the evening. With Henderson at the wheel, the three head out of town and turn just past Wal-Mart. During the drive, Shepard asks McKinney about their destination. McKinney offers this response: "Guess what? We're not gay, and you're going to get 'jacked. It's Gay Awareness Week." McKinney asks for Shepard's wallet, and Shepard gives it to him. Then come blows from the butt of a Smith & Wesson .357-caliber magnum; it is unloaded and weighs three pounds. They continue down a dirt road, through sagebrush, until the rutted road dead-ends at a rough-hewn fence. A house is under construction nearby.

Henderson ties Shepard's hands behind his back and binds them to the rail fence. It is only a few yards long and serves no purpose. With his head and body crumpled near the ground, Shepard is helpless. Meanwhile, McKinney takes Shepard's patent-leather shoes (just as his attackers had taken his shoes in Morocco). Yet more blows from the "Dirty Harry" gun and even some kicking rain down on Shepard, either because his assailants believe he has seen the license-plate numbers or because he mouths off to them. Shepard begs for his life, but McKinney, the leader, beats him while Henderson, the follower, stands back and laughs. In total, Shepard takes about 18 blows to the head.

Leaving the victim for dead, the roofers head back to town with Shepard's size-seven shoes, his wallet, and a credit card—and with expectations of burglarizing his residence. Somehow they get distracted downtown by two Hispanic teenagers, high school dropouts—Jeremy Herrera and Emiliano Morales. They are walking nearby, having just slashed a tire for the hell of it. The roofers and the teenagers begin to banter, and soon the roofers begin cursing them. McKinney bashes Morales on the skull, getting yet more blood on the .357 magnum. Herrera bashes McKinney in the head with a big stick he has handy. When the police show up in response to a vandalism call, McKinney and Henderson run away, leaving the truck behind. In it are Shepard's credit card and shoes—and the .357 magnum covered in blood.

Meanwhile, back at the fence, Shepard loses blood, and the early morning temperature falls to near freezing.

At about 1:30 A.M. Wednesday, McKinney comes home to his 18-year-old girlfriend, Kristen Price, and their child. He is disoriented and covered in blood. "I've done something horrible," he tells Price. He says he thinks he may have killed somebody. At about 2 A.M., Morales arrives at Ivinson Memorial Hospital in Laramie, but his injuries require his transfer to Poudre Valley Hospital in Fort Collins. (Treating Morales's cut skull requires 21 staples.)

As dawn brightens into day, no one shows up at the house under construction close to where Shepard lies because workers have the day off.

In the afternoon, McKinney and his girlfriend and Henderson and his 20-year-old girlfriend, Chasity Pasley, a university student, ponder what to do. Price takes McKinney at about 5 P.M. to Ivinson, where he is admitted with a hairline fracture to the skull; he too gets sent to the Fort Collins hospital. Price and Pasley concoct alibis for the two men and drive 50 miles to Cheyenne to dispose of McKinney's bloody clothes. The victim's wallet gets hidden in a bag of dirty diapers in the McKinney kitchen.

At 6:30 in the evening, Aaron Kreifels, a U.W. freshman, is riding his mountain bike on the old, rutted road the McKinney pickup had traveled many hours earlier. He struggles through deep sand and falls to the ground, his front wheel broken. Getting up, he notices something out of the corner of his eye. At first, he thinks it is a scarecrow, but then he realizes it is an unconscious person. He races to the nearest house.[4]

On Thursday, police find the incriminating items in the McKinney truck and Shepard's wallet at McKinney's home. On Friday, McKinney becomes the last of four suspects to be taken into custody when authorities arrest him hours after he is released from Poudre Valley Hospital, where he was down the hall from Shepard. Matthew is suffering from hypothermia and is comatose, his brain stem badly damaged. As a result, such involuntary functions as heartbeat, breathing, and temperature are at risk. His other injuries include knee and groin bruises and head, neck, and facial cuts. Hospital specialists discover that Shepard is HIV positive.

On Friday readers of the *Denver Post* learn that a diminutive gay student "who wanted to dedicate his life to human rights" has been savagely beaten and left to die for up to 18 hours on a wooden fence outside Laramie. Readers also learn much else: He was found "tied to a fence 'like a scarecrow' "; braces on his teeth highlight his boyishness. In the *Post* an uncle speaks of Shepard as "a small person with a big heart" who looks, in his battered state, like "something you might see in a war."

The campus newspaper on Friday publishes a special edition. The editor says "Equality State" means nothing anymore because she lives in a state where a young man was brutally beaten because he is gay. While distributing copies, another editor hears the appellation "faggot-lover."[5]

On the same day, a court hearing attracts gay-rights and anti-hate-crime activists from Fort Collins and Denver. The roofers get hit with charges of kidnapping, aggravated robbery, and attempted first-degree murder and their girlfriends with charges of accessory to attempted first-degree murder. The men's bonds are $100,000 and the women's $30,000. Except for Price, all remain in custody.[6]

On Friday night, Judy and Dennis Shepard arrive from Saudi Arabia, having stopped in Minneapolis to pick up their son Logan. Doctors tell them Matthew will never come out of the coma. Meanwhile, strangers overwhelm the hospital with calls, inquiries, and flowers. The hospital establishes and publicizes a Web site on Shepard's condition, promising to update it at 9 A.M. and 9 P.M. daily.

On Saturday, the University of Wyoming and Colorado State University conduct homecoming events. As the Wyoming parade kicks off, about 100 students, university employees, and townspeople line up at the end of a long string of floats and marching bands. They are there to protest the attack on Shepard; eventually their numbers grow to 500, perhaps to as many as 800.

The Colorado parade includes a float whose riders occasionally display a scarecrow draped in antigay epithets, supposedly the result of vandalism. (About a week later, Fort Collins, a university town, votes down, by nearly a two-to-one margin, a proposal to expand the city's antidiscrimination statute to include protection for gays and lesbians.)

Over the weekend, newspapers across the nation quote various authorities and observers: U.W. President Philip Dubois calls the attack an "isolated incident," and Wyoming Governor Jim Geringer terms the beating a "heinous crime." Jim Osborn, head of the gay organization to which young Shepard belongs, says that one event "should not be used to qualify or typify an entire state." Marv Johnson, executive director of the Wyoming American

Civil Liberties Union, says, "Wyoming is not a hospitable place for gays and lesbians."[7]

McKinney's father and Price tell the *Denver Post* that Shepard embarrassed young McKinney in front of his friends by making two passes at him at the Fireside. McKinney and Henderson never set out to kill the student, only to rob him, Price and the elder McKinney insist. The father faults the news media for blowing the matter "totally out of proportion because it involved a homosexual." Had a heterosexual been involved, he says, the story would never have made the national news. The father deplores the viciousness of the attack, saying it should never have happened. Price agrees and adds, "It just got out of hand, I guess."

"All Americans deserve protection from hate," President Bill Clinton says in a prepared statement. The president and House Minority Leader Richard Gephardt liken the Shepard beating to the racial killing in Jasper, Texas, of James Byrd, Jr., who was decapitated when dragged in chains behind a pickup truck on June 7, 1998. Clinton specifically endorses the Hate Crimes Prevention Act proposed a year earlier in Congress. Hate crimes, based on race, religion, or national origin, would be expanded to include sexual orientation, gender, and disability. Nineteen states have hate-crime laws that do not include sexual orientation as a basis for tougher penalties.[8]

At 12:53 A.M. Monday, five days after the robbing, the bludgeoning, and the abandonment, Matthew Shepard dies in a hospital room surrounded by his family. Judy Shepard, in a formal statement, says, "Go home, give your kids a hug, and don't let a day go by without telling them you love them." Once again, President Clinton calls for Congress to pass hate-crime legislation.

At a news conference, Governor Geringer condemns the assault on young Shepard and questions the usefulness of hate-crime laws. "We're very open to changing our law where it's not strict enough or where it's not comprehensive enough. But how do you enhance a penalty when a death has occurred? If capital punishment is the result, how do you enhance that? You can only do it once."[9]

Aaron James McKinney and Russell Arthur Henderson, in court for a 6 P.M. hearing, learn that charges against them have been increased from attempted first-degree murder to first-degree murder, which in Wyoming carries a possible death sentence. The kidnapping and aggravated robbery charges remain unchanged. Bail, previously set at $100,000 in cash, is now denied. Charges against the girlfriends, first accused of being accessories to attempted first-degree murder, soon omit the adjective "attempted." If convicted, they may face three years in jail and a fine of $3,000.[10]

On Tuesday the governor meets with Matthew's father and quotes him as having said he does not want his son's death to become a "media circus." But news of Shepard's death creates widespread sympathy, thousands of head-

lines, and dizzying rhetoric. Hate-crime statistics appear repeatedly. The Poudre Valley Hospital's special Web site begins receiving 30,000 hits an hour.

Coverage in the *Rocky Mountain News* on Tuesday includes these headlines: "Suspects' Old Pals Shun Them Now; 'He's a Punk,' Says Ex-Friend
of McKinney" and "Coming Out a Liberating, but Scary Choice." On the
same day, a *New York Times* story includes pro- and antigay sentiments and
this statement: "While some gay leaders saw crucifixion imagery in Mr. Shepard's death, others saw a different symbolism: the Old West practice of nailing
a dead coyote to a ranch fence as a warning to future intruders."

The *Times* story also presents typical statements. "Hate-crimes laws have
nothing to do with perpetrators of violent crime and everything to do with
silencing political opposition," says Steven A. Schwalm, an analyst with the
Family Research Council, a Washington group dedicated to defending faith,
family, and freedom. "It would criminalize pro-family beliefs. This basically
sends a message that you can't disagree with the political message of homosexual activists." In the view of John Paulk, a man featured during the summer in advertisements about how he and his wife "overcame" homosexuality
through religion, "We have every right to speak out against an agenda that
is contrary to Biblical norms."

In balancing such views, the *Times* presents yet more comments. Hate-
crime laws on the books in 40 states have not impinged on freedom of speech,
in the view of Brian Levin, a criminal justice professor who directs the Center
on Hate and Extremism in Pomona, New Jersey. "We want to deter the
broken windows and simple assaults before they escalate," he says. "With
other crimes, violence is a means to an end; with hate crimes, the violence
becomes an unstoppable goal." Beatrice Dohrn, legal director of the Lambda
Legal Defense and Education Fund, says Shepard's "horrible suffering and
death cannot be dismissed simply as the fault of deranged, isolated individuals." She believes his assailants "are among millions of Americans who con-
stantly hear the message that gay people are not worthy of the most basic
equal treatment."

While debate rages over coffee cups, in governmental offices, and in newspapers and magazines around the world, about 800 mourners attend Shepard's funeral in St. Mark's Episcopal Church on Friday, October 16, in Caspar.
Hundreds more fill a nearby Presbyterian church to hear an audio feed of the
service. U.S. Secretary of Veterans Affairs Togo West, Jr. attends the funeral
on behalf of President Clinton. Outside, the weather is bitterly cold.

A human chain is formed around the church to preserve the dignity of the
occasion, and 68 Wyoming law officers are on hand with bomb-sniffing dogs.
As the service begins, protesters stand outside the church likening gays to
something less than dogs. One sign reads "Matt in Hell," another "No Tears
for Queers." Among the protesters are the Reverend Fred Phelps, a fervently
antigay pastor from Topeka, Kansas, and some of his followers.

Inside St. Mark's, an Episcopal minister and cousin of Shepard preaches the homily. "Matthew is loved by God, and it is that love that has radiated out of this tragedy," she declares. She calls it love "more powerful than any voice of hate."[11]

The next day the *Denver Post* tells the story of McKinney and Henderson. It is one of broken homes, problems at school, experimentation with and possible dependence on drugs and alcohol, chronic resistance of authority, and recurring displays of runaway tempers. Family and friends who knew or know them say they could never have predicted that one day they would stand accused of murder. They concede that McKinney may have drunk too much, smoked too much pot, driven badly, and committed petty crimes. Speaking of Henderson, some say he may have partied a lot, acted as if he did not have to follow the rules, and had his own problems with the law, but he was never considered dangerous.

Readers learn much about McKinney from the comments of friends and relatives. He flunked the sixth grade and started getting into fights in the eighth grade. Bill McKinney, Aaron's father, discloses that the boy started running with the wrong crowd in junior high. At age 14, he spent three months in a youth detention center in Laramie for stealing a cash register from a local sports-card store. When the father got custody of the boy after his ex-wife died in 1993, he took him to Cheyenne. But when Bill McKinney lost his job, he sent his son to live with his late ex-wife's husband in Laramie. Young McKinney was pretty much alone at 17, about the time he met Henderson. McKinney and Henderson soon quit school. McKinney enrolled in a night-school program, but outstanding library fines kept him from getting a diploma. Henderson got him a job with a roofing outfit.

Before long, McKinney and Price started dating, and in June 1997 they moved in together. They became close friends with Henderson and his girlfriend, Pasley. When Price became pregnant, she and McKinney moved to Florida to live with her mother. However, in April 1998 McKinney was extradited back to Laramie to be tried for allegedly robbing a Kentucky Fried Chicken restaurant. He was in jail when his son was born in May. He pleaded no contest to stealing $2,500 in cash and checks.

Henderson, once a quiet, studious loner, was reared by his grandmother and rarely spoke of his parents. He held a 3.5 grade-point average in high school until he started hanging out with school dropouts who worked. Friends and acquaintances called him arrogant, a problem neighbor, a man with a volatile temper.

In Wyoming and far beyond, Shepard's death continues to be big news. In New York City on October 19, a demonstration begins at a 6 P.M. rally in front of the Plaza Hotel on 59th Street near Central Park. It swells to 5,000 people on Fifth Avenue, blocking traffic. A confrontation begins between activists and police. Demonstrators hurl water bottles and candles at police and chant, "Shame, shame, shame." Police swing clubs and make more than 100 arrests, causing them to hastily commandeer transit buses. The size of the event in midtown surprises both organizers and police. It shows how the Shepard killing has galvanized lesbians and homosexuals in New York and around the country, unlike any other single event in recent years.[12]

These events are not unique, the *New York Times* reports. Candlelight vigils are taking place across the country, from Washington to Raleigh, North Carolina, to Lubbock, Texas. San Franciscans lower to half staff the giant rainbow flag in the Castro district that symbolizes the gay-rights movement. Discussions of the crime fill the Internet. For every Web site memorializing Matthew, another gleefully celebrates his death.

"The Democratic-controlled State Assembly [of New York] has repeatedly passed bills that would outlaw anti-gay crimes," the *Times* reports, "but the Republican-controlled State Senate has failed to act on them." A magazine editor summarizes for the *Times* the impact of the Shepard killing on the gay-rights movement: "There was that sense of connecting the dots. Between the well-publicized murders, the less-publicized hate crimes that we hear about across the country, Trent Lott's words calling homosexuality a disease, and small acts of intolerance, there were all sorts of indications. But the murder of Matthew Shepard brought the picture into relief."

Back in Laramie on December 2, McKinney and Henderson plead not guilty at separate hearings. On December 9, the girlfriends, Price and Pasley, also plead not guilty. A prosecutor asks for a joint trial of the men, presumably because the evidence will be virtually the same against both and many witnesses will have to testify twice. But defense attorneys worry that the proof may be very strong against one and very minimal against the other. The judge rules for separate trials. In denying a request for a gag order, he reminds the lawyers not to make statements to reporters that might prejudice a legal proceeding. Basically, lawyers can talk about what motions they have filed, actions they have taken, and facts available in the public record, the executive director of the Wyoming Press Association explains.

Before mid-December, the Shepard family announces the formation of the Matthew Shepard Foundation "to help people abandon ignorance, prejudice, and hate." Another purpose is to help people "move beyond tolerance to embrace and rejoice in diversity." There is already a Matthew Shepard Memorial Fund.[13]

On January 10, 1999, Henderson's 40-year-old mother is found dead at about 8:30 A.M. along a snow-covered rural road. She had been drinking and had died of hypothermia, the coroner rules. Authorities do not permit her incarcerated son to attend the funeral, fearing that he might be harmed.

In February the district judge denies a Court TV request for live, uninterrupted coverage of Henderson's scheduled trial, citing his concern for the privacy of witnesses and jurors. A scheduling conflict involving one of the attorneys causes the judge to move the trial from March 22 to April 6. A few days later the Laramie City Council decides not to consider a bias-crimes ordinance until after the trials of Henderson and McKinney.

Before the end of March, prospective jurors complete a 20-page questionnaire that includes questions about the death penalty, psychiatrists, firearms, and much more, including whether they have seen or read media reports about the case and what they consider are the three most pressing problems of the justice system. No questions concern homosexuality. A public defender files an unsuccessful motion to keep Bibles out of jurors' hotel rooms. Sheriff Gary Puls says security at the courthouse will be tight.

On March 21, the *Rocky Mountain News* reports that "the most publicized murder case in Wyoming history returns to the national spotlight this week." The next day the *Denver Post* says jury selection "will set the stage for a case guaranteed to be watched around the world." According to the *Post*, "experts" say homophobia could reduce jury sympathy of Shepard, but the more likely possibility is that the urge to defend Wyoming's honor could inspire a rush to condemn Henderson as the exception and not the Cowboy State rule.

Outside the courthouse, the Reverend Phelps and 12 of his followers protest against homosexuals. Also on hand are counterprotesters. But there is no Henderson trial. On April 5, two days before the scheduled start of his trial, Henderson pleads guilty to felony murder and kidnapping. A plea bargain allows him to sidestep the premeditated first-degree murder charge. The agreement calls for a sentence of two life terms. The judge orders Henderson to serve the terms consecutively.

In the courtroom Henderson's grandmother expresses sorrow for the Shepard family's tragic loss and says, "You have shown us such mercy and we are so grateful." This suggests that the Shepards may have had some say in approving the arrangement that will keep Henderson off death row.

Matthew's parents describe their son as a caring, generous young man. Judy Shepard describes seeing in the hospital "an emotionless, unaware young man" whom she could identify as her son only by a bump on his left ear and the clear blue pupil of one of his partially opened eyes. "You murdered my son," she tells Henderson. "I hope you never experience a day or night without experiencing the terror, humiliation, the hopelessness, and helplessness that he experienced that night." Among other things, Dennis Shepard says, "There's a hole in my life that I can never fill."

A day or so later, a television reporter obtains two letters said to have been written by McKinney to Henderson. One letter says that Shepard was so frightened that he tried to buy off his attackers with $200 he had at his home and so provided his address. According to the correspondence, McKinney had no intention to kill anyone and did not single out Shepard because he was gay. In other statements attributed to McKinney, he identifies himself as a "drunk homofobick" who "flipped out." "I thought it would be a good idea to tie him up and take his shoes so that he would have a hard time getting away," a letter says. "As I began to leave he mouthed off to the point that I became angry enough to strike him more with my gun."[14]

In May defense attorneys do not file a motion to change the location of his trial by the deadline the judge had imposed. Seemingly, they have decided to keep his trial in Laramie. The judge grants a prosecution motion to seal McKinney's court file. On May 21, another judge sentences Henderson's girlfriend, Chasity Pasley, to 15 to 24 months for trying to cover up the crime.

Meanwhile, the Shepard story stays in the headlines, mostly because of public debate, rallies, and fund-raisers. On June 1, Elton John performs a benefit concert at the University of Wyoming, raising more than $250,000 for the Matthew Shepard Foundation and other antihate organizations. The concert is about ending hate, the entertainer tells his audience.

Back in Saudi Arabia, Judy Shepard spends her time with the foundation and tries to respond to 10,000 pieces of mail and more than 80,000 e-mail messages. She has already testified before Congress in support of the federal hate-crime bill. Having passed the Senate, it is stalled in the House.[15]

As the anniversary of the Shepard beating approaches, gay leaders plan quiet remembrances rather than marches and rallies, not wanting to over-emphasize the Shepard murder. On the university campus at Laramie, a vigil begins at 6:30 P.M., and a concert by the folk group Peter, Paul, and Mary begins an hour later.

Monday, October 11, marks the opening day of McKinney's death-penalty trial. At the outset, a defense attorney tells prospective jurors that his client was too drunk and high on drugs to know what he was doing. "This is not a case of who committed the crime," he says, nor is it one in which "we are going to contend Aaron McKinney was insane." He says McKinney should be convicted of second-degree murder or possibly manslaughter. Just as in the Henderson case, prosecutors and defense attorneys argue that robbery was the primary motive. Judge Barton Voigt dismisses a prospective juror after he approaches the Shepards during the noon recess and offers his con-dolences. Outside, Shepard's friends and acquaintances, wearing white smocks and angel wings, outnumber antigay protesters from a Kansas church.

The actual start of the trial gets delayed because Colorado State–Wyoming football fans occupy all hotel rooms in town, leaving jurors no place to be sequestered. Court-appointed attorneys for McKinney invoke the "homo-sexual panic" defense: Shepard's sexual advance triggered a five-minute drunken rage that killed him. A defense attorney says McKinney experienced sexual abuse at ages 7 and 15, both involving males. Witnesses testify that neither Shepard, Henderson, nor McKinney appeared to be drunk on the night of the beating despite claims by the defense.

The coroner testifies that Shepard was struck at least 20 times and suffered six skull fractures. Price, McKinney's girlfriend, says the two assailants decided in the restroom to pretend they were gay so they could get Shepard in the truck and rob him. Her testimony counters defense contentions that the robbery was not planned and that McKinney went into a drunken, drug-induced rage after a sexual advance that triggered his memories of a childhood homosexual assault. Price says she saw no sign that McKinney had been using drugs around the time of the beating, although she reveals that he and she had often shared methamphetamines in the past.

On Wednesday the judge scolds and stuns the defense: He tells defense attorneys he was not pleased to learn during jury selection and opening statements of a proposed voluntary intoxication defense. Moreover, he may disallow that and the "gay panic" defense. "I need someone to convince me that a case can be raised in Wyoming without a statute," he declares. A defense attorney says no "gay panic" defense has been asserted, only that Shepard made a homosexual advance. "It goes to [the defendant's] state of mind at the time, and that is admissible," the attorney argues. The jury does not hear this exchange, but McKinney, wearing a dark suit over a bulky bulletproof vest, does. A former Cody, Wyoming, bartender, a final witness, testifies by telephone that he once punched Shepard into unconsciousness after he made homosexual advances toward him. Henderson does not testify.

The prosecution ends its case on Friday and the defense on Monday. Fewer than a half dozen defense witnesses are called. Also on Monday, the presiding judge rejects the "gay panic" defense, ruling that it amounts to a diminished-capacity or temporary-insanity defense, neither of which is allowed under Wyoming law.

The jury of seven men and five women deliberate for about eight hours on Tuesday and for another two hours on Wednesday. They acquit the defendant of first-degree murder but find him guilty of second-degree murder, kidnapping, and aggravated robbery. If McKinney is to get the death penalty, the jury's decision in that regard must be unanimous.

In a surprising development the next day, the judge announces a sentencing agreement that will send McKinney to prison for two consecutive life terms, one for murder and the other for kidnapping. This follows communication between Judy Shepard and defense attorneys and then her request that prosecutors not pursue the death penalty.

Before his formal sentencing, McKinney tells the Shepards he is "truly sorry."

In an emotional 25-minute statement, the murder victim's father tells the jury that it showed the world that Laramie and Wyoming will not tolerate hate crime. "Yes, this was a hate crime," he declares, "pure and simple." He tells McKinney that he and his wife believe in the death penalty and that he "would like nothing better than to see you die." Continuing, he says, "However, this is a time to begin the healing process, to show mercy to someone who refused to show any mercy."

The trial ends, and a week later Kristen Price pleads guilty to a reduced charge of interfering with a police investigation; she is sentenced to 180 days in jail, 120 of which are suspended and the other 60 credited for time already served. Chasity Price, having been cooperative during five months in prison, sees her sentence suspended.

Meanwhile, the Shepard story and debates about hate-crime laws and gay rights continue. The Shepards, as national figures, speak out about tolerance and related matters. Singer-songwriter Melissa Etheridge popularizes an intensely emotional number called "Scarecrow." The A&E Network airs a documentary titled *American Justice: The Matthew Shepard Story. The Laramie Project,* a theatrical examination of homophobia, the cowboy culture, and the Shepard chronology, attracts sold-out audiences. In May 2002, HBO airs a two-hour movie adaptation of *The Laramie Project* with an ensemble cast that includes Peter Fonda and Amy Madigan. A week later, NBC broadcasts a made-for-television movie, *The Matthew Shepard Story,* with Stockard Channing and Sam Patterson as the parents who must decide whether to demand the death penalty.

The name Shepard in headlines during and after October 1998 inspired politicians, civil rights activists, and pundits to debate hate-crime laws with renewed vigor. Columnists George Will and Richard Cohen, stoked by early news of the Shepard beating, were among the first to join the debate. In the simplest terms, it was between conservatives and liberals, gays and antigays.

In mid-October, Cohen blasted political and religious conservatives for their homophobia. He cited the frequent lynching of African Americans years ago as "a product of racist rhetoric and belief" that turned them into something not quite American, not quite human. How is Senate Majority Leader Trent Lott's remark comparing homosexuals to kleptomaniacs much different? he asked. To call homosexuals sinners is "to separate them from you and me—to put them beyond the pale." Antigay politicians inadvertently legitimize the sort of hate that left Shepard tied to a fence and near death, he declared.

Will deplored the congressional practice of using "the criminal law as a moral pork barrel for indignation gestures." Hate-crime laws stipulate that some crime victims are especially important. Will questioned whether juries can distinguish causation from correlation. Before passing laws that will make inquisitorial questioning routine in millions of cases involving violent and nonviolent behavior, Will recommended that everyone consider that, according to the FBI, in 1996 only 12 murder cases were classified as hate crimes.

In time Congress pondered whether to add crimes motivated by the victim's sexual orientation, disability, or gender to those already covered—those involving race, color, religion, and national origin. Arguments for and against hate-crime legislation continued to appear with great passion in editorials, letters to the editor, and interview stories.

Among the most interesting, most compelling arguments for hate-crime laws were these: Statutes are needed to protect people who are disproportionately targeted for violence. Hate-crime legislation does not punish anyone's beliefs or "thoughts" until those thoughts become violent actions. It symbolizes and protects the values of society. Because hate crimes have a more severe impact on society and the victim, they should be punished more severely. Enhancement penalties were not invented with the advent of hate-crime laws; they have been around for years (for instance, the law more severely punishes violence against children, the president, and police officers). People who commit hate crimes are less concerned about whom they attack than what class the victim represents. Hate crime is a form of terrorism. It represents violence not against one victim but against an entire class of people. Hate crimes are perpetrated to send a message. Gays seek equal rights, not special rights.

Opposing arguments were just as interesting and compelling: All violent crimes are hateful. Hate-crime laws have the potential to infringe on the First Amendment guarantee of free speech. Hate-crime statutes work by elevating the punishment, but in a capital case, such as murder, there is no room to elevate it any higher. Criminals should be punished for their deeds, not for their thoughts. It would be naive to imagine that a hate-crime law could protect a Matthew Shepard any better than the laws already in place. So far, Attorney General Janet Reno, who advocated expanding the law, had yet to cite a single example of a case where federal intervention would have been necessary because local and state authorities decided not to prosecute. Hate laws are great for making privilege legitimate, commanding conformity, and legislating political correctness. In enforcing hate-speech and hate-crime laws, who defines "hate"? When people are committing a crime, they are not going to be deterred by a hate-crime law; the death penalty does not even deter murder. Hate-crime laws are simply "feel-good fluff."

If the wisdom or folly of having or expanding hate-crime legislation aroused debate and passion among liberals and conservatives, then so did the role of the news media in the Shepard case and its aftermath. Media coverage began on the day after the discovery of the beaten victim when the Albany County Sheriff's Office called a small press conference. On hand were representatives from the Associated Press (AP) and the Wyoming and Colorado media, two friends of young Shepard, and Bob Beck, director of Wyoming Public Radio. After giving basic information, Sheriff Puls, under questioning, indicated that the victim may have been beaten because he was gay and that he had been found tied to a fence like a scarecrow.

The sheriff was asked to explain exactly what the scarecrow reference meant. The radio director believed everyone present got the impression of "being tied up spread-eagled, splayed out." After all, the biker who found Shepard had said that he at first thought the victim was a scarecrow flopped on the ground, maybe some kind of Halloween joke staged a few weeks early. The idea that Shepard had been strung up in a manner akin to a crucifixion became the starting point for the reporting and reaction that followed. The initial reporting was never corrected, Beck said.

Shepard's friends at the press conference further alerted the media to the story and gave statements. One friend unhesitatingly seized on the attack as a political opportunity, linking the assault to the Wyoming legislature's refusal to pass a hate-crime bill. The day after the press conference, media interest increased exponentially.

On Friday afternoon when those involved in the crime appeared in court for the first time, it was "wall-to-wall cameras" in a small room in the court-house basement. The reading of the charges had to be delayed while everyone moved upstairs to the much larger district court.

On Saturday, Beck tried to do his reporting job while juggling requests for interviews. He felt a growing frustration about the sloppiness he saw around him. Part of the problem was that the news media did not have all the infor-mation they needed. At first, the sheriff was very up front, but then "nobody's talking," Beck declared. City officials, unprepared for the media onslaught and angry that Laramie was being depicted in some reports as a hate-crime capital, began to restrict access. The media, especially the tabloids, needed to turn things around quickly, but on being stonewalled by the city and many of its residents, they began to conduct interviews in bars.

Beck found that many reporters were critical of Laramie for not having a head trauma unit, not having gay bars, not pushing back homecoming. He found the tone of the questioning hostile. He considered it an example of pack journalism. The lead investigator in the case held a press conference early on, but he found that it made little difference. As time wore on, the court limited press access. Assessing the performance of Wyoming Public Radio, Beck said, "I'm not saying we didn't make mistakes, because we prob-ably did. But I finally got so weary of it I said, 'if we can't confirm it ourselves, we don't go with it.' It was just too wild."[16]

The first stories published contained reporter or source errors. On October 10, 1998, *The Gazette* of Montreal published a brief story, attributed to the AP and Reuters, that contained three errors: It listed Shepard's age as 22 and told of two passersby discovering his body and three U.W. students being arrested. (Shepard's age was 21, a lone cyclist found him, and only one U.W. student was arrested.) Many early stories mentioned burns on Shepard's body, but after two or three weeks, no references to burns appeared anywhere. Perhaps the most serious error was the statement or suggestion that Shepard was tied spread-eagled to a post.[17]

Editorialists offered diverse and conflicting opinions within days of the first news stories. The *New York Times* argued that Shepard's death made clear the need for hate-crime laws. The *San Francisco Chronicle* editorialized that because hate crimes against gays were very much a reality, Congress and state legislatures "in Shepard's name" needed to quickly expand hate-crime laws to include sexual orientation. In the view of the *San Diego Union-Tribune,* hate-crime legislation acts as a practical deterrent and sends its own message to society, one that is eloquently clear: "Hate, when it becomes violence, will not be tolerated."

But pushing for tougher hate-crime legislation, the *Washington Post* found, was a misguided effort because murder laws already are "amply tough to punish a sadistic murder committed for whatever reason." The *Seattle Times* warned of "serious constitutional issues to be considered" because the criminal act itself must be punished, not mere thought. In the view of the *Houston Chronicle,* "no law can prevent those who hate from committing crimes against those whose skin color and/or sexual preference is different from their own." Swift prosecution and severe sentences for all crimes of violence, the *Boston Herald* contended, "will do more to deter hate crimes than statutes that try to calibrate penalties according to motive."

The day after Shepard's death, a reporter for the *Caspar Star-Tribune* announced his homosexuality in a column and confirmed it by saying, "Matt was very short and hard to hug." He was soon interviewed on NBC and MSNBC and quoted in the *New York Times.* An October 15 editorial cartoon by Herblock elicited harsh criticism from a fellow editorial board member of the *Washington Post,* in turn prompting the cartoonist to defend his work passionately in a letter to the editor. The cartoon depicted a woman standing next to the Matthew Shepard headstone, facing Trent Lott and a man holding a ledger marked "Christian Politics" and asking, "Would you explain again how a young man like this might have cured himself of his 'sin'?"

Gannett White House correspondent Deborah Mathis and her syndicate received more than 10,000 calls in one day protesting a column in which she criticized the "anti-homosexual crowd" for complicity in Shepard's murder. James Dobson, Focus on the Family founder and president, mentioned the Mathis piece on his radio show, gave out phone numbers, and precipitated the avalanche of calls, many from places where the column never appeared. None of more than 100 client newspapers registered a single negative comment with the syndicate.[18]

The news media came under severe criticism after October 22, 1999, when the *Washington Times* told of the grim murder of a 13-year-old boy under this headline: "Media tune out torture death of Arkansas boy: Homosexuals charged with rape, murder." The AP, prodded by the *Times* story, did not assign or move the story on the national wire until 33 days after the death. The AP story said that, according to police, two men blindfolded, gagged, repeatedly raped, and sodomized Jesse Dirkhising with various objects before he suffocated to death. Critics said the story omitted a lot of horrifying details. The belated *Times* and AP reports did not trigger a rush of catch-up stories, but they did ignite a firestorm of media criticism, especially on Web sites.

Several complaints echoed repeatedly: The liberal media practice a double standard. The Shepard case got hyped for political reasons—to build support for inclusion of homosexuals in a federal hate-crime law. The Dirkhising case got ignored also for political reasons—squeamishness about publicizing something that could further anti-gay prejudice.

The complaints perplexed media defenders who classified the Shepard murder as a hate crime and the Dirkhising killing as a sex crime. On November 14, 1999, the *Washington Post* ombudsman argued that the Shepard murder was news because it prompted debate on hate crimes and because of the degree to which there is still intolerance of gay people in this country—it was much more than a murder story. The Dirkhising murder was a routine story reported as a news brief on October 30. The *Post*'s crime-news policy calls for not covering murders beyond the Washington area unless it was a mass murder or one that has caused a large local sensation or "has raised a larger social issue." The Shepard and Byrd murders were "a special kind of killing" that told a segment of society that its physical safety is at risk. These crimes sparked public expressions of outrage that themselves became news, the ombudsman said.

"Some of the gay-baiting right's argument about media bias holds up," Andrew Sullivan, a gay spokesman, declared. He faulted the *Boston Globe,* the *New York Times,* and the *Los Angeles Times* for ignoring the Dirkhising murder completely. Had that killing been covered instantly and with the same attention to gruesome detail as the Shepard murder, wouldn't it, too, have prompted a national conversation? he asked.[19]

The death of Matthew Shepard gave a face to the hate-crime movement and galvanized gays everywhere, but it also galvanized those who denounce homosexuality. Shepard—and Byrd—sparked debate and soul-searching and presumably created a better-informed public.

On June 20, 2000, the U.S. Senate voted 57 to 42 to expand the 1968 federal hate-crime statute involving religion, national origin, and race to include new categories specifically related to offenses motivated by sexual orientation, disability, or gender. Thirteen Republicans joined with 44 Democrats to help pass the measure cosponsored by Democrat Edward Kennedy and Republican Gordon Smith. Because the Supreme Court tends to severely limit congressional power to pass laws on subjects normally a state responsibility, the expanded measure requires that the crime involve some interstate connection and that states get the first chance to prosecute. House Republican leaders said that they would not schedule a vote on the issue and that state laws suffice.

The next year, with a new Congress and a new president in place, Kennedy and Gordon renewed their hate-crime expansion efforts. Indications were that the House Republican leadership and the Bush White House would contend that existing laws are adequate.[20]

Twenty-six states and the District of Columbia have hate-crime laws that include sexual orientation, 18 have hate-crime laws that do not explicitly include sexual orientation, and five have no hate-crime laws at all: Arkansas, Indiana, New Mexico, South Carolina—and Wyoming.[21]

NOTES

1. Melanie Thernstrom, "The Crucifixion of Matthew Shepard," *Vanity Fair,* March 1999, 209–14, 267–75, and JoAnn Wypijewski, "A Boy's Life," *Harper's,* September 1999, 61–74.

2. Information about the crime, the backgrounds of the killers, the trial, and related happenings is taken largely from the Denver dailies; Thernstrom, "The Crucifixion of Matthew Shepard"; Wypijewski, "A Boy's Life"; and Beth Loffredo, *Losing
Matt Shepard: Life and Politics in the Aftermath of Anti-Gay Murder* (New York:
Columbia University Press, 2000).

3. *Washington Post,* 10 October 1998.

4. *Denver Post,* 15 October 1998.

5. *New York Times,* 12 October 1998.

6. *Denver Post,* 10 October 1998; *Washington Post,* October 10, 1998.

7. *Denver Post,* 9, 10 October 1998; *New York Times,* 10 October 1998.

8. *Rocky Mountain News,* 11 October 1998.

9. *Denver Post,* 13 October 1998.

10. Ibid., 14 October 1998.

11. Ibid., 17 October 1998.

12. *New York Times,* 21 October 1998.

13. *Rocky Mountain News,* 14 December 1998.

14. Ibid., 7 April 1999.

15. *Los Angeles Times,* 14 September 1999.

16. Loffredo, *Losing Matt Shepard,* 4–6.

17. *Editor & Publisher,* 24 October 1998, 9; 31 October 1998, 8–9.

18. Ibid., 24 October 1998, 9.

19. *New Republic,* 2 April 2001, 8.

20. *Houston Chronicle,* 21 June 2000, 28 March 2001; *Hartford Courant,* 28 June
2000.

21. Human Rights Campaign, http://hrc.org, 28 August 2001.

THE SUMMATION

Ladies and gentlemen of the jury, as mentioned at the beginning of these proceedings, a trial is the stuff of news, rich in drama. Without question, the stakes are high, often life or death. I tell you now, it is no overstatement that some trials—those you have just read about—contain the elements of a Shakespearean play.

As you have surmised from the 10 exhibits put forth, a jury renders a legal judgment, but the larger court of public opinion determines the final verdict in terms of the social and historical significance of the crime, the trial, and the accused. This proved true for those poor souls in Salem Village so many years ago; it is true for those who murdered the young, innocent Matthew Shepard 207 years later.

Previous juries already have spoken. Their call was to assign guilt or innocence to the accused. That is not your charge, nor is it the reason you are reading this. The task before you is far more onerous. Yours is to assign guilt or innocence to the public and, not incidentally, to history. Historians such as our 10 authors attempt to explain the context of a period so that you, the reader, can better understand the actions of those who constructed our past. Nevertheless, even as historians unravel past events and interpret them through modern lenses, it ultimately falls to you to determine what it all means. The defense and prosecution have spoken in historical terms. Their jobs are finished. Now yours begins. I ask you to decide what that evidence means. That is your charge, one that should not, and cannot, be taken lightly. Do not forget, even for a moment, that justice, unlike truth, is but an elusive shadow.

Through the wonder of linear communication and with the blessings of Johann Gutenberg, you have revisited 10 tragic events. Perhaps some were crimes. Perhaps not. Perhaps some were important. Perhaps not. That is for you to decide.

For we now have reached the crux of our proceedings. The facts have been laid forth, but what do they mean? Our historians (and litigators perhaps?) have presented the evidence and in each case have explained its significance as they see it. If I may be so bold, allow me to summarize their findings.

Without question, the Salem Witch Trials were like a modern-day train wreck. We stop and look, shake our head with chagrin even while something in us is drawn to the destruction, then we turn our heads away and wonder why something like that happens. Ultimately, the witch hysteria was born of fear, nourished by a skewed belief system, and died when enough people questioned that system. It completed the break between the Church and magic,[1] and it can be argued—although perhaps a stretch—that the witch hysteria in Salem marks the beginning of the end of the vise-like grip religion held on everyday colonial life. What it did impact, however, was the degree to which the clergy and the Church influenced public opinion. From a legal standpoint—which certainly provides commentary on social conditions—the trials, to whatever degree, helped further the concept of fairness in legal proceedings, a point worth noting throughout eighteenth-century America on the colonies' journey toward independence and the creation of its own unique system of governance.

The timing of the *Amistad*'s arrival could not have been better. Although the *Amistad* mutiny case did not strike an overwhelming blow against the institution of slavery, it played a pivotal role in determining the direction the country would take in shaping its basic doctrines regarding freedom. The case raised numerous questions regarding slavery and racial prejudice and their relevance in determining nineteenth-century liberties—questions that politicians, journalists, and the American public had avoided discussing for years. By forcing the key issues to the forefront of the antislavery struggle, abolitionists compelled leaders to stop evading the situation.

Not only did the case incite interest in whether a human being could be declared property, it also permitted the abolitionists to demonstrate that the Africans could be both intelligent and civilized. The *Amistad* mutiny case thrust the issues of slavery and racial equality into the public arena, providing a legal and political platform to discuss the morality of slavery and the momentum to nudge the country closer to a solution.

America generally viewed Indians as mostly wild and barbarous heathens. The only way to make an Indian "safe" was to make him like a white man— and a Christian as well. The Sioux uprising affected the American psyche in several ways, all negative for the Indians. All Indians, but particularly the Sioux, were seen as bloodthirsty, savage, brutal enemies never to be trusted. The frontier was a dangerous place where constant vigilance was necessary.

Any brutality toward Indians was justified. Any guilt about taking Indians' lives was assuaged following the brutality against whites in the uprisings.

Fact of life in the early twentieth century: Capitalism is the greatest mechanism founded by human beings to produce great wealth. It is also an accepted fact in society's lower strata that working people are not enjoying the benefit of such capital accumulation. As a consequence, a virtual kaleidoscope of remedies were being offered to correct the imbalance, any one of which would have upset the best-laid plans and desires of those who occupied the country's boardrooms. Of all the characters who threatened the system, "Big Bill" Haywood and the miners represented the greatest threat. They publicly disavowed the benefits of capitalism and turned their efforts to destroying the system, intent on replacing it with a nonprofit communal society. Many at the top rung of the social ladder wanted Haywood out of the way. What better way than a capital offense and a murder trial?

The Ed Johnson lynching was but one of a series of beatings, mutilations, and lynchings in the United States in the last years of the nineteenth century and through the mid-twentieth. In most cases, local citizens, and often local law officials, refused to recognize the importance or the relevance of constitutionally guaranteed protections for the accused. The U.S. Supreme Court under Chief Justice Earl Warren, acting in the late 1950s and 1960s, finally made firm and clear in decisions like the 1966 *Miranda* decision that if states and state officials would not protect the rights of an individual, then the federal courts would. Ed Johnson's death, the apparent complicity of Sheriff Joseph Shipp, and the resulting Supreme Court contempt ruling set a precedent that echoes down through the years. People accused of crimes have a right to a fair trial, and, importantly, law officers have an obligation to protect that right as well as an obligation to ensure the physical safety of the accused.

In 1920 Detroit, blacks reaffirmed what they already suspected: They were unwelcome in white neighborhoods. When they did purchase homes in those areas, they risked their lives. Their eviction from white sections contradicted the intent of the framers of the Constitution, who affirmed John Locke's view that nature endowed every human being with natural rights to life, to liberty, and to property. The abolition of slavery, on paper, elevated the black man to the same level of human dignity as other American citizens. Segregation was a counterbalance to that. The Sweet trial raised that issue and at the same time marked a place for itself in the black struggle for civil rights.

The seven-year legal ordeal and execution of alien Italian anarchists Nicola Sacco and Bartolomeo Vanzetti in the 1920s created an international cause célèbre that put American justice and its legal system on trial. Were they guilty of armed robbery and murder? Or were they judicially railroaded into the electric chair for their radicalism during an anti-immigrant season of cultural nativism and paranoia? Their case became an international rallying point for a disparate array of artists, agitators, intellectuals, journalists, and radicals and a dizzying array of ideologies and sentimentalities. Their execution became a focal point for their disillusionment and a moment of cultural despair in twentieth-century America.

The Clay Shaw trial was a kind of gateway to postmodernism where nothing was real, nothing was true, and nothing meant anything. Kennedy embodied hope for America's future. Young, good-looking, vital, well married, and progressive, he carried on his shoulders a kind of utopic burden. With Kennedy, many could see a shining future. Dallas not only ended all that but also crushed it cruelly. While not everyone was decimated by the loss of Kennedy as president, many Kennedy foes were shaken by the assassination. Then, of course, Jack Ruby took away whatever solace or sense of justice or satisfaction people might have had from seeing Lee Harvey Oswald tried and ostensibly convicted of extinguishing the bright and shining light.

The Shaw trial was all they had left—the only shot anyone would ever have at making someone accountable for the horrible act. But by then times had changed drastically. The Summer of Love ended badly. Bobby Kennedy and Martin Luther King, Jr. were freshly dead. Most dreams of Camelot only made people incredulous that they had once thought it possible. By then, most people appeared to believe that Oswald did not kill Kennedy or did not kill Kennedy alone, but it is not clear that most people had any real conviction that Jim Garrison would conclusively solve the murder. But the assassination had created television as a powerful news medium, and the trial was one of the first real spectacles of the television age and part of its significance.

Part of the spectacle was the creating of celebrity, which it did for Jim Garrison, who started the investigation as a popular parish attorney and ended it as a worldwide figure of some notoriety, if not note. But even more than that, the trial helped create a self-sustaining aura of suspicion, mistrust, and deceit surrounding the federal government. People harbored various conspiratorial theories and ideas that involved the government before Garrison became known, and Garrison's own almost paranoid theories and ideas fed voraciously into that. Once this door opened, it never shut, and, in fact, as more records become available and more people write about what they believe to be true, Garrison's conspiratorial paranoia escalates exponentially (as witnessed by hundreds or even thousands of books, articles, Web sites, and other media offerings). So many people have so much invested in so many different scenarios, all claiming to have ample supporting evidence, that "truth" appears not to have much meaning.

By the time Manuel Noriega was convicted in July 1992, other events, such as the fall of the Soviet Union and celebrity sex trials, eclipsed the court proceedings for the short, pock-faced, military dictator from a Central American country. But the social significance of the Noriega trial remains the subject of legal speculation. Did the United States have a right to bring a foreign head of state to justice? Should Noriega be a prisoner of war, as he remains? Were Noriega's rights violated when his telephone calls to his attorneys were recorded? And, most important, was it worth the loss of American lives and the expenditure of millions of dollars to keep Noriega in the federal prison system until at least 2007?

Discovering the motivating factors for the Noriega trial may provide its social significance. Is American justice sometimes defined by what makes for good government policy at the time? Was this trial an attempt to justify the loss of 23 American lives in a questionable military action? Was it an attempt to conceal an agreement just short of criminal in order to catch criminals? Is the social significance as simple as this: Can Americans trust what the government does in the name of national interests, and can they trust what the government says about its actions and motives in such situations? Finally, and no less important, can Americans put faith in a news media system that fails to articulate these questions?

The brutal murder of Matthew Shepard precipitated worldwide publicity and debate about justice, tolerance, and the concept of hate crimes. The clamor was especially intense in the United States as city councils, legislatures, and Congress pondered whether crimes perpetrated against gays and lesbians should carry stiffer penalties than the same crimes directed against society in general. Strong, compelling arguments were made on both sides, and the discussions, even when they did not bring about change, at least precipitated thinking and the dissemination of fact and opinion.

The Shepard murder and its aftermath required almost everyone to defend traditional positions or to argue for the acceptance of new concepts and attitudes in the case of homosexuals. Many of the major forces in American society were caught up in the debate, especially the church, law enforcement, the justice system, government, and the news media. The case caught the public's imagination, stirred emotions, and galvanized gay and antigay forces throughout the country. Neither side won the debate or effected dramatic change, but the indications are that the Shepard case allowed homosexuals to gain more public sympathy and to make slight advances in their campaign for acceptance and protection.

So, ladies and gentlemen of the jury, these are the finding of our 10 litigators. Their conclusions, of course, represent their declaration of truth and are not an attempt to trespass on your judicial soil. Any pronouncements in that regard fall on you. You have witnessed witchcraft, religion, slavery, and socialism. You have been presented a racist America, a capitalistic America, and an anarchist America. You have seen murder, deceit, ignorance, and avarice covering a time span of 207 years.

Ten trials. That we know. But—and here's the rub—how many crimes were committed? And who committed them? An unfinished mural has been placed before you. On it you see many faces—John Proctor and Abigail Williams, Sengbe Pieh and Lewis Tappan, Ed Johnson and Nevada Taylor and Joseph Shipp, Frank Steunenberg and John Haywood, Ossian and Henry Sweet, Nicola Sacco and Bartolomeo Vanzetti, Clay Shaw and Jim Garrison, Manuel Noriega and Frank Rubino, Mathew Shepard and Aaron McKinney and Russell Henderson. You see the Coeur d'Alene, the Ku Klux Klan, the Waterworks Improvement Association, the University of Wyoming, the towns of Salem, Caldwell, Detroit, Chattanooga, and Laramie. Also there, muted, painted in indistinct, hushed tones, are those you judge: ethereal entities that come in and out of focus but whose power on everyone and every place in the mural is undeniable. They are public opinion and its sister(s), the mass media.

It is for you to bring the mural into focus by determining what the evidence means. Sift through the cavalcade of facts, plethora of opinions, and ubiquitous media reports to determine the guilt the public and, not incidentally, the mass media should bear in these events. Moreover, please consider this: Your decision is much more than an academic exercise. It is a historical pronouncement. History, as I suspect you already know, is without guilt or innocence. Those who create it are not so fortunate.

Take your time. We patiently await your verdict.

Lloyd Chiasson Jr.
with the assistance of the contributors

NOTE

1. Hans Sebald, *Witch-Children, from Salem Witch-Hunts to Modern Courtrooms* (Amherst, N.Y.: Prometheus Books, 1995), 68.

BIBLIOGRAPHY

Albert, Steve. *The Case against the General: Manuel Noriega and the Politics of American Justice*. New York: Macmillan, 1993.

Anderson, Gary C. *Little Crow: Spokesman for the Sioux*. St. Paul: Minnesota Historical Society Press, 1986.

Anderson, Gary C., and Alan R. Woolworth, eds. *Through Dakota Eyes: Narrative Accounts of the Minnesota Indian War of 1862*. St. Paul: Minnesota Historical Society Press, 1988.

Anderson, Maxwell. *Four Verse Plays*. New York: Harcourt Brace & World, 1959.

Andrews, Eliza Frances. *Journal of a Georgia Woman, 1870–1872*, edited by S. Kittrell Rushing. Knoxville: University of Tennessee Press, 2002.

Appeal to Reason.

Atlanta Journal and Constitution.

Avrich, Paul. *Sacco and Vanzetti: The Anarchist Background*. Princeton, N.J.: Princeton University Press, 1991.

Babcock, Willoughby M. "Minnesota's Indian War," *Minnesota History* 38, no. 3 (September 1962).

Barber, John W. A History of the Amistad Captives. New Haven, Conn.: E. L. and J. W. Barber, 1840.

Baton Rouge State-Times.

Bernhard, Virginia, Betty Brandon, Elizabeth Fox-Genovese, and Theda Perdue, eds. *Southern Women: Histories and Identities*. Columbia: University of Missouri Press, 1992.

Best, Joel, David G. Bromley, and James T. Richardson, eds. *The Satanism Scare*. New York: Aldine de Gruyter, 1991.

Blegen, Theodore C. *Lincoln's Secretary Goes West: Two Reports by John G. Nicolay on Frontier Indian Troubles 1862*. La Crosse, Wis.: Sumac Press, 1965.

Boston Evening Transcript.

Boston Globe.

Boston Herald.

Boyer, Paul, and Stephen Nissenbaum. *Salem Possessed: The Social Origins of Witchcraft.* Cambridge, Mass.: Harvard University Press, 1974.

Boyer, Paul, and Stephen Nissenbaum, eds. *The Salem Witchcraft Papers.* New York: Da Capo Press, 1977.

Brewer, George D. *The Fighting Editor or Warren and the* Appeal. Girard, Kans.: Author, 1910.

Bryant, Charles S. *A History of the Great Massacre by the Sioux Indians in Minnesota, Including the Personal Narratives of Many Who Escaped.* Cincinnati: Rickey & Carroll, 1864.

Buckley, Kevin. *Panama: The Whole Story.* New York: Simon and Schuster, 1991.

Buhle, Paul M. "The *Appeal to Reason* and *The New Appeal.*" In *The American Radical Press,* ed. Joseph R. Conlin. Vol. 1.. Westport, Conn.: Greenwood Press, 1974.

Burr, George Lincoln, ed. *Narratives of the Witchcraft Cases 1649–1706.* New York: Charles Scribner's Sons, 1914.

Cable, Mary. *Black Odyssey: The Case of the Slave Ship Amistad.* New York: Penguin Books, 1977.

Cantril, Hadley. *The Invasion from Mars: A Study in the Psychology of Panic.* Princeton, N.J.: Princeton University Press, 1940.

Caporael, Linnda. "Ergotism: The Satan Loosed in Salem?" *Science* 192, no. 4234 (2 April 1976).

Carlebach, Michael L. *American Photojournalism Comes of Age.* Washington, D.C.: Smithsonian Institution Press, 1997.

Carley, Kenneth. *The Sioux Uprising of 1862.* St. Paul: Minnesota Historical Society Press, 1976.

———, ed. "Chief Big Eagle's Story." *Minnesota History* 38, no. 3 (September 1862).

Charleston Courier.

Chattanooga Daily Times.

Chattanooga News.

Chiasson, Lloyd, Jr. *The Press in Times of Crisis.* Westport, Conn.: Greenwood Press, 1995.

Christian Science Monitor.

Clodfelter, Michael. *The Dakota War: The United States Army versus the Sioux, 1862–1865.* Jefferson, N.C.: McFarland & Company, 1998.

Conlin, Joseph R., ed. *The American Radical Press.* Vol. 1. Westport, Conn.: Greenwood Press, 1974.

Coward, John M. *The Newspaper Indian: Native American Identity in the Press, 1820–1890.* Urbana: University of Illinois Press, 1999.

CrimeLibrary.com/Sacco/Saccomain.htm.

Curriden, Mark, and Leroy Phillips, Jr. *Contempt of Court: The Turn-of-the-Century Lynching That Launched a Hundred Years of Federalism.* New York: Faber and Faber, 1999.

Darrow, Clarence. *The Story of My Life.* New York: Charles Scribner's Sons, 1932.

Davey, William. *Let Justice Be Done.* Reston, Va.: Jordan Publishing, 1999.

Davis, John H., *Mafia Kingfish: Carlos Marcello and the Assassination of John F. Kennedy.* Ontario: Signet/Penguin Books, 1989.

Denver Post.

Detroit News.

Doppelt, Jack. "No Longer News: The Trial of the Century That Wasn't." *ABA Journal,* (January 1993): 56–59.

Dos Passos, John. *The Big Money.* New York: New American Library, 1969.

Dos Passos, John. *Facing the Chair: Story of the Americanization of Two Foreignborn Workmen.* Boston: Sacco-Vanzetti Defense Committee, 1927. Reprint, New York: Da Capo Press, 1970.

Drake, Samuel G. *Annuals of Witchcraft in New England.* New York: Benjamin Blom, 1869.

Editor & Publisher.

Edwards, Laura F. *Gendered Strife and Reconstruction: The Political Culture of Reconstruction.* Urbana: University of Illinois Press, 1997.

———. *Scarlett Doesn't Live Here Anymore: Southern Women in the Civil War Era.* Urbana: University of Illinois Press, 2000.

Ehrmann, Herbert B. *The Case That Will Not Die: Commonwealth vs. Sacco and Vanzetti.* Boston: Little, Brown, 1969.

———. *The Untried Case: The Sacco-Vanzetti Case and the Morelli Gang.* New York: Vanguard Press, 1933.

Eisenstein, Elizabeth. *The Printing Revolution in Early Modern Europe.* New York: Cambridge University Press, 1983.

Ellis, Richard N. *General Pope and U.S. Indian Policy.* Albuquerque: University of New Mexico Press, 1970.

Emancipator.

Epstein, Edward Jay. *Between Fact and Fiction: The Problem of Journalism.* New York: Vintage Books, 1975.

———. *Counterplot.* New York: Viking Press, 1969.

———. "Epitaph for Jim Garrison: Romancing the Assassination." *The New Yorker,* 30 November 1992.

———. http://edwardjayepstein.com/archived/garrison2htm.

Famous American Trials. http://www.law.umkc.edu/faculty.

Feinberg, Matilda. "Clarence Darrow at His Best." *Chicago Law Record* 41 (1960): 460–66.

Fleming, Thomas J. "Take Hatred Away and You Have Nothing Left." *American Heritage* 20 (December 1968): 74–80.

Folwell, William W. *A History of Minnesota.* Vol. 2. St. Paul: Minnesota Historical Society Press, 1924.

Foner, Philip. *History of the Labor Movement in the United States.* Vol. 2. New York: International Publishers, 1975.

Frankfurter, Felix. *The Case of Sacco and Vanzetti: A Critical Analysis for Lawyers and Laymen.* Boston: Little, Brown, 1927.

Friedman, Josh Alan. "Jack Ruby: Dallas' Original J.R." at http://www.wfmu.org/LCD/20/ruby.html.

Garrison interview. *Playboy,* October 1967.

Garrison, Jim. *On the Trail of Assassins.* New York: Warner Books, 1988.

Ghent, W. J. *The* Appeal *and Its Influence in the Charity Organization Society.* New York, 1 April 1911.

Graham, John. *Yours for the Revolution: The* Appeal *to Reason, 1985–1922.* Lincoln: University of Nebraska Press, 1990.

Gramling, Oliver. *AP—The Story of News*. New York: Farrar and Rinehart, 1940.

Grosjean v. American Press Co. 297 U.S. 233 (1936).

Hale, John. "A Modest Inquiry." In *Narratives of the Witchcraft Cases 1648–1706,* ed. George Lincoln Burr. New York: Charles Scribner's Sons, 1914.

Hammer, Joshua. "The "Gay Panic" Defense." *Newsweek,* 8 November 1999.

Harris, David. *Shooting the Moon: The True Story of an American Manhunt Unlike Any Other, Ever*. New York: Little, Brown, 2001.

Hawthorne, Nathaniel. *House of Seven Gables*. Cambridge, Mass: Houghton Mifflin, 1924.

Hays, Arthur G. *Let Freedom Ring*. New York: Horace Liveright, 1928.

Haywood, William D. *Bill Haywood's Book*. New York: International Publishers, 1929.

Heard, Isaac V. D. *History of the Sioux War and Massacres of 1862 and 1863*. New York: Harper and Bros., 1863.

Herald of Freedom.

Holland, Max. "The Power of Disinformation: The Lie That Linked CIA to the Kennedy Assassination." *Studies in Intelligence,* no. 11 (fall–winter 2001). On-line at http://www.jfkassassination.net/sii.htm.

http://amistad.mysticseaport.org.

http://amistad.mysticseaport.org/library/court.

http://projects/ftrials/SaccoV/SaccoV.htm.

http://www.law.umkc.edu/faculty/projects/ftrial/amistad/AMI_LTR.HTM.

Hutchinson, Thomas. *The History of the Colony and Province of Massachusetts-Bay (1764)*. Edited by Laurence Shaw Mayo. Cambridge, Mass.: Harvard University Press, 1936.

Il Proletario.

In Re Slaughter-House Cases. 83 U.S. 36 (1872).

Independent Commission of Inquiry on the U.S. Invasion of Panama. *The U.S. Invasion of Panama: The Truth behind Operation "Just Cause."* Boston: South End Press, 1991.

Industrial Union Bulletin.

Jackson, Brian. *The Black Flag: A Look at the Strange Case of Nicola Sacco and Bartolemeo Vanzetti*. Boston: Routledge & Kegan Paul, 1981.

Jaffe, Carolyn. "The Press and the Oppressed—A Study of Prejudiced News Reporting in Criminal Cases: The Problem, Existing Solutions and Remaining Doubts." *Journal of Criminology and Political Science* (March 1965).

James, Rosemary, and Jack Wardlaw. *Plot or Politics?* New Orleans: Pelican Press, 1967.

Janesville Daily Gazette.

Jensen, Richard J. *Clarence Darrow: The Creation of an American Myth*. New York: Greenwood Press, 1992.

Joint Committee on the Conduct of War. "Report of Maj. General John Pope." *Supplemental Report of the Joint Committee on the Conduct of War*. Washington, D.C.: Government Printing Office, vol. 2, 1865.

Jones, Howard. *Mutiny on the Amistad*. New York: Oxford University Press, 1839.

Jones, Robert H. *The Civil War in the Northwest*. Norman: University of Oklahoma Press, 1960.

Justice.

Kempe, Frederick. *Divorcing the Dictator: America's Bungled Affair with Noriega*. New York: G. P. Putnam and Sons, 1990.

Kim, Richard. "The Truth about Hate Crimes Laws." *The Nation*, 12 July 1999.

Kirkwood, James. *American Grotesque*. New York: Simon and Schuster, 1970.

Kretch, Joseph W. *Clarence Darrow, Attorney for the Damned*. Charlotteville, N.Y.: SanHar Press, 1972.

Lacayo, Richard. "The New Gay Struggle." *Time*, 26 October 1998.

Lambert, Patricia. *False Witness*. New York: M. Evans and Company, 1998.

Leo, John. "Not Fit to Print." *U.S. News & World Report*, 16 April 2000.

Loffredo, Beth. *Losing Matt Shepard: Life and Politics in the Aftermath of Anti-Gay Murder*. New York: Columbia University Press, 2000.

Lopez, Steve. "To Be Young and Gay in Wyoming." *Time*, 26 October 1998.

Los Angeles Times.

Lukas, J. Anthony. *Big Trouble*. New York: Touchstone Books–Simon and Schuster, 1997.

Marbury v. Madison. 5 U.S. 137 (1803).

Martin, B. Edward. *All We Want Is Make Us Free: La Amistad and the Reform Abolitionists*. Lanham, Md.: University Press of America, 1986.

Mather, Cotton. *Memorable Providences Relating to Witchcrafts and Possessions*. Boston, 1689.

Mather, Increase. *Cases of Conscience Concerning evil Spirits personating Man, Witchcrafts, infallible Proofs of Guilt in such as are accused with that Crime, All Considered according to the Scriptures, History, Experience, and the Judgment of many Learned men*. Boston, 1692.

Mayo, Lawrence Shaw, ed. *The History of the Colony and Province of Massachusetts-Bay (1764)*. Vol. 2 Cambridge, Mass.: Harvard University Press, 1936.

McClure's.

McCormack, Ross. "The Industrial Workers of the World in Western Canada, 1905–1914." In *Canadian Working Class History*, ed. Laurel Sefton MacDowell and Ian Radforth. Toronto: Canadian Scholars Press, 1992.

McKerns, Joseph P. "Descent into Hell: The Red Crisis." In *The Press in Times of Crisis*, ed. Lloyd Chiasson, Jr. Westport, Conn.: Greenwood Press, 1995.

Meyer, Roy W. *History of the Santee Sioux: United States Indian Policy on Trial*. Lincoln: University of Nebraska Press, 1980.

Milburn, George. "The *Appeal to Reason*." *American Mercury* 23 (1931).

Miller, Mark. "The Final Days and Nights of a Gay Martyr." *Newsweek*, 21 December 1998.

Minkowitz, Donna. "Love and Hate in Laramie." *The Nation*, 12 July 1999.

Minnesota in the Civil and Indian Wars, 1861–1865, vol. 2, *Official Reports and Correspondence*. St. Paul, Minnesota, 1893.

Montreal Gazette.

Morning Courier & New York Enquirer.

Morison, Samuel Eliot, Henry Steele Commager, and William E. Leuchtenburg. *Growth of the American Republic*. 6th ed. New York: Oxford University Press, 1969.

Mother Earth.

Munn v. State Of Illinois. 94 U.S. 113 (1876).

Murphy, Sharon. "American Indians and the Media: Neglect and Stereotype." *Journalism History* 6, no. 2: 39–44.

Near v. State of Minnesota Ex Rel. Olson. 283 U.S. 697 (1931).

New Haven Daily Herald.

New London Gazette.

New Orleans States-Item.

New Orleans Times Picayune.

New York Advertiser & Express.

New York American.

New York Colored American.

New York Commercial Advertiser.

New York Evening Post.

New York Evening Star.

New York Journal of Commerce.

New York Morning Herald.

New York Sun.

New York Times.

New York World.

Newsweek.

Nord, David Paul. "The *Appeal to Reason* and American Socialism, 1901–1920." *Kansas History* 1, no. 2 (1978).

Norfolk Beacon.

Noriega, Manuel, and Peter Eisner. *The Memoirs of Manuel Noriega: America's Prisoner.* New York: Random House, 1997.

O'Connor, Richard. *Heywood Broun: A Biography.* New York: G. P. Putnam's Sons, 1975.

Oehler, Charles M. *The Great Sioux Uprising.* New York: Oxford University Press, 1959.

Owens, William A. *Black Mutiny: A Revolt on the Schooner Amistad.* Baltimore: Black Classic Press, 1997.

Perrett, Geoffrey. *America in the Twenties: History.* New York: Simon and Schuster, 1982.

Phelan, James. "A Plot to Kill Kennedy? Rush to Judgment in New Orleans." *Saturday Evening Post,* 6 May 1967.

———. *Scandals, Scamps, Scoundrels: The Casebook of an Investigative Reporter.* New York: Random House, 1982.

Porter, Katherine Ann. "The Never-Ending Wrong." *The Atlantic,* June 1977.

Posner, Gerald. *Case Closed: Lee Harvey Oswald and the Assassination of JFK.* New York: Random House, 1993.

Quint, Howard H. "The Challenge and *Wilshire's Magazine.*" In *The American Radical Press,* ed. Joseph R. Conlin. Vol. 1. Westport, Conn.: Greenwood Press, 1974.

Reitzes, Dave. "Who Speaks for Clay Shaw." Four-part on-line series. http://mcadams.posc.mu.edu/shaw1.htm.

Richmond Enquirer.

Robinson, Doane. *A History of the Dakota or Sioux Indians.* Minneapolis: Ross & Haines, 1956.

Rocky Mountain News.

Rosenthal, Bernard. *Salem Story: Reading the Witch Trials of 1692.* New York: Cambridge University Press, 1993.

Rosmond, Babette. *Robert Benchley: His Life and Good Times.* Garden City, N.Y.: Doubleday, 1970.

Rovere, Richard. *Senator Joe McCarthy*. New York: Harper Colophon, 1959.

San Diego Union-Tribune.

San Francisco Chronicle.

Schultz, Duane. *Over the Earth I Come: The Great Sioux Uprising of 1862*. New York: St. Martin's Press, 1992.

Scott, Anne Firor. *Making the Invisible Woman Visible*. Chicago: University of Illinois Press, 1984.

Sears, D. O. "Black Invisibility: The Press and the L.A Riot." *American Journal of Sociology* 76 (1971): 698–72.

Seattle Times.

Sebald, Hans. *Witch-Children, from Salem Witch-Hunts to Modern Courtrooms*. Amherst, N.Y.: Prometheus Books, 1995.

Sentman, Mary Alice. "Black White Disparity in Coverage by *Life* Magazine from 1937–1972." *Journalism Quarterly* 61 (1983): 501–8.

Sewell, Samuel. *The Selling of Joseph, a Memorial*. Boston, 1700. Reprinted from an original in George H. Moore, *Notes on the History of Slavery in Massachusetts* (New York, 1866).

Shoaf, George H. *Fighting for Freedom*. Los Angeles: Simplified Economics, 1953.

Shore, Elliott. *Talkin' Socialism: J. A. Wayland and the Role of the Press in American Radicalism, 1890–1912*. Lawrence: University of Kansas Press, 1988.

Siegenthaler, John. *A Search for Justice*. Nashville: Aurora Publishers, 1971.

Silverman, Kenneth. *The Life and Times of Cotton Mather*. New York: Columbia University Press, 1985.

Sinclair, Upton. *Boston*. New York: Albert & Charles Boni, 1928.

———. *The Brass Check*. 9th ed. Long Beach, Calif.: Author, 1928.

Smith, Rex Alan. *The Moon of Popping Trees*. New York: Reader's Digest Press, 1975.

St. Louis Post-Dispatch.

St. Petersburg Times.

Starkey, Marion L. *The Devil in Massachusetts: A Modern Enquiry into the Salem Witch Trials*. New York: Knopf, 1949.

Stemple, G., III. "Visibility of Blacks in News and News-Picture Magazines." *Journalism Quarterly* 48 (1971): 337–39.

Stone, Irving. *Clarence Darrow for the Defense*. Garden City, N.Y.: Doubleday, 1941.

Stone, Melville. *Fifty Years as a Journalist*. Garden City, New York: Doubleday, Page, 1921.

Streisand, Betsy, et al. "A Death on the Prairie." *U.S. News & World Report,* 26 October 1998.

Sullivan, Andrew. "Murder in Wyoming: Did the Usual Suspects Kill Matthew Shepard?" *The American Spectator,* December 1998.

Sunday Times (London).

The Comrade.

The Economist. "The Misogyny, Ergot, or Envy? The Salem Witch-Trials." 16 May 1992.

The Evening Journal.

The Sacco-Vanzetti Project. http://www.saccovanzettiproject.org/pages/summary.html.

The Socialist.

Thernstrom, Melanie. "The Crucifixion of Matthew Shepard." *Vanity Fair,* March 1999.

Time.

Times (London).

Toronto Star.

Upham, Charles. *Salem Witchcraft, with an Account of Salem Village and A History of Opinions on Witchcraft and Kindred Subjects.* 1867. 2 vols. Reprint, Williamstown, Mass.: Corner House, 1971.

U.S. v. Shipp. 203 U.S. 563 (1906).

U.S. v. Shipp. 214 U.S. 386 (1909).

USA Today.

Wall, Joseph. *Iowa: A Bicentennial History.* New York: Norton, 1978.

Washington Post.

Washington Times.

Wayland, J. A. *Leaves of Life.* 1912. Reprint, Westport, Conn.: Hyperion Press, 1975.

Weinberg, Arthur, and Lila Weinberg. *Clarence: A Sentimental Rebel.* New York: Atheneum, 1987.

Weinberg, Kenneth G. *A Man's Home, a Man's Castle.* New York: McCall Publishing, 1971.

West, Nathaniel. *The Ancestry, Life, and Times of Henry Hastings Sibley.* St. Paul, Minn., 1889.

WFMU Web site. http://www.wfmu.org.

Williams, Roger M., and Michael Parks. "The Clay Shaw Trial: Reporter-Participants." *Columbia Journalism Review,* spring 1969, 38–41.

Wilshire's Magazine.

Woolf, Alan. "Witchcraft or Mycotoxin? The Salem Witch Trials." *Journal of Toxicology: Clinical Toxicology* 38, no. 4 (June 2000): 457–460.

Wypijewski, JoAnn. "A Boy's Life." *Harper's,* September 1999.

Young, William, and David E. Kaiser. *Postmortem: New Evidence in the Case of Sacco and Vanzetti.* Amherst: University of Massachusetts Press, 1985.

INDEX

ABOUT THE EDITOR AND CONTRIBUTORS

ELIJAH F. AKHAHENDA is associate professor of communication studies at St. Mary's University in San Antonio, Texas. A graduate of Wheaton College in Illinois and Southern Illinois University at Carbondale, he was formerly director of graduate communication studies at St. Mary's University and director of journalism at Southern University at New Orleans. He has published book chapters and articles on portrayal of minorities in the media as well as a chapter on the history of public relations in the United States in *Three Centuries of American Media*. His latest work on the bombing of the American embassy in Kenya and its implications for national unity for the country, *When Blood and Tears United a Country*, is forthcoming from University Press of America.

LLOYD CHIASSON JR., a former reporter with dailies in Vermont and Louisiana, is a professor in mass communication at Nicholls State University in Thibodaux, Louisiana. A journalism historian specializing in literary journalism and the role of the press in society, he received a master's degree from the University of Arizona and a doctorate from Southern Illinois University. Dr. Chiasson coauthored *Reporter's Notebook*, a journalism interactive computer textbook, and served as editor and coauthor of *The Press in Times of Crisis, The Press on Trial*, and *Three Centuries of American Media*. In 1999, Dr. Chiasson visited Latvia as a Fulbright scholar where he taught at the University of Latvia and Riga Stradina University.

ROBERT DARDENNE, a former reporter with daily newspapers in Louisiana, New York, and Mexico, holds a Ph.D. from the University of Iowa.

His professional and academic interests include news history, alternative reporting and writing approaches, the potential of narrative, community, and
diverse perspectives in reporting. At the University of South Florida in St.
Petersburg, he teaches media theory, contemporary news issues, mass media
and society, and a variety of reporting, writing, and other courses. He is
coauthor of *The Conversation of Journalism: Communication, Community
and News,* author of the monograph *A Free and Responsible Student Press,*
and author of several chapters and articles on various topics in journalism
history. Dardenne spent the 1999–2000 academic year as a Fulbright professor teaching journalism and in Shanghai and lecturing throughout China.
A longtime member of "Speak Up, Tampa Bay," a group that encourages
public dialogue and operates Hillsborough County public access television,
he is active locally in efforts to involve news media in community-building
projects.

ALFRED N. DELAHAYE is professor emeritus of journalism at Nicholls
State University. He worked as managing editor of the *Houma Courier* and
the *Terrebonne Press* before becoming director of publications and public
relations at Nicholls State University. In retirement, Dr. Delahaye has taught
reporting and technical writing classes, has authored a chapter on the Lind-
bergh kidnapping case in *The Press on Trial,* and is author of *Nicholls State
University: The Elkins-Galliano Years, 1948–1983,* the first of a two-part history of Nicholls State University.

NANCY MCKENZIE DUPONT is an associate professor and head of broadcast journalism in the Department of Communications at Loyola University
in New Orleans. After 17 years as a television news professional, Dr. Dupont
began teaching in 1993. She earned her master's degree at Loyola in 1994
and her doctorate at the University of Southern Mississippi in 1997. Dr.
Dupont's research interests are journalism history, international broadcast-
ing, and television news objectivity. She has published several book chapters
as well as articles in *Louisiana History* and the *Journal of Radio Studies* and
has presented numerous papers at national conferences, such as those for the
American Journalism Historians Association, the Association for Education
in Journalism and Mass Communication, the Southwest Education Council
for Journalism and Mass Communication, and the Popular Culture Association. She is also a regular contributor to the annual Symposium on the 19th
Century Press, the Civil War, and Free Expression.

ARTHUR J. KAUL is a professor of journalism and associate director of the
School of Mass Communication and Journalism at the University of Southern
Mississippi. He has published articles and essays on media history and ethics
and literary journalism in *American Journalism, Critical Studies in Mass
Communication, Journal of Mass Media Ethics,* and numerous books and has

edited a volume on post–World War II literary journalism for the *Dictionary of Literary Biography*.

JOSEPH P. MCKERNS is an associate professor of journalism at Ohio State University. He holds a Ph.D. from the University of Minnesota, an M.A. from Ohio State University, and an A.B. from the University of Notre Dame. He is the author of two texts and has written articles on the history of the American news media published in numerous scholarly journals. McKerns is a past president of the American Journalism Historians Association and past editor of *Journalism Monographs*.

KITTRELL RUSHING is head of the Department of Communication at the University of Tennessee at Chattanooga. His current research interests include media of the nineteenth century and the abolitionist press. He is editor of a diary of nineteenth-century writer and scholar Frances "Fanny" Andrews. He also authored a chapter on the Chicago Haymarket riot in the late nineteenth century for *The Press on Trial*.

DAVID R. SPENCER is a professor of journalism and media studies at the University of Western Ontario in London, Canada. His research interests include study of the late Victorian and early twentieth-century radical, reformist, agrarian, and trade union presses in both Canada and the United States. He is a past president of the American Journalism Historians Association and a past chair of the History Division of the Association for Education in Journalism and Mass Communications.

BERNELL E. TRIPP received her doctorate in mass communication from the University of Alabama, and she is currently an associate professor of journalism at the University of Florida. She has written a book, *Origins of the Black Press, 1827–1847*, and numerous conference papers and book chapters on the abolitionist press and the nineteenth-century African American press. Dr. Tripp is the 2001–2002 president of the American Journalism Historians Association.